Gender and War in Twentieth-Century Eastern Europe

Indiana-Michigan Series in Russian and East European Studies

Alexander Rabinowitch and William G. Rosenberg, eds.

EDITED BY NANCY M. WINGFIELD
AND MARIA BUCUR

Gender and War in Twentieth-Century Eastern Europe

INDIANA UNIVERSITY PRESS
Bloomington and Indianapolis

This book is a publication of

Indiana University Press
601 North Morton Street
Bloomington, IN 47404-3797 USA

http://iupress.indiana.edu

Telephone orders 800-842-6796
Fax orders 812-855-7931
Orders by e-mail iuporder@indiana.edu

The paper used in this publication meets the minimum requirements of American National Standard for Information Sciences—Permanence of Paper for Printed Library Materials, ANSI Z39.48-1984.

Manufactured in the United States of America

Library of Congress Cataloging-in-Publication Data

Gender and war in twentieth-century Eastern Europe / edited by Nancy M. Wingfield and Maria Bucur.
p. cm. — (Indiana-Michigan series in Russian and East European studies)
Includes bibliographical references and index.
ISBN 0-253-34731-9 (cloth : alk. paper) — ISBN 0-253-21844-6 (pbk. : alk. paper)
1. Europe, Eastern—History, Military—20th century. 2. Sex role—Europe, Eastern. I. Wingfield, Nancy M. (Nancy Meriwether) II. Bucur, Maria, date. IV. Title: Gender and war in 20th century Eastern Europe. Series.
DJK48.5.G46 2006
940.3082'0947—dc22

2005029505

1 2 3 4 5 11 10 09 08 07 06

For Codruţ, Danny, David, Dylan, and Nick

Contents

Acknowledgments

While attending a conference celebrating women's history in eastern Europe in Minsk, the capital of post-Soviet Belarus, in autumn 1999, we began contemplating projects worth pursuing as a group of committed gender historians. Taking a break from the conference, we visited the nearby museum dedicated to the Great Fatherland War that was replete with gender connotations. Together with several people who would later contribute to this volume, we walked through the exhibits, discussing ways in which the narratives contained there might be changed if we spread some gender pixie dust over the musty exhibits.

These discussions materialized in a group of three panels at the annual meeting of the American Association for the Advancement of Slavic Studies (AAASS) in Crystal City, Virginia, in 2001. The positive comments of our audiences and the enthusiasm of Janet Rabinowitch, herself a historian and now the director of Indiana University Press, encouraged us in our conviction that gender and war in twentieth-century eastern Europe was a subject deserving of further study. This volume is the result.

We would like to thank our contributors for their fine work. Their insightful articles have resulted in a volume that we believe makes an important contribution to the study of gender and war. We would also like to thank our referees for their excellent suggestions, and Janet Rabinowitch for her helpful advice in shepherding this volume through the publication process. We owe special thanks also to Krassimira Daskalova and Cynthia J. Paces for encouraging this project, to Marsha Rozenblit for her comments on one of our panels at the AAASS, and to Daniel Unowsky for stepping in and reading one of our presenter's papers at the same conference.

Again, we dedicate this collection to the men in our lives, all of whom support us in our academic endeavors. Thank you, Codruţ, Danny, David, Dylan, and Nick.

Nancy M. Wingfield
Maria Bucur

Gender and War in Twentieth-Century Eastern Europe

1 Introduction: Gender and War in Twentieth-Century Eastern Europe

Nancy M. Wingfield and Maria Bucur

> Harboring a secret, foreign will
> I must humbly do my heroic deed;
> With deadly iron on the field of war
> I'm sent to plow a bloody rut.
> (. . .)
> And the heart, burning, loving angered
> Foresees the eternal light in pitch-black hell:
> For the world to come I go into battle,
> For the life to come I go to death.
> Poliksena Sergeevna Solovi̇ëva, 1915[1]

The essays in this collection grow out of two fundamental questions: What does it mean to "gender the front"? And why it is particularly fruitful to bring gender to the front in twentieth-century eastern Europe? At the most basic level, gendering the front means deconstructing the notion that wartime heroism is exclusively masculine. More generally, gendering the front means defining war as a historical subject that encompasses more than battlefields and "the cult of the fallen soldier."[2] The tragic stories of these soldiers came to define the drama of the wars writ large. Thus, historians inscribed heroism as exclusively masculine, while broadening its definition across classes. During the last two decades, however, social, cultural, and gender historians of western Europe and the United States especially have expanded and redefined the meaning of war. They have transformed a variety of topics into essential components for understanding war. Among other issues, gender and social historians have analyzed social/class hierarchies, work, social and political activism, the home front experience, and women's experience. Cultural historians, working to deconstruct essentialist assumptions about social/class hierarchies, have focused on representations of these same experiences. They have challenged the very categories of home front versus fighting front as hierarchically inscribed with historical significance on the basis of culturally embedded assumptions about heroism and sacrifice, both of which have traditionally been gendered masculine, albeit only implicitly. Cultural historians have also looked beyond the immediate causes and consequences of war (questions of "why" and "what"), suggesting that questions focusing on "how" provide great insights into war as a transformative historical event with repercussions across society. We join historians who have challenged this assumption and explore the gender fluidity of the home and fighting front categories on the eastern fronts during the two world wars.[3]

Given the enormous English-language literature on the two world wars, it is perhaps surprising how small the share of studies on eastern Europe is. Moreover, the literature of the world wars in eastern Europe has heretofore focused almost exclusively on traditional diplomatic-military questions.[4] Only recently have historians of the region turned their attention to cultural and social aspects of war, and gender analysis has remained marginal in this new trend. Yet, the particularities of the eastern European context suggest both the need to incorporate gender into the study of the world wars in eastern Europe and the integration of this region into the broader narrative of war in twentieth-century Europe. The eastern European experience of world wars—where the fighting fronts were more mobile and fluid than in western Europe during World War I and more brutal during World War II—renders the conclusions historians have drawn based solely upon the western European experience more difficult to sustain.

Complicating the effort to gender the front in the east is the overriding centrality of the tension between nationalism and trans-nationalism or internationalism. During the course of World War I many of those who had originally fought for the preservation of Austria-Hungary found themselves moving to support its destruction by the war's end. Indeed, the war destroyed the two multinational empires—the Habsburg and Ottoman—that had heretofore dominated eastern Europe, and replaced a third—the Romanov—with a different sort of multinational empire altogether. A series of nominally national states—in fact, often multinational states governed as nation states—replaced these empires in the newly reconfigured eastern Europe. The violence of World War I affected all citizens of the region as they were forced to shift civic identities virtually overnight from transnational to national, for example, from Habsburg into Hungarian or Romanian and from Russian into Latvian or Lithuanian.

The concern of political elites with consolidating the national identity of the nascent states of eastern Europe crowded out most other issues raised by the experience of World War I. Thus, economic, political, and social-welfare projects were framed primarily in ethno-national terms. While women might have benefited from these programs, they were not necessarily the target audience.[5] The new governments granted feminist demands for political enfranchisement only insofar as they strengthened the ethno-national majority. Moreover, in many of these states by the end of the nineteenth century masculinity had gained an inescapably national—and contested—component. The re-inscription of male gender identity and the construction of male national identity were, in fact, inextricably linked.

World War II had unique characteristics in eastern Europe, most notably the double occupation of much of this geographically vulnerable region by the Nazis and Soviets and the level of violence and moral degradation both civilians and soldiers experienced—a revolution from abroad, according to Jan Gross—

Figure 1.1. Red Army Soldiers Cast in Bronze Stand Guard over Their Fallen Comrades in Prague. Photo by Nancy M. Wingfield.

including the large Jewish population and its subsequent genocide, as well as the postwar Soviet domination of official history in most of the area.[6] One significant outcome of this war was the transformation of the nationalist interwar states into members of the communist bloc. Hungary, Poland, and Romania were changed into "brotherly" communist states. Thus, Soviet ideological concerns initially dominated the official memory of World War II not only in that country but elsewhere in communist bloc, although Soviet ideological concerns sometimes produced rather different results at home than in the satellites. Until 1989 the state continued to play a greater role in shaping public memory of the two world wars than in western Europe. In commemorating the Great Fatherland War, the state relied on clichés about male heroism and strength that were at least questioned, if not rejected in the postwar west.[7]

The authors in this volume employ gender as a central category of analysis for a number of themes that help expand our understanding of war in twentieth-century eastern Europe, both in its immediate experiential form and in its long-term outcomes. They explore the links between the civilian and military war effort on the so-called home and fighting fronts. Heretofore, many historians have equated the fighting front with the masculine and the home front with the feminine. Like other recent scholarship, this collection takes issue with these divisions. On the one hand they are still significant for situating contemporary representations of wartime experience. On the other hand, we want to problematize this division as a stable category of analysis. The broad thematic focus of the essays can be divided into these categories: wartime experiences challenging traditional gender roles; postwar restoration of gender order; collaboration and resistance; the body; and memory and commemoration.

The first step, however, is to render women visible. While such an attempt might at first glance seem to contradict the goal of gendering history, this is not the case. What historians have constructed as universal is, in fact, masculine. Making women visible underscores this point. Nowhere is this clearer than in the construction of wartime heroism. Expanding upon our feminist predecessors from the 1970s, whose aim was to shed light on an "authentic" female experience, we seek to demonstrate how this experience has been culturally constructed and is therefore contingent upon a specific context.

There is a rich historiography on the efforts to mobilize women for the wartime workforce in western Europe. Some of this literature explores changes, albeit temporary, of gender roles in the workplace; the feminization of certain professions; and the growth of women's identification with the workplace. In contrast, almost nothing has been published on efforts to mobilize women in eastern Europe with the exception of the Soviet Union, where there is a long historiography of women's participation in the "Great Patriotic War." Even there, however, gender has seldom been employed as an analytical category in accounts of World War II.[8] Our volume provides several case studies of such changes in the workforce and discusses both the links between these developments and the longer trends in female employment and professional advancement, as well as the limitations of these experiences in reshaping employment opportunities for women in the postwar period.

While much has been written about female volunteers on the fighting front as nurses and military personnel during World War I in the western European context, there is little comparable literature concerning eastern Europe.[9] World War II saw increased female participation in all aspects of combat—in the case of Czech women, for both eastern and western allies. The historiography on this

Figure 1.2. Grave of Female Red Army Soldier in Prague. Photo by Nancy M. Wingfield.

topic is well developed for both western Europe and the Soviet Union.[10] Yet, the experience of the fighting front remains represented as exclusively masculine elsewhere in eastern Europe and rather clearly separated from the home front. Thus wartime heroism and masculinity on the battlefield are inextricably linked in the collective memory of the two world wars there.

Although there was fluidity between the home front and the fighting front,

Figure 1.3. Romanian Soldiers Dancing the Hora, World War I. Courtesy of the National Military Museum, Bucharest.

civilians and soldiers had very different experiences and understandings of the war. Gender was an important dimension of how these differences played themselves out. Women on the home front initially experienced a period of economic and emotional vulnerability. But during both world wars they also learned to become more self-reliant, often taking on traditionally masculine roles. Several contributors underscore the leading role of women as heads of household, breadwinners, and protectors of their children and property. While this experience proved to be short-lived, with the return of soldiers from the fighting front, women had learned to question traditional gender roles in civilian life and the workplace. Although it was assumed that the families would benefit from men's return, postwar reunification with fathers, brothers, and spouses was fraught with tension, because family relations had been realigned during the war.[11] Indeed, rather than benefiting the family, sometimes the return of the soldier undermined traditional familial ties.

The experience of men on the home front, especially during World War I, departed from what was becoming the new masculine norm during wartime—fighting for one's country as a soldier. Men had to justify their participation in the war in ways that forced them to redefine their gender roles. Veterans turned participation in combat into an important element for separating "true men" from the rest, thus upending traditional masculine class and educational hierarchies. Although populist, men's combat experience narrowed the field of masculine prowess.[12]

Male combatants participated in both wars to fulfill their traditional obligations of protecting women at home and living up to masculine norms of heroism. But their experiences of death, destruction, and disempowerment forced men to question their *own* masculinity while reinforcing the link between masculinity and violence. The intensity of their traumatic experiences—as witnesses, victimizers, and victims—rendered at least some combatants unable to reconnect with the women and men who lived through the war on the home front. These tensions remained deeply buried under the apparent restoration of gender hierarchies in the wake of the two wars. While the essays in this volume do not argue against the basic premises of Margaret and Patrice Higonnet's "double helix" thesis of a restoration of gender hierarchies,[13] they emphasize instead the kinds of struggles over gender hierarchy in which men and women engaged during and after wars. We are focusing on the buried intensity of the conflicts themselves rather than their more obvious political and social outcomes.

During both world wars women sometimes chose, albeit in small numbers, to participate in combat. As they moved beyond the auxiliary roles, like nursing and administration, becoming pilots and sharpshooters, they defied the masculine norms that identified heroism and courage with men. Although asserting their agency in extraordinary ways, these female combatants proved unable to change gender norms. Fellow soldiers, civilian politicians, mothers, and wives at home could only make sense of their heroic actions as manly (read: unfeminine) and out of the ordinary (read: abnormal). Although often revered by their entire home nations, these female heroes have been poorly integrated into the popular narrative of the wars. They literally stand outside the mainstream. The case of the Romanian Ecaterina Teodoroiu during World War I exemplifies this. A wartime volunteer who joined the army because her brothers were also fighting, she was twice wounded and later perished in battle. Though a mature woman of twenty-three, and engaged to be married, her contemporaries immortalized her as a "young girl" and a "virgin," as a means both to explain her heroism without disturbing established masculinist norms and to decouple other women's actions on the home front from wartime heroism.[14]

Trauma was an important element in the growing chasm between men and women during the wars. Soldiers—mostly male—confronted irrational mass killings on the battlefront. Some were unable to come to terms with this violence in any other way than by committing violent acts upon their return home, for instance, by beating their wives. More often than not, doctors and other observers chose to interpret such behavior as predictable outbursts in line with prewar gender roles. The gendered aspect of male combat trauma remained ignored and men dishonored only themselves by their actions.

In contrast, civilians—mostly female—were subjected to often grotesque sexual violence.[15] However, these same women were often stigmatized as having dishonored their family and nation in the act of being sexually abused. They were thus silenced and their traumatic experiences degraded. Women then were the double victims of physical violence and public condemnation. Moreover, as civilians increasingly became wartime targets, they suffered extreme privation. In some cases, starvation not only caused the loss of youth and beauty, it even erased physical gender differences, making it "difficult to distinguish males

Figure 1.4. Ecaterina Teodoroiu as Androgynous Symbol, World War I. Courtesy of the National Military Museum, Bucharest.

from females."[16] Females lost their womanhood as starvation caused their bodies to disappear as women's bodies.

The rise of the total state, which became involved in all aspects of social life, both public and private, is another significant aspect of war in the twentieth century that gender analysis helps illuminate. In the wartime attempt both to mobilize their populations and to control the energies that mobilization released, state institutions expanded their economic, political, and social reach. European governments developed welfare programs to cope with women's economic vulnerability, the childcare needs of those in the work force, and social assistance for veterans, war widows, and orphans. At the center of these policies were concerns with maintaining gender hierarchies while mobilizing women for the war effort, yet even many recent accounts of mobilization fail to address gender.

Propaganda efforts were central to state activities to mobilize the entire population. Visual propaganda, including film, cartoons, newsreels, posters, and postcards, utilized well-worn masculine and feminine cliches. At the same time, the real experience of both men and women increasingly confounded these cliches and challenged the propaganda. Eastern European propaganda efforts in World War I were limited and generally unsuccessful in comparison to western Europe.[17] This is especially the case with regard to gender. During World War II, the states of eastern Europe paid more attention to the need for propaganda and even to gendered aspects of mobilization, especially in the Soviet Union.

One method of mobilizing populations to support the war effort was to draw a clear line between individuals who could become heroes and those who could not. The war made it easier to exclude people who were unwilling or unable to cooperate fully with the war effort. Among the excluded during World War I were pacifists and the international wing of the socialist movement. Some feminists aroused suspicion by virtue of their prewar criticism of governmental policies. Others attempted to paint themselves loyal to the war effort by aping the state's xenophobic, nationalist rhetoric. During World War II, eastern European governments—both independent and occupation—employed even more xenophobic and racist language than during the previous war. This rhetoric also narrowed the scope of masculine and feminine roles, not only for the "undesirable" but also for the "normal" population. Thus, the activities of feminists and left-wing activists outside the Soviet Union were deemed disloyal, even if they were members of the dominant ethno-national group.

While identity and ideological conviction were the basis for excluding entire groups of men and women, collaboration with the enemy was another important criterion. Yet, not all collaborators were deemed equal. Wartime and postwar regimes treated men and women differently, an aspect of retribution that has heretofore received little attention in recent volumes addressing the topic in eastern Europe.[18] Both the criminal acts of collaboration and their punishment were gender specific. Since female patriotism was so closely identified with procreation, their sexual liaisons with the enemy were considered a far greater crime than the similar trespasses of men. Indeed, women who fraternized with the enemy were doubly culpable, for they were betraying both their family and their nation.

By using gender as a category of analysis, we can arrive at a more nuanced understanding of the subjective nature of wartime experience and its representations. We do not claim, however, that there are authentic as opposed to questionable representations of experience. Rather, the essays in this volume examine power differences among individual voices as well as between individuals and institutions. Indeed, the foregrounding of subjective representations invites questions about the very categories that historians often take for granted in these pages: feminine/masculine, patriotism/treason, public/private. Deconstructing these categories helps underscore their fluidity.

Yet our deconstruction is not meant to deny their usefulness. As much as individuals understand and represent gender roles in subjective ways, they are still constructing their individualized discourse based on cultural norms and symbols. By the same token, these subjective representations become the basis for future narratives about war. Thus, while men and women spoke a great deal about their wartime actions to demonstrate self-sacrifice and heroism, their personal recollections of such actions generally used metaphors and language that often reinforced their gendered understanding of heroism. When, however, these representations challenged well-accepted norms, such texts were often subsequently discarded from institutionalized narratives of wartime experience.

Thus, collective memory of the world wars is both selective and essentially gendered. Public discourse about the wars encoded heroism as male and paved the way to commemorative practices that celebrated and reinforced already existing gender dichotomies. Beginning with World War I, war memorials throughout Europe overwhelmingly mourned the loss of all combatants' lives and increasingly emphasized the heroism of the common soldier rather than high-ranking officers. Despite this "democracy of death," the deaths of auxiliary personnel, many female—for example, volunteer nurses—were seldom memorialized on the myriad public markers put up in towns and villages throughout many of the former belligerent countries. These frequently took the form of an obelisk or a single soldier standing erect and unwounded, "an image of bodily continuity that seeks to displace or overcome the memory of bodies violated and destroyed," although destruction is, as Kirk Savage argues, the defining premise of warfare.[19] These monuments often listed the names of the native sons who died in battle.[20] The difference in degree of public recognition of sacrifice is in part due to the far greater number of soldiers who died in combat. Yet, one cannot take for granted the choices made in representing heroism as exclusively masculine. These choices served to reinforce gender dichotomies and render women's experiences of the wars unheroic and less worthy of public attention.

The silencing of women's voices becomes even more apparent when examining the selective incorporation of individual wartime memories into collective narratives. Although women left behind vivid recollections, diaries, and other autobiographical writings about their wartime experiences, their voices have been largely omitted from official histories. Even in reconstructing the experience of civilians, public historians and curators have privileged men's autobiographical writings.[21]

Although commemorative traces of war are predominantly male, there is a strong female presence in the performative aspect of commemorations. Indeed, men have predominantly been the choreographers of official commemorations of the two wars. In some cases, women have been permitted to remember the war in public, though not necessarily their own experiences. Women have, how-

Figure 1.5. Soviet Male Soldier—Savior of Helpless Women and Children, Sofia, Bulgaria. Photo by Maria Bucur.

ever, played the role of oracle, transmitting stories of male heroism from one generation to the next.

* * *

The essays by Alon Rachamimov, Maureen Healy, and Eliza Ablovatski examine different aspects of both challenges to gender roles and restoration of gender order in the post-World War I world. All of them address the connection between politics and prescribed or stereotyped gender images. Rachamimov explores the influence of maternalism on women's war service, while Healy provides a gendered reading of Austrian veterans' acts of domestic violence in the wake of World War I and shows the perceived vacuum in Austrian society through the absence of real and symbolic fathers. Ablovatski analyzes attempts by the political right in post-revolutionary Hungary to marginalize the "unruly" women of the left in their narratives, while the left wing memorialized these same women as martyrs of the failed revolution. She demonstrates how memoirs of revolution simultaneously reflect stereotypes and carve out active roles for women.

Alon Rachamimov examines women in a traditional role, nursing, in a nontraditional setting. The arrival of Habsburg nurses in Russia during World War I constituted the first time nurses from the home country were included as part of the Red Cross inspection team of prisoner of war (POW) camps on the eastern front. Certainly the nurses themselves, all from aristocratic families, were part of a traditional, soon to be obsolete, system. Their participation in the war as nurses was rooted in nineteenth-century social thinking about the role of upper-class women in charitable endeavors. But their presence changed the dynamic of the interaction between Red Cross officials (now women) and the POWs, as well as of relations between the combatant countries. These were among the first women to act as representatives of their country in the Great War at such a high international level.

Rachamimov analyzes a situation that is anomalous in a variety of ways. The female nurses were in a position of power over the POWs because of both their class background and their institutional affiliation. Some of these nurses commented about the breakdown of social norms in POW camps, criticizing, for example, a lack of discipline among both the officers and the ranks and a failure to maintain distinction between friend and foe.

Maureen Healy employs the term *Umarbeitung* (adaptation), a reference to the tailoring of military uniforms to civilian use, as a metaphor for the "cleansing of the war out of the warrior." Healy highlights the process of demobilization and transformation from soldier to civilian, which was made especially difficult by both Austria's defeat and the postwar economic situation, which resulted in mass unemployment among demobilized soldiers. Healy notes that the difficult transition to normalcy and "order" in Britain and France following World War I took place against the backdrop of victory, while in Austria fears about disordering gender relations became part of the explanations for the very loss of the war. Indeed, Austrians had blamed the absence of male authority for wartime social phenomena as varied as food riots, juvenile delinquency, rising crime, and women's "sexual depravity." Everywhere, women were denounced for fraternizing with enemy soldiers; and increasing numbers of women turned to prostitution to survive. Moreover, wider societal concerns about the homecomers, the *Heimkehrer*, included fear that soldiers, especially those returning from revolutionary Russia, would bring with them criminality, infectious diseases, political instability, and social deviance. Impoverished POWs from Russia were held in "Bolshevik quarantine" within Austria to prevent the spread of ideological contagion.

Some returning veterans were wounded physically, while others were wounded psychologically; these emasculated men were part of a crisis of masculinity that occurred on two levels: to real men within their families and to the family writ large as the paternal pillars of prewar society. Thus, both the rebuilding of individual men and the rebuilding of the family were necessary for restoring the gender order in defeated Austria. Some men, however, failed to undergo successful *Umarbeitung:* they were violent both on the streets and within their own families. The Austrian men in this story reflect a partial history of defeat from below.

In her essay Eliza Ablovatski analyzes attempts to reestablish traditional gender roles as part of the postwar, postrevolutionary "national and Christian" consolidation of power in Hungary. She explores how the Hungarian myth of threefold suffering—world war, revolution, and territorial loss—was reflected in perceptions, which also depended on preexisting stereotypes, of the revolutionary and counterrevolutionary woman. Both the political left and right employed the events of 1919 as a foundation myth. In the eyes of the conservatives, revolutionary women in Hungary, like those of the 1871 Paris Commune, were both politically dangerous and physically degenerate.[22] They were also sexually dangerous. These same conservatives, who demonized revolutionary women for their presence in the masculine and political public realm, considered their own, totally depoliticized women, to be of flawless moral character. Indeed, the noble Red Cross nurses of Rachamimov's essay are employed in this rhetoric as the epitome of the national feminine idea: ministering to the soldier. In contrast, revolutionaries stressed reports of White officers' depravity and sexual abuse of revolutionary women, which became part of the left's myth of martyrdom.

Melissa Feinberg, Benjamin Frommer, and Mara Lazda challenge preconceived notions about collaboration and resistance. Feinberg's and Frommer's essays offer compelling analyses of these issues in Bohemia and Moravia, whose unique situation during World War II as the Nazi-dominated Protectorate of Bohemia and Moravia made the line between collaboration and resistance particularly subtle.

Melissa Feinberg argues that in the World War II Protectorate of Bohemia and Moravia the domestic sphere, too, was part of the world of occupation and that the kitchen was a site of collaboration and resistance. And because few Czech men spent the war in the military, but rather worked in factories, the gendered division of fighting front versus home front was not part of the Czech wartime experience. Thus Czech men and women both experienced occupation, and their response to the issue of collaboration and resistance was framed in terms of the struggle for the survival of the nation.

Feinberg employs a case study of a prominent group of right-wing Czech women—all members of an organization named the Women's Center—who sought to realize the goal of equality in gender difference. She analyzes the group's guide to menus showing how to make the best use of the wartime rationing system to demonstrate how their mixed goals fit into the ideological landscape of the Protectorate. The Women's Center's attempts to help Czech women keep the nation physically and spiritually healthy and protect it from the ravages of war and occupation demonstrate the complicated and sometimes contradictory behavior of Czechs vis-à-vis their German occupiers in what they considered the interest of the Czech nation.

Benjamin Frommer, noting that the history of collaboration has usually been written without women, argues that women were not only victims, but sometimes also perpetrators. Extending the study of collaboration beyond leaders and organizations, Frommer examines the aid that nonaffiliated women provided the occupiers. He concentrates on the most typical—and stereotypical—female collaboration: denunciation and fraternization, focusing on the role of sex and gender in the designation and prosecution of denouncers and fraternizers in wartime and postwar Czechoslovakia. The gender-differentiated treatment of collaboration in post–World War II Czechoslovakia illustrated in Frommer's essay reflects how subjective the state institutions and their representatives were in interpreting universal concepts such as treason and justice.

Although familial ties led some women into collaboration, more often husbands and wives were victims of spousal denunciation for a variety of nonideological reasons, among them greed, infidelity, and jealousy. Men appear to have practiced denunciation for many of the same reasons as women, but denunciation and woman became conflated in the popular imagination and remain so in today's scholarly accounts. While denunciation was the most common wartime crime for which women were tried, Czechoslovak courts were more likely to punish men for it.

Fraternization, however, was the worst form of collaboration, and the most detested variety was sexual. Not only did contemporary mores demand a higher standard of female behavior, but women who fraternized were considered to be aiding in the Nazi program of Germanization, whose ultimate goal was to annihilate the Czech nation. In the climate of retribution that characterized the immediate postwar era, not only were German women and Czech women who fraternized with Germans brutalized; legally intermarried Czech women faced discrimination ranging from intimidation to outright violence. The reverse was not true for intermarried Czech men, whose German wives were to be treated benevolently according to the citizenship decree.

Mara Lazda focuses on the relationships among gender, the total wartime state, and the Latvian nation in the context of the family. She analyzes how the Soviet and Nazi regimes defined familial relationships to build loyalty and recruit supporters in the wartime regime as well as to counter Latvian attempts to resist the new order. Both Soviet and Nazi wartime policies also regulated familial relationships.

The Soviet regime sought to erase associations with interwar Latvia, and the promotion of new Soviet-Latvian gender roles severed ties to the ethnic Latvian nation. The formulation of gender and power in the language of familial relationships softened the militarism of occupation and established the hierarchy of the Soviet state. The Soviet "liberation" of women from the constraints of interwar Latvian gender structures, the regime claimed, legitimized occupation. Soviet deportation policies carried out in this first year of occupation, however, conflicted with this propaganda. In practice the Soviets restructured family relationships through deportation in which the separation of family members was an integral part of the deportation process. Latvians considered this policy an attack on their nation, and in response they often "adopted" fellow nationals as family-members-in-exile.

The Nazi occupation followed the Soviet mass deportation by a few weeks. In contrast to the Soviets, the Nazis attempted to manipulate traditional gender roles and conceptions of the family that Latvians associated with interwar independence to promote National Socialism's anti-Semitic, race-based ideology. Controlling family relationships provided a means for the Nazis to monitor racial categories and expression of Latvian independence. In practice the Nazis sought to control marriages between Germans and non-Germans in Latvia in the context of military and economic needs.

In their contributions Melissa Bokovoy, Maria Bucur, Katherine R. Jolluck, and Lisa A. Kirschenbaum examine issues of gender and memory in the context of war and violence. All four essays demonstrate how language and the body inscribe narratives of war in gendered ways and consider how women's memories of the world wars have been treated in the official narratives of wars. Women were present in commemorative rituals, participating actively in the shaping of collective memory of the war, as Bokovoy's essay demonstrates. While Bokovoy examines state appropriation of female mourning for political-national purposes, Bucur and Kirschenbaum employ memoirs to analyze how women's memories challenged these same narratives. Bokovoy and Bucur both address how language and memory are gendered, while Jolluck and Kirschenbaum examine the body as a site of history, narrative, and memory.

Melissa Bokovoy looks at the role of gender in the ritual articulation of myths in creating a usable national history. Serbian women were central in the creation, promotion, and preservation of the idea that the Wars of Liberation (1912–1918) continued the centuries-old struggle of the Serbs against the Turks. These women were designated as bearers of national memories due to their role as mothers. They drew upon the myth of the Kosovo Maiden and the Mother of the Jugovicí in the Serbs' century-long battle for independence from the Ottoman Empire.

Serbian men and women both experienced World War I as refugees, prisoners of occupation, victims, and mourners of the dead. Women's experiences, however, were relegated to a secondary role or largely ignored in the commemorative practices that emerged in Yugoslavia during the interwar period. These commemorations focused on fallen soldiers as ideal national citizens who sacrificed their lives for the Serbian nation. Serbian intellectuals and politicians employed women's mourning of these soldiers—husbands, sons, fathers, and brothers—to privilege Serbian sacrifice for the creation of the Yugoslav state.

In her contribution, Maria Bucur examines the differences between women's and men's remembrances of wartime experiences to bring out the gender dimensions of the act of memory writing. She also analyzes the selective ways in which these memoirs have been incorporated into larger narratives about the war, to highlight the gendered identification of wartime heroism as exclusively masculine, and the parallel invisibility of women's actions and experiences. In the Romanian case, even experiences linked to the everyday life of occupation by the Central Powers in World War I, which was statistically an overwhelmingly female experience, have been presented in the major historical narratives primarily from a masculine perspective, with women augmenting the story only from the margins. Bucur explores how Romanian women's narratives from World War I were relatively well received initially, eliciting much discussion in the interwar press, but were eventually marginalized as representations of both the home front and the fighting front experience. Bucur questions the accuracy of these accounts and calls for a reexamination of the female experience as historically essential for understanding life in wartime, especially with regard to issues of survival, collaboration, and resistance under occupation.

Following the Soviet invasion and annexation of eastern Poland in autumn 1939, hundreds of thousands of Polish citizens were forcibly resettled in the interior of the Soviet Union. In her contribution, Katherine R. Jolluck examines the response of Polish women, who came from all walks of life, to the violence inflicted upon their bodies in this exile. Women could openly discuss the non-gender-specific hardships they endured, for example beatings or near starvation, depicting the effects of these experiences on their bodies and their efforts to cope with them. Indeed, they appropriated the traditional Polish male notion of suffering for their martyred nation.

Following the invasion of the Red Army, many Polish women went into forced Soviet exile. Focusing on these women as the double victims of physical violence and public opprobrium, Jolluck analyzes the traumatic impact of female subjection to wartime violence, highlighting their silence concerning transgressions of social norms regarding their bodies.

Exiled women's sexuality became a weapon in the hands of men in authority as Soviet men regularly transgressed the boundaries of the Polish women's bodies. These gender-specific offenses against their bodies elicited a different response from these women than non-gender-specific offenses. The author designates the three categories of offenses employed specifically against women—mixing, invasion, and sexual exploitation—arguing that as the level of abuse escalated, the women could no longer interpret these abuses as crimes against the nation. Besmirched in their own eyes, these Polish women no longer spoke of the offense as a crime of the enemy; indeed, most could no longer speak of the offense at all. These acts of violence against the female body constituted acts of violence against gender identity and proved profoundly silencing.

Lisa A. Kirschenbaum addresses the issue of the role of the starving body in gender identity and memory during wartime. In her essay, Kirschenbaum focuses on the siege of Leningrad, which was neither the only siege of World War II nor even of the Soviet Union. Leningrad was different, however, due to the blurring of the distinction between the fighting front and the home front. This line was blurred not only by the physical proximity of Leningrad, which had become a city of women, to the front, but also by the bodily effects of starvation. Soviet wartime and postwar accounts minimized the extent of starvation and employed images of women and children as victims of Nazi violence rather than of starvation. The official story provided a comforting framework for constructing personal memory and survivors' accounts, which often accept the view that Leningraders should be considered active soldiers rather than civilian victims. Certainly, the starving body, as Kirschenbaum notes, represented a potential challenge to the notion of heroic and meaningful sacrifice by the civilian heroes of the Leningrad front, by complicating and even contradicting the "heroic" narratives constructed by the state and often adopted by the survivors.

Wartime narratives represented Leningrad women as both vital to the war effort and indestructibly feminine, inextricably tied to the world of children and family. Starvation, however, destroyed the visible markers of gender identity, and undermined "natural" male views of women as objects of desire, rendering them old and wrinkled. Reminiscences of spring 1942, a time of rebirth that presaged ultimate Soviet victory, mention hair salons full of women getting manicures and hot waves. While the disappearance of the physical markers of gender became an important symbol of the horrors of the siege, few survivors wanted to examine too closely what starvation did to their own bodies. Recovery from starvation was marked by the return of femininity and youth. In the end, the memory of the resilience and sanctity of the human body as a site of gender identity proved less painful, for the state and survivors, than the degradation and destruction of the body.

In highlighting gender as a category of analysis, the case studies in this collection expand our understanding of war not only in twentieth-century eastern Europe, but throughout Europe more broadly, because consideration of the eastern fronts may enhance conclusions about the world wars based only on the west. Rather than portraying women solely as victims of war, with their insistence that women do have agency, some essays contradict the traditional privileging of male wartime agency. Moreover, some authors also highlight the fact that female agency does not necessarily represent a positive force. Indeed, women, like men, behaved in a variety of ways, some of which reflected their own narrow and personal interests, rather than confirming traditional images of female nurturing. Other authors highlight continuity in women's roles under the changed circumstances of war and postwar, underscoring the fact that not all women's wartime activity is necessarily empowering in the long term.

Blurring the boundaries between fighting front and home front, these essays confirm the broad reach of total war and its devastating effect on all segments of society.

Notes

1. From "To the War," in Margaret R. Higonnet, ed., *Lines of Fire: Women Writers of World War I* (New Haven: Yale University Press, 1987), 481–82. Aside from this translation, all other translations are by the respective contributors to this volume, unless otherwise noted.

2. The term is George L. Mosse's from, "The Cult of the Fallen Soldier," in *Fallen Soldiers: Reshaping the Memory of the World Wars* (New York: Oxford University Press, 1990), 70–106.

3. For example: Margaret H. Darrow, *French Women and the First World War: War Stories of the Home Front* (New York: New York University Press, 2000); Belinda J. Davis, *Home Fires Burning: Food, Politics, and Everyday Life in World War I Berlin* (Chapel Hill: University of North Carolina Press, 2000); Margaret R. Higonnet et al., eds., *Behind the Lines*; Miranda Pollard, *Reign of Virtue: Mobilizing Gender in Vichy France* (Chicago: University of Chicago Press, 1998).

4. These volumes are legion. In English: Jan Tomasz Gross, *Polish Society under German Occupation: The Generalgouvernement, 1939–1944* (Princeton: Princeton University Press, 1979); Gross, *Revolution from Abroad: The Soviet Conquest of Poland's Western Ukraine and Western Belorussia* (Princeton: Princeton University Press, 1988); Vojtech Mastny, *The Czechs under Nazi Rule: The Failure of National Resistance, 1939–1942* (New York: Columbia University Press, 1971); Mastny, *Russia's Road to the Cold War: Diplomacy, Warfare, and the Politics of Communism, 1941–1945* (New York: Columbia University Press, 1979); H. Louis Rees, *The Czechs during World War I. The Path to Independence* (Boulder, Colo.: East European Monographs, 1992).

5. Women do figure in the histories of the early Soviet Union, but there the war in general (and women's contributions to it) were largely forgotten.

6. The Jewish experience of World War II has by and large had a separate historiography. Though some of the individual essays in this collection make reference to this topic, we hope our discussions here will in fact generate greater interest in the gender aspects of that experience.

7. Jay Winter, *Sites of Memory, Sites of Mourning: The Great War in European Cultural History*, reprinted ed. (Cambridge: Cambridge University Press, 2000).

8. Recent work examining gender includes: Katherine Hodgson, *Written with the Bayonet: Soviet Russian Poetry of World War II* (Liverpool: Liverpool University Press, 1996); Hodgson, "The Other Veterans: Soviet Women's Poetry of World War II," in John Garrard and Carol Garrard, eds., *World War II and the Soviet People* (New York: St. Martins, 1993); Anna Krylova, "Healers of Wounded Souls: The Crisis of Private Life in Soviet Literature and Society, 1944–1946," *Journal of Modern History* 73, no. 2 (June 2001): 307–32.

9. A welcome exception is Melissa K. Stockdale's recent article on the "Women's Battalion of Death," " 'My Death for the Motherland is Happiness': Women, Patriotism, and

Soldiering in Russia's Great War, 1914–1917," *American Historical Review* 109, no.1 (February 2004): 78–116.

10. Recently there has been focus on Soviet women's contributions on the battlefield (and lack of recognition of the same): K. Jean Cottam, "Soviet Women in Combat in World War II: The Ground Forces and the Navy," *International Journal of Women's Studies* 3, no. 4 (1980): 345–57; Juliane Furst, "Heroes, Lovers, Victims: Partisan Girls during the Great Fatherland War," *Minerva: Quarterly Report on Women and the Military* 18, no. 3–4 (2000): 38–75; David M. Glantz, "Women in War: The Red Army's Experience," *Journal of Slavic Military Studies* 12, no. 1 (1999): 208–12; Reina Pennington, "'Do Not Speak of the Services You Rendered': Women Veterans of Aviation in the Soviet Union," *Journal of Slavic Military Studies* 9, no. 1 (1996): 120–51; Pennington, "The Propaganda Factor and Soviet Women Pilots in World War II," *Minerva: Quarterly Report on Women and the Military* 15, no. 2 (1997): 13–41.

11. For example Elizabeth D. Heinemann, *What Difference Does a Husband Make?: Women and Marital Status in Nazi and Postwar Germany* (Berkeley: University of California Press, 1999); Susan Kingsley Kent, *Making Peace: The Reconstruction of Gender in Interwar Britain* (Princeton: Princeton University Press, 1993); Mary Louise Roberts, *Civilization without Sexes: Reconstructing Gender in Postwar France, 1917–1927* (Chicago: University of Chicago Press, 1994).

12. See Mosse, *Fallen Soldiers.*

13. Margaret R. Higonnet and Patrice L.-R. Higonnet, "The Double Helix," in *Behind the Lines,* 31–47.

14. Maria Bucur, "Between the Mother of the Wounded and the Virgin from Jiu. Romanian Women and the Gender of Heroism during the Great War," *Journal of Women's History* 12, no. 2 (Summer 2000): 30–56.

15. The scholarship on the Shoah has delved into the gender dimensions of these traumatic experiences during World War II. Much less has been written, however, about other civilians in eastern Europe. Our volume offers several case studies that will enhance the spectrum of understanding such experiences. Though we do not engage in any comparisons with the scholarship on the Shoah, we hope such comparisons will become the subject of future studies in the spirit of critically understanding these experiences in the broad context of the war.

16. Cynthia Simmons and Nina Perlina, eds., *Writing the Siege of Leningrad: Women's Diaries, Memoirs, and Documentary Prose* (Pittsburgh: University of Pittsburgh Press, 2002), 14.

17. On the use of Allied propaganda against the Habsburg Monarchy during World War I: Mark Cornwall, *The Undermining of Austria-Hungary: The Battle for Hearts and Minds* (New York: Palgrave Macmillian, 2000). On Russian World War I propaganda: Hubertus F. Jahn, *Patriotic Culture in Russia during World War I* (Ithaca: Cornell University Press, 1995).

18. See the relevant essays in István Deák et al., eds., *The Politics of Retribution in Europe: World War II and its Aftermath* (Princeton: Princeton University Press, 2000).

19. Kirk Savage, "The Politics of Memory: Black Emancipation and the Civil War Movement," in John R. Gillis, ed., *Commemorations: The Politics of National Identity* (Princeton: Princeton University Press, 1994), 131.

20. For "democracy of death": Thomas W. Laqueur, "Memory and Naming in the Great War," in *Commemorations,* 150–51. On war memorials more generally: Alan Borg, *War Memorials: From Antiquity to the Present* (London: Leo Cooper, 1991); James M.

Mayo, *War Memorials as Political Landscape: The American Experience and Beyond* (New York: Praeger, 1988). On war monuments and gender representations: Daniel Sherman, *The Construction of Memory in Interwar France* (Chicago: University of Chicago Press, 2001).

21. Among the best-known examples is Paul Fussell, *The Great War and Modern Memory*, reprint ed. (New York: Oxford University Press, 2000). Also Denis Winter, *Death's Men: Soldiers of the Great War*, reprint ed. (New York: Penguin USA, 1993).

22. On the Commune, see Gay Gullickson, *Unruly Women of Paris: Images of the Commune* (Ithaca: Cornell University Press, 1996). On the vilification of women in the political realm: Lynn Hunt, ed., *Eroticism and the Body Politic* (Baltimore: Johns Hopkins University Press, 1991); Hunt, *The Family Romance of the French Revolution* (Berkeley: University of California Press, 1992); Joan B. Landes, *Visualizing the Nation: Gender, Representation, and Revolution in Eighteenth Century France* (Ithaca: Cornell University Press, 2001).

Part One. *Challenging Gender Roles/Restoring Order*

2 "Female Generals" and "Siberian Angels": Aristocratic Nurses and the Austro-Hungarian POW Relief

Alon Rachamimov

In the course of World War I enemy forces captured an estimated 2.77 million Austro-Hungarian soldiers.[1] This astonishingly high number constituted about one third of the 8.32 million men mobilized by Austria-Hungary during the war, and about 11 percent of the total male population of the Dual Monarchy.[2] The great majority of these prisoners—2.11 million—were captured by Russian forces in the years 1914–1916. Expecting a short war, none of the belligerents made any advance preparations to lodge, feed, clothe, and medically treat this massive influx of enemy soldiers. The long columns of prisoners sent to the rear joined the estimated 4–5 million refugees, who either fled the war zone or were forcibly removed and now clogged the roads for hundreds of miles. Thus, in addition to fighting a war on a massive and unprecedented scale, the belligerent countries on the eastern front had to deal with what would be called today a "humanitarian crisis" on a tremendous scale. The endeavor to assist the multitude of displaced, interned, and distraught people required enormous financial, physical, and emotional mobilization at a time when all three resources were in great demand. And as the case often is with assistance, it involved not only succor, but also control, distrust, and frictions along class, national, and gender lines.[3] Until recently this humanitarian crisis and the various aid programs it engendered failed to attract the interest of historians and found little room in the ever-expanding historiography on the Great War.[4]

This essay focuses on one of the most important assistance projects during World War I—the Austro-Hungarian POW relief effort—and on its most visible representatives, a group of aristocratic Red Cross nurses sent to Russia during the war. Assigned the auxiliary appellation of "nurses," these women were expected to do almost everything *except* personally treat the sick and the wounded. They were supposed to report on the loyalty of the "imperial and royal" (*kaiserlich und königlich*-k.u.k.) captured soldiers, re-enforce hierarchy and discipline in the camps, negotiate with high-ranking officials in Russia, assess authoritatively the living conditions in scores of POW camps, distribute large amounts of money according to local needs, and embody the maternal caring and the good will of their monarchical home state. These aristocratic women were delegated considerable powers and responsibilities vis-à-vis millions of their male compatriots in a situation that was highly exceptional for the time.

The detailed diaries, memoirs, and reports left by these aristocratic delegates reflect the different strategies they chose for handling the complexities and many contradictions of their mission. Their accounts reveal how their presence as "female generals"—as one delegate put it—challenged and disturbed established gender hierarchy in a way that could not be masked under the convenient familial designation of "sisters" (*Schwestern*).[5] None of these women could truly conform to the ideal-typical representation of a nineteenth-century nurse, and none managed to win the confidence of more than a section of the POW population.[6] It was no coincidence that only the Swedish Red Cross nurse Elsa Brändström, the daughter of the Swedish Ambassador in Petrograd, who had focused primarily on alleviating the material needs of the prisoners, won the gratitude, devotion, and trust of the prisoners as "The Angel of Siberia." A veritable Elsa Brändström cult developed in many of the POW camps (especially officer camps) and continued on during the 1920s and 1930s among POW veteran associations. The Brändström myth celebrated not only the Swedish nurse's enormous philanthropic work during and after the war, but also her adherence to what seemed to be traditional, nonthreatening forms of benevolence.

Prisoners of war are by definition "in the power of the hostile government."[7] The home state usually has no direct contact with its captive soldiers and can rely only on indirect means to assist them. One way in which a home state can make an impact on the well-being of prisoners is by forging agreements with the enemy government on the distribution of relief. This option requires a shift in the perception of war from something which would be resolved quickly to a longer affair, in which imminent repatriation of prisoners is unlikely; it also requires that both belligerent governments see moral and political value in such an agreement; and it requires that neutral governments and benevolent institutions (most often the Red Cross) become involved as intermediaries and facilitators.[8]

In Austria-Hungary's case, the recognition that the end of the war was nowhere in sight came during the winter of 1914–1915 after four months of failed combat against Serbia and Russia.[9] The realization that the war was there to stay had been accompanied in the Austro-Hungarian War Ministry by an awareness that all was not well with its POWs in Russia. Whereas during the first few months of the war POWs generally expressed content with their treatment and living conditions in captivity, a noticeable deterioration began taking place in the winter of 1914–1915.[10] Typhus and cholera outbreaks were reported in a few camps and prisoners wrote home about extreme overcrowding and lack of sufficient clothing.[11] Soldiers who went to war in their summer uniforms found themselves suddenly dealing with a Russian winter without appropriate apparel. According to Brändström, in the beginning of 1915 few prisoners had overcoats,

60 percent of them had worn-out shoes, and twenty percent had no shoes whatsoever, requiring them to wrap "their feet in straw and rags."[12]

The grievances of Austro-Hungarian and German POWs in Russia and similar complaints of Russian POWs in Austria-Hungary and Germany expedited discussions of a proposal for POW relief, which had been sitting on the desks of the respective foreign ministries since September 1914.[13] According to the proposal, material aid from the home country would be distributed among its captive soldiers, and Red Cross delegations would be permitted to inspect POW camps in Russia, Germany, and Austria-Hungary. The delegations would be permitted to talk directly to prisoners and allowed to distribute money, clothing, and food according to their judgment.[14]

What makes the relief action on the eastern front unique in twentieth-century warfare was the inclusion of Red Cross nurses from the home country in the inspection teams. Historian Reinhard Nachtigal argued that only the "old-European, aristocratic solidarity which linked three warring empires" could have enabled such a POW relief effort, and indeed all the nurses sent by the home states were upper-class women from some of the most prominent families of the three monarchies.[15] The decision to send aristocratic women to distribute relief was rooted in nineteenth-century social thinking about the role of upper-class and upper-middle-class women in charitable endeavors. As Roger Chickering argued with regards to Germany, these women were the anchors of "many charitable organizations, whose local networks comprised women's clubs of assorted confessional and political colorations."[16] Before World War I affluent women fulfilled many of the functions later assumed by the welfare state.[17] In fact, the coming of total war in 1914 exponentially increased the demand for these volunteers and allotted them, at least temporarily, greater responsibilities and powers. On account of their status, available time, connections, and political reliability these upper-class women were now entrusted also with official duties formerly reserved to men. As a rule these duties were linked with provision of succor (broadly defined) and understood as a stopgap measure for the duration of the war. Inspired by patriotism, a sense of class duty, and the wish to combat the social ravages of total warfare, these women now performed on two distinct planes: they undertook various tasks according to specific needs, while simultaneously assuming a role of substitute mothers and sisters, mending the torn fabric of society.

From the perspective of interned soldiers, the Red Cross nurse "was a piece of the *Heimat*, a representative of his far-off mother."[18] Yet, as the Austro-Hungarian superintendent for POW affairs Heinrich von Raabl-Werner made clear, these nurses were expected to do more than just embody the maternal side of a patriarchal regime:

> They [Austro-Hungarian nurses] were expected to provide concrete suggestions for improvement . . . negotiate directly with the authorities . . . defeat strong prejudices which gained a foothold [among the prisoners] through systematic agitation! In ad-

dition to strengthening the spiritual constitution of the prisoners and intensifying their connection to the homeland through visitations and distribution.[19]

As agents of their state these upper-class women were expected to accomplish a great deal. Most of them left detailed accounts of their struggles to do so, the most moving of which is perhaps Nora Kinsky's *Russian Diary* published posthumously in 1976.[20] Although different in tone and emphasis, the Austro-Hungarian delegates pointed out repeatedly that their ability to fulfill their complex duties rested to a large extent on the material means at their disposal. Therefore, it is necessary to say a few general words about the Austro-Hungarian POW relief effort.

From the perspective of the Austro-Hungarian War Ministry there were two distinct components to the POW relief program. The first focused on material relief and was aimed at relieving the most acute shortages in clothing and medication. The second centered on a series of visitations and was geared toward boosting morale, reporting and correcting ill-treatment, reviewing living conditions, and assessing the Habsburg loyalty of the Austro-Hungarian POWs in Russia. While the first component was handled primarily by the Swedish Red Cross Society and to a lesser extent by a number of other intermediaries—the American YMCA, the Danish Red Cross and the Relief Committee for Military and Civilian Prisoners in Tientsin (today Tianjin), China (*Hilfsaktion für Kriegs-und Zivilgefangene in Tientsin*)—the second component was entrusted primarily to nurses from Austria-Hungary under the umbrella organization of the Danish Red Cross.[21] It is crucial to remember, however, that although Austro-Hungarian War Ministry officials differentiated between "material relief" and "visitations," the prisoners themselves usually did not. Austro-Hungarian POWs expressed amazement at times that "their" nurses could come all the way from Austria-Hungary and bring them very little or no material relief at all.[22]

In terms of actual material support, the Austro-Hungarian relief effort fell well short of the needs of its prisoners, although in absolute numbers it was not insignificant. Between October 1915 and March 1918, the Dual Monarchy dispatched via Sweden 43 trains (each of 28 cars) carrying a total of 375,000 uniforms, 1,195,000 pairs of underwear, 300,000 blankets, 150,000 pairs of boots, and 5,000 Red Cross packets.[23] In addition, between 1915 and 1918 Austria-Hungary sent medicinal supplies worth 8 million Austrian crowns to Russia and food worth almost 15 million Austrian crowns. Altogether, the official aid sent directly from the Dual Monarchy to its POWs was worth 85.5 million crowns or roughly 42 crowns per prisoner.[24] Heinrich von Raabl-Werner emphasized after the war that "only a person who takes into consideration the terrible clothing shortages at home could truly appreciate the difficulties of organizing such an effort; it is alone justified by the fact that it saved thousands from the Russian death."[25]

Nevertheless, the k.u.k. POW relief effort was still relatively parsimonious. According to Holger Herwig, already during the first year and a half of the war Austria-Hungary spent an estimated 20–22 billion crowns on financing its military endeavor, which makes the sum of eight million crowns in three years for POW medication shockingly small.[26] The funds assigned for POW relief were just a drop in the ocean in the context of wartime expenditures, especially when considering that a sizable portion of the young Austro-Hungarian male population found itself in captivity. The inadequacy of the Austro-Hungarian relief was highlighted by Germany's much more generous relief effort. Germany provided 4.4 times more per capita than the Habsburg Monarchy provided. Moreover, German citizens sent more money to their POWs in Russia than k.u.k. citizens (15 vs. 8 million) and purchased more Red Cross parcels in Denmark; altogether, German citizens bought more than 100,000 standard Red Cross parcels for German POWs in Russia compared to a paltry 5,000 parcels purchased by Austro-Hungarian citizens. Johann von der Wülbecke, a German noncommissioned officer (NCO) in the east Siberian POW camp of Berezovka, reported that the discrepancy in the number of parcels created "ugly confrontations," with the Austro-Hungarian POWs demanding an equal share.[27] Thus, the material relief coming from Germany created two standards of care among prisoners of war in Russia: a modest Austro-Hungarian one and a relatively generous German one. It indicated both symbolically and practically that Germany cared more about its soldiers in captivity than the Habsburg Monarchy did.

Relief distribution in Russia was hampered also by serious logistical difficulties. The Swedish Red Cross, which handled most of the on-the-spot relief distribution, was significantly understaffed. There were never more than forty-eight Swedish Red Cross delegates in Russia at any given time, dealing with all aspects of relief administration for both Austro-Hungarian and German POWs. Altogether, between the years 1915 and 1920, seventy-seven different Swedish Red Cross officials were involved in relief apportioning, led by Brändström.

The Swedish Red Cross gained more recognition from POWs than any other relief agency. Although understaffed, it appeared ubiquitous and steadfastly present in Russia throughout World War I. Brändström, in particular, became "a symbol of sisterly love, noble humanity and self-sacrifice and willingness to help."[28] The unthreatening nature of Brändström's mission (she was a neutral delegate, not an official from the home country); her focus on archetypal "maternal" activities such as clothing, feeding, and healing; and her unwavering commitment to assisting POWs during and after the war all lent themselves to mythologizing. The sense of fragility and impotence felt by many of the prisoners, especially the officers, translated into the depiction of Brändström as a saint and a protective goddess. In the tellingly titled book "Violated Men" (*Vergewaltigte Menschen*), published in 1926 under the auspices of the Austrian Federal Association of Former POWs (*Bundesvereinigung der ehemaligen österreichischen Kriegsgefangen*-B.e.öK), Brändström appeared as a Nordic warrior goddess combating a host of demonic creatures that threaten a chained and prostrate prisoner (see fig. 2.1).[29] Her right arm extended in a soothing gesture over the head of the prisoner, Brändström resolutely holds the Swedish shield in her left arm and pushes the demons away. Noticeably she was depicted without a sword or any other offensive weapon.

Figure 2.1. Brändström as a Nordic Warrior Goddess. Source: J. Kowalewski, et al., *Vergewaltigte Menschen. Blätter aus dem Felde und der Kriegsgefangenschaft* (Vienna: Reisser, 1926), 336.

Figure 2.2. Brändström as an Angel Tending to POWs. Source: J. Kowalewski, et al., *Vergewaltigte Menschen. Blätter aus dem Felde und der Kriegsgefangenschaft* (Vienna: Reisser, 1926), 336.

Another painting—accompanied by a laudatory poem—compared Brändström to rays of sun that illuminated the darkness of captivity (see fig. 2.2). In an infirmary barrack packed with decrepit and despondent prisoners, Brändström is portrayed as bringing assistance and hope. The wounded prisoners, crippled and in rags, attempt to reach the Swedish nurse and touch her. She appears not to be afraid to grasp an ailing POW with her left hand, although her gaze is directed at the viewer of the painting and not at the prisoners. She is thus represented as an important part of the narrative, yet in a certain way also outside of it. Her extended hand invites the viewer in, a bridge between those at home and the POWs. The caption underneath the scene inquires whether "the sun is finally coming into our lives?" and an accompanying poem commemorates Brändström as morning light which follows a dark night. During the early 1920s Brändström was considered a leading candidate for a Nobel Peace prize. Today largely forgotten, Brändström still awaits the first scholarly treatment of her life and work and an attempt to disentangle myth from reality.

Alongside the Swedish Red Cross, material relief reached the prisoners in Russia via two additional channels: the American YMCA and Elsa von Hanneken's Relief Committee. Von Hanneken's Relief Committee was an impromptu benevolent society, which grew in size and importance during the war. Established originally in October 1914 by German and Austro-Hungarian residents of Tientsin, the committee relied on von Hanneken's extensive connections among the colonial forces in China and obtained the official backing of the

American Red Cross society. While relying initially on privately raised funds, in the spring of 1915 the Tientsin committee became a conduit through which Germany and Austria-Hungary channeled relief funds. All in all Germany sent money in the value of 1,716,800 Swedish crowns to Tientsin, while Austria-Hungary transferred funds worth 3,527,000 Swedish crowns. The fact that both states were willing to allocate sizable sums to what was basically a private initiative in far-away China attests to the degree class and gender permeated wartime philanthropy.

The Relief Committee had the credentials of a serious and trustworthy endeavor first and foremost because it was led by an upper-class woman wielding influence and authority, though not in an official capacity. Von Hanneken managed to organize a group of sixty German and Austro-Hungarian volunteers—all "work-happy Ladies and Gentlemen," in her words—and created a remarkably efficient organization.[30] The Relief Committee purchased clothing, food, and medications, and supported hundreds of thousands of prisoners in eastern Siberia and the Russian pacific maritime region. The "odd Chinese clothes" the Relief Committee sent to Russia became the butt of many jokes among the POWs, but in three and a half years of activity the organization managed to forward an estimated 180,000 of these funny uniforms. The Tientsin Committee's ability to be so effective rested in the final analysis on the readiness of the Russian authorities to view it as a benevolent organization and not as an operation run by enemy subjects. Von Hanneken made clear that she received Russian support both before and after the revolution.[31] The Russian postal service hired additional employees to staff its Tientsin branch and took great pains to ensure that virtually all money transfers arrived safely in POW camps. The achievements of POW relief agencies—like von Hanneken's Relief Committee—depended on their ability to present themselves as vital yet nonthreatening, and to generate an atmosphere of trust and good will. Having upper-class women at the forefront of these efforts became an important factor of their success.

The mission of the Swedish Red Cross and other charitable organizations was complex in terms of logistics yet simple in terms of its goals. Their task was first and foremost to alleviate the physical and mental suffering of captivity. The mission of the Austro-Hungarian nurses was not as logistically challenging but was much more complex in terms of its goals. The Austro-Hungarian nurses were expected to inspect camps, usually in a day or less for each camp, press local Russian military authorities to rectify the most urgent problems, distribute money and tobacco, assess the POWs' Habsburg loyalty, and boost morale. As if this were not enough, these nurses were counted on to symbolize monarchical care by virtue of their upper-class background and their gender. They were thus expected to be exceptional in their personal abilities and qualities, and to know how and when to use their patrician background and femininity.

The first round of visitations began in the fall of 1915 and included three German and three Austro-Hungarian nurses. The three German delegates—Countess Alexandrine Uexküll, Erika von Passow, and Magdalene von Walsleben—had arrived in Russia already in October 1915, almost two months before their colleagues from the Dual Monarchy. The Austro-Hungarian delegation had to wait until the final ratification of the visitation agreement by Russia and the Habsburg Monarchy and left Vienna for Russia only on 10 November 1915. According to the official criteria formulated by the k.u.k. War Ministry, each delegate had to possess four principal qualifications: first, she had to be a nurse; second, she had to be able to converse in a few of the Monarchy's languages in addition to German and French; third, she had to be impeccably loyal to the Habsburg state, which meant being either of an aristocratic background or married to a career officer (in 1916 a qualification was added stating that delegates could not be married, meaning they could not be wives of career officers); finally, she was prohibited from having relatives in Russian captivity (a qualification added in 1916).[32]

The preference for upper-class women undoubtedly reflected the overwhelming predominance of the nobility in diplomatic assignments throughout Europe. In this sense, upper-class women were perceived not only as unquestionably loyal, but also as the most likely to possess the necessary educational and social skills to handle such a delicate mission. Still, the fact that the War Ministry preferred the nurses to be as unattached as possible—i.e., unmarried and without relatives in captivity—hints that these envoys were not expected to be able to juggle personal and official commitments very well. Yet, if one examines the background of the Austro-Hungarian delegates, it is clear they were chosen *because* of personal connections and not because they perfectly matched official qualifications. Countess Anna Revertera, who headed the k.u.k. delegation, was selected because of her extensive network of Russian acquaintances; her mother was a Russian princess from the Buturlin family and her father served in the Austrian legation in St. Petersburg. Ilona von Rosty (born Countess Forgách) lobbied to be included in the delegation because her son was a POW officer in the camp of Krasnoyarsk. She was thus added as a representative of the Hungarian Red Cross and by extension of the Hungarian half of the monarchy. The only member of the delegation who actually possessed some experience as a nurse was Käthe von Mihalotzy, who had worked in the Vienna Radetzky Military Hospital since the beginning of the war. According to von Mihalotzy, she was also told by the head of the Austrian Red Cross Society, Baron Spiegelfeld, that "it was highly desirable that one of the three ladies selected for this mission would be an officer's wife."[33] Still, traveling to Russia for an extended period raised a dilemma for von Mihalotzy: with her colonel husband stationed at the front, she had to leave her daughters in Vienna for three months. After much deliberation she decided to take this assignment as "a great work of compassion."[34]

Before leaving for Russia the delegation was briefed by Austro-Hungarian Red Cross and War Ministry officials. Anna Revertera wrote a few years after the war that "the information supplied before the departure . . . proved to be inadequate."[35] The briefing included an introduction to the three Danish officers who would accompany the nurses during their sojourn in Russia, a review of international law pertaining to the treatment of POWs, a brief synopsis of what was known about conditions in Russian POW camps, and a visit to a few POW camps in Austria-Hungary to see how Russian prisoners were treated.[36] While the delegation was making its preparations to leave, reports appeared in newspapers regarding the trip, and the three women were swarmed by relatives of POWs, who presented them with letters and money to take to their loved ones in Russia. According to von Mihalotzy, "the many letters that we were expected to take, but which according to our instructions we were forced to decline, would have required a whole wagon."[37] Von Mihalotzy's poignant portrayal encapsulates the tensions embedded in the mission from its inception between the expectations and anguish of the prisoners and their families and the good will, limitations, and weighty burden felt by the three hastily trained delegates.

On 10 November 1915 the delegation took the train from Vienna to Berlin. There they were updated about the activities of the three German nurses who were already in Russia and heard a lecture about the dietary needs of the prisoners. News of their stay in Berlin circulated again among the families of POWs, and once more they were inundated with requests to take letters and money to Russia.[38] From Berlin they traveled to Denmark, where they had an audience with the Danish queen and meetings with the Austro-Hungarian ambassador and his staff, and with Danish Red Cross officials. Revertera, von Mihalotzy, and von Rosty continued their journey via Sweden and Russian Finland to Petrograd, where they arrived in the last week of November 1915.

In Petrograd the delegation was delayed a week and half due to last-minute disagreements between Russia and Austria-Hungary. The two most important points of contention were whether before leaving Petrograd the delegations would have to submit a binding list of all the camps they intended to visit and whether the Austro-Hungarian nurses could themselves determine who would go to which part of Russia.[39] Anna Revertera described "tempestuous meetings" with Russian officials and intense behind-the-scenes negotiations needed to iron out these disagreements. The compromise reached at the beginning of December allowed the Austro-Hungarian delegations "to visit all camps without having to submit preapproved routes."[40] As Revertera correctly pointed out, this leeway enabled the delegations to put camp commanders on their toes and could not have been achieved without having powerful people "in the court, society and military authorities on our side."[41] However, the Austro-Hungarian delegations were less successful in deciding their own areas of inspection and had to accept the Russian allocation; von Rosty was assigned to the Moscow and Kazan military districts and also received the huge Siberian camp of Krasnoyarsk, where her son was interned; von Mihalotzy was assigned the Turkestan military district and the large European camps in the Samara-Orenburg region; and Revertera received the gigantic area of western and central Siberia (except the camp of Krasnoyarsk) and was expected to inspect it within eight weeks.

All three nurses placed their main emphasis on reporting unsatisfactory material conditions in internment facilities. Due to extreme hurry they usually relied on the POW medical personnel to give them accurate descriptions and "to disregard strenuous efforts [of Russian camp personnel] to throw dust in the eyes of the visitors."[42] When a comprehensive medical report could not be provided, the delegates organized their own inspection procedures, which placed them in unaccustomed power relationships. Upon visiting the rank-and-file camp in Kazalinsk, von Mihalotzy instructed the men to stand in military formation so she could inspect the condition of their shoes and clothing. The prisoner in charge shouted an "attention" order, which made von Mihalotzy "feel at first embarrassed."[43] "I reminded myself," she wrote, "of a female general, but got quickly used to this idea, like so many other things in this not-so-easy assignment."[44] The fact that she could assume military authority, and even more remarkably, in her mind, be acknowledged as possessing such authority by the men, struck her as exceptional and worth reporting. No less revealing perhaps was her self-characterization as a "female general," especially when one takes in consideration that her husband, a career officer, was "merely" a colonel. This mission made her feel unusually empowered, despite her initial sense of transgression.

As had the Swedish and American inspectors before them, the delegates censured locations with deficient lodgings, inferior food, and unfair wage practices for working POWs. Accompanied by Danish and Russian officers, the nurses attempted to rectify some of the most grievous problems. In Totskoe, the Russian camp with the worst prisoner mortality, von Mihalotzy's delegation bought clothing and blankets to alleviate the terrible shortages and purchased crates of medical supplies from a local veterinarian.[45] The impression some camps left on the nurses was devastating. Revertera felt revolted by the underground earth barracks prevalent in central Siberia and dreaded the physical and psychological impact they had on the prisoners. Von Mihalotzy stated that "if I lived three lifetimes, I would still not forget the impressions [from Totskoe]."[46] The profound sense of shock echoes the jolt felt by many POW officers upon seeing how some of the rank and file lived in captivity. Officer Ladislaus Baczy, for example, wrote to a Hungarian member of parliament: "their condition is simply indescribable. They are covered with filth, water constantly drips from above and the whole crowd is infected with typhus."[47] The shock expressed by the nurses thus had less to do with their gender and more with their class position and advantaged background. Coming in direct contact with large-scale misery, as existed in some rank-and-file camps during World War I, deeply affected visitors whose daily life had usually been sheltered from such experiences.

According to the nurses, the Austro-Hungarian POWs always responded positively to their efforts to pull strings to amend shortcomings. Von Raabl-Werner thought that Revertera was especially adept in utilizing her personal connections to that purpose, including direct access to the governor of Siberia and to the head of administration at the General Staff (*Glavnoe Upravlenie General'nogo Shtaba*), General Mikhail Beliaev.[48] However, the other goals of the mission proved to be more difficult for the delegates, particularly the distribution of money and "charitable gifts" (*Liebesgaben*). The nurses brought with them approximately 4.5 million Austrian crowns (about 1.8 million Romanov rubles) for the purpose of on-the-spot allocation.[49] The Austro-Hungarian War

Ministry preferred that money not be given to individual POWs but rather be allocated for communal projects in each camp. If it was distributed individually, officer POWs were to receive 30 to 50 rubles as a loan (to be paid back by their families in Austria-Hungary), while the rank and file were to receive 3 to 5 rubles as gifts. Each nurse could determine whether to treat ensigns, cadets, one-year volunteers, and NCOs as separate groups deserving special consideration or as officers and rank and file.

The question of how this small pecuniary pie was divided became one of the thorniest and most aggravating issues for the prisoners. To exacerbate the dilemmas of distribution even further, the nurses ran out of money in the middle of their trips. The dreadful conditions in Totskoe made a dent in von Mihalotzy's budget, and inaccurate information about the POW camp of Troitskii-Tashkent caused her to bring Christmas gifts (tobacco and soap) for 600 instead of 16,000 men.[50] Since bestowing gifts was a vital way to demonstrate the care and commitment of the home state, the nurses had to face POW resentment in many cases.[51]

Each of the nurses interpreted the problematic issue of POWs' loyalty quite differently. When she had time and permission, von Mihalotzy attempted to strengthen the emotional link between POWs and their home state through public meetings, sing-alongs, and religious ceremonies. Taking advantage of a sentimental atmosphere in the days prior to Christmas, she seems to have cultivated a sense of homesickness among the prisoners. On 5 December 1915 she celebrated dinner and "Nikolo" (St. Nicholas' Day) with a group of officers in the camp of Kuznetsk. In Perovsk she sat down with a group of Hungarian officers, who had been captured in Przemyśl, listening to violin music and singing folk songs. "When we left," she reported, "we were accompanied by boisterous *eljen* calls and the tunes of the Rakoczy March."[52] On 24 December 1915 the delegation visited all three camps in the city of Tashkent, bringing with them a Christmas tree: "We went from camp to camp; everywhere they waited for us to light up candles. It was touching to see, and from the addresses to hear, the joy it brought these poor people, to see a nurse from the homeland in their midst." In the officers' camp she heard recitals of a string quartet and the "so-called Bukhara vocal quartet."[53]

From her account it seems she felt more comfortable with POW officers, related to them better and lavished on them more time and attention than on the rank-and-file prisoners. It is unknown how the rest of the von Mihalotzy mission would have proceeded; on that same night she came down with symptoms of typhus and was hospitalized in the private lodgings of a Russian general. According to von Mihalotzy two well-known Austrian POW physicians and three Russian doctors treated her devotedly. She was strong enough to leave Tashkent in the beginning of February and was surprised with a parting concert. In her absence, the Danish officer Captain Fritz Cramer conducted the inspection of other Central Asian camps.

In contrast to von Mihalotzy, Revertera adopted a more confrontational approach to the issue of Habsburg loyalty. From her first stop in Perm on 10 December 1915 she noted the places where she found signs of disloyal or "Russophile" attitude, especially among officers: "A number of officers [in Perm] lived in a big building in the middle of the city, loyal officers beside Russophiles. A terrible, passionate and stormy conflict raged in the minds of everyone: on the one hand wounded fatherland love and on the other open treason."[54] Revertera does not specify why she considered some of the officers traitors, but she did collect names, which infused her mission with considerable tension.[55] It is not clear whether she had been officially asked to do so, but in a letter to the head of the Austrian Red Cross, Baron Spiegelfeld, she wrote that "a number of soldiers requested that their loyalty be registered in Vienna: Serbs, Czechs, Italians etc."[56] Evidently, her presence induced prisoners from "suspect" nationalities to make sure she reported their loyalty to the state.[57] In Irbit on 16 December she encountered open hostility to her visit from officers and rank and file alike: "Despairing, I left that place with what was for me still a strange feeling of indescribable shame and disgrace that came from the ranks of these derelicts of duty [*Pflichtvergessenen*]."[58]

As was common among Austro-Hungarian officials in Vienna, Revertera constructed a hierarchy of loyalty among various Habsburg nationalities. Using the Russian authorities' treatment as an indicator, she placed the Austro-Germans and Magyars at the top of the ladder and Czechs at the bottom:

> [The Russian authorities'] hand weighs heavily on the brave, patriotic Austro-Germans and passionately patriotic Magyars. The Czechs, who as Slavs are easily won over by anti-Austrian propaganda, are consequently also the unmistakable darlings of the Russians. They enjoy all privileges as soon as they go over, the easiest work and the warmest fire are always reserved to them, whereas their loyal [*kaisertreuen*] comrades hunger and freeze. The Poles, owing to their political situation as a connecting link between all belligerents, have their own special position in captivity. They find brothers among Russian soldiers and among the commandants of the same race. The Bosniaks, Croats and other Slavic men fight alongside their Austrian and Hungarian comrades, and share freely in their misery rather than partake in the advantages of deserters. Often they request me with touching simplicity to take from them the name "Slavs," the source of shame in their lives. . . . Shortly before my departure [from Tomsk] I saw some of the Slavic rank and file doing their schoolwork, learning German. . . . in their childish, clumsy handwriting, I saw the most precious autograph of the Austro-Hungarian fatherland.[59]

Revertera's loyalty rankings had little to do with the prisoners' actions and thoughts, and more with who they were and how the Russians treated them. Her perception of what a loyal Slav is—one who wants to shed his Slavic identity—was firmly rooted in late nineteenth-century colonialist and racist discourses, which idolized the simple, childlike, and loyal "natives." Her conflation of German *Kultur* with Austro-Hungarian patriotism left very little room for other forms of dynastic patriotism.

Ironically, her own account of conversations with prisoners suggests that many POWs were indeed attached to the person of Francis Joseph. She reported several cases of Slavic POWs expressing their love of the emperor in places she considered "Russian propaganda camps" (Irbit and Tiumen).[60] In Petropavlovsk she was approached by three Czech NCOs who asked in the name of other Czech POWs why she took a greater interest in the fate of non-Slav prisoners. She replied that all prisoners were dear to her, that she herself was half Russian, and that Francis Joseph cared for POWs regardless of nationality: "Upon hearing this [the Czech rank and file] were deeply touched; the greetings of their old emperor were received with tears and joyful outbursts."[61]

Using her excellent personal contacts in Russia, Revertera managed to extend her stay to five months instead of the prearranged eight weeks. She was thus able to visit more Siberian camps than originally planned, returning to Petrograd only on 5 May 1916. Upon returning to Vienna in June, she was informed that Francis Joseph would like to see her immediately. Arriving in Schönbrunn in the midst of the Brusilov offensive catastrophe, Revertera expected to see a broken old man. However, she found Francis Joseph in sharp wits, and he questioned her attentively about the condition of the prisoners in Russia, complaining that he never seemed to get straight answers from bureaucrats. He was particularly interested in the condition of his officers in captivity. Revertera informed him that officers would be able to enjoy walks outside camp if he would allow them to give their word of honor not to escape, but Francis Joseph thought that to give one's word of honor to the enemy "was unmilitary . . . and contrary to the Austrian tradition."[62] The issue that was most on his mind was the loyalty of the officers: "Is it true," he asked according to Revertera, "that a few of my officers are fighting against me?" She answered briefly in the affirmative, "without giving names and details. Every word burnt my lips. . . . and he cried with the unspeakable tears of old age. The tears flowed over the wrinkled cheeks and could not be stopped. They poured with mightier strength as I told him about the heroism of the faithful, their misery in Siberian prisons and their never failing loyalty."[63]

The moving finale in Schönbrunn encapsulated in many ways the entire mission. The emotional and almost personal sense of attachment to the officers was punctuated by concerns regarding their loyalty and honorable behavior. Revertera and the Emperor were apparently less concerned with the fate of the rank and file, who constituted the vast majority of the POWs and truly experienced dreadful living conditions.[64] In Revertera's narrative Francis Joseph comes across as a premodern sovereign deeply distressed about the fate of his captured warriors, rather than a head of state who had sent millions of his citizens to fight and eventually be captured by the enemy. Arguably, it was exactly this premodern sense of attachment to the army and its officers that enabled this unique visitation program on the part of the three conservative monarchies in the first place, and it was the notion of the Emperor as a caring paterfamilias, which led to the dispatch of upper-class women as symbols and messengers of monarchical care.

However, it was the same class-imbued spirit that brought some of the nurses, especially Revertera, into clashes with the prisoners. Revertera's account of her stay in Russia emphasized power, connections, and control rather than care and nurturing. Of all of the Austro-Hungarian nurses she deviated the most from the traditional image of a merciful nurse and acknowledged considerable pride in confronting Russian officials and camp personnel. She behaved as the high-ranking official representative she undoubtedly was and faced POW ill will as a consequence.

The first round of visits was considered a success.[65] The Austro-Hungarian and German nurses visited altogether 123 camps, which contained according to official count 272,919 Austro-Hungarians and 47,953 Germans.[66] At the request of the Russian Empress-Mother, the Red Cross societies of the three belligerents proceeded to negotiate a second round of visitations, which was to begin in April 1916 and include six nurses from each country.[67] However, the sinking of the Russian hospital ship *Portugal* by a German submarine in the Black Sea led to a suspension of the negotiations. The Russian demand for a formal apology for the 115 people killed had been accepted by Austria-Hungary but not by Germany, resulting in a suspension of visits until July 1916. Only after the intercession of Prince Carl of Sweden did the Russian government agree to allow a second round of visitations.

The Austro-Hungarian nurses sent to Russia during the second tour were all new faces. Although Revertera's reappointment was at first approved by the Austro-Hungarian War Ministry, the overwhelmingly negative feedback to her mission from POWs resulted in her removal.[68] As with the first round of visits, the women chosen came from prominent backgrounds: the doyenne of the second round, Princess Kunigunde von Croy-Dülmen, was related to the Russian Benckendorffs, and her cousin Count Alexander von Benckendorff served as the Russian ambassador in London. Like Revertera, she was expected to use her extensive Russian contacts to cut through red tape. Two additional members of the Habsburg aristocracy were the Hungarian countess Pauline von Stubenberg-Palffy and her Bohemian niece, Countess Nora Kinsky. Although chosen already in March 1916 on account of her language skills and work among wounded Austro-Hungarian soldiers, the twenty-six-year-old Kinsky became involved even more deeply in the fate of the prisoners when her brother Zdenko and her fiancé, Count Ferdinand Wilczek, were captured during the Brusilov offensive in June 1916.[69]

Alongside von Croy-Dülmen, von Stubenberg-Palffy, and Kinsky, two additional nurses were added as representatives of the Hungarian Red Cross Society: Countess Magda Cebrian and Sister Andorine von Huszár. In comparison to the first tour, the nurses received relatively smaller areas to cover; von Croy-Dülmen was assigned the Moscow-Yaroslavl-Tver areas and a few large camps along the Trans-Siberian line (Omsk, Tomsk Novo-Nikolaevsk); von Stubenberg-Palffy received the problematic Ufa, Kazan, and Orenburg regions; Kinsky was allotted eastern Siberia; and the two Hungarian nurses, Cebrian and von Huszár, divided between them respectively west and central Siberia (except those camps allocated to von Croy-Dülmen).

Leaving Austria-Hungary in late June 1916, the nurses traveled again via Berlin and Stockholm, arriving in Petrograd on 7 July 1916.[70] Like their predecessors, they were bogged down in the Russian capital due to disagreements on routes and jurisdictions, and once again the time was used for an extensive briefing by Swedish, Danish, and American officials. Their stay was also utilized to spark old contacts with Russian dignitaries and visit the Russian Tsarina in Tsarkoe Selo on July 27. The Empress and her daughter Grand Duchess Olga received the two delegations separately (first the German and then the Austro-Hungarian), wearing nurses' uniforms.[71] Kinsky commented briefly in her diary about "how sad Her Majesty appeared," but was nonetheless impressed by the magnificence of the palace gardens. The visit apparently did result in a telegram from the empress to her protégé Prime Minister Stürmer, urging him to let the nurses finally leave Petrograd. It was precisely their gender and aristocratic background that enabled these nurses to seek the patronage of key figures in the Russian regime and obtain authorizations that might not have been granted to women from humbler backgrounds. Likewise, men of the same station could not have been engaged during wartime in a similar dialogue with the Russian political and military elite without appearing "unpatriotic." The combination of class and gender made this relief mission possible, despite its many limitations.

In certain respects the second mission's task was easier. The dreadful shortages in clothing and medications had already been partly relieved before their arrival, and the most severe outbreaks of typhus and other epidemics were luckily behind them. Moreover, the Austro-Hungarian nurses brought more money and medical equipment than their predecessors. This time they came with 15.5 million Austrian crowns for distribution as personal gifts, loans, and collective projects, as well as six truckloads of medical supplies.[72] The delegations began departing gradually from Petrograd in early August 1916, but four of the nurses—two German and two Austro-Hungarian—had to wait until early September for their final authorizations.

In the meantime they were granted permission to inspect hospitals and internment facilities in the Petrograd area and obtained a first glimpse of the task in hand. Kinsky, one of the Austro-Hungarian nurses left in the capital, wrote in her diary of her excitement about starting her mission and the "thrill to see finally our compatriots!"[73] On 13 August 1916 she met 125 wounded and sick POWs in hospital 108 in Petrograd: "A Rumanian Honvéd captain was moved to tears because he could speak Rumanian with me, he could not speak a word in any other language."[74] The fact that Kinsky spoke nine different languages fluently—an astonishing number even for the traditionally polyglot Habsburg aristocracy—enabled her to approach prisoners in their mother tongues and reach them on a more personal level.[75] She thought that even when she criticized prisoners they did not react badly to her words because they had been expressed in their mother language. As a Bohemian aristocrat, Kinsky made an extra effort to connect with Czech-speaking prisoners—who otherwise had been regarded with considerable suspicion by Revertera and the k.u.k. War Ministry—and had not once throughout her inspection tour labeled them as "disloyal."

On 5 September 1916, Kinsky and von Huszár finally left Petrograd, the last nurses to do so. Kinsky, who had been assigned east Siberia and the Russian Pacific maritime region (*Primorskaia*), took with her fifty tightly handwritten pages about her mission along with her diary, in which she scrupulously documented her actions and impressions. Writing primarily in French, Kinsky also composed certain sections of her diary in Czech, German, and Hungarian in an attempt to confuse Russian agents and accidental snoops.

From the beginning of her journey Kinsky did not encounter the same grievous conditions her predecessors discovered in some POW camps. Although she was often critical of medical facilities and Russian disciplinary procedures, she nonetheless considered many of the camps decent and unproblematic. One does not find in her account any camp even remotely approximating von Mihalotzy's and Revertera's respective descriptions of Totskoe and Yekaterinburg. What bothered Kinsky most was the lack of discipline she perceived among all ranks of Austro-Hungarian POWs, and the apparent sloth and demoralization among officers:

> We passed the day with the officers in Skotovo. Neither order nor discipline. That is sad. The camp is not far from the [Pacific] ocean, the view is pretty, but the barracks are too small and there is not enough room for the officers. . . . I have found the moral condition of the officers much worse than that of the rank and file. It is quite understandable that they suffer more in captivity than the rank and file. The scarcity of work is terrible for them.[76]

The next day she visited both the officer and rank-and-file camp in Rasdolnoe, "finding many 'intellectuals' extremely stupid and without any discipline to speak of."[77] Four days later the delegation visited the camp of Spasskoe, where she discovered to her dismay that one-year volunteers and intellectuals were given separate quarters by the commandant: "They were unpleasantly surprised when I did not give them more money than regular soldiers."[78] Nonetheless, commented Kinsky, the intellectuals treated her nicely and they all drank miserable coffee together.

Kinsky's insistence on discipline was rooted in her belief that the personal and the mental health of the prisoner, as well as his attachment to the Habsburg Monarchy, depended on retaining as much military structure as possible. The fact that POW officers were exempt from any work under the Hague Convention resulted in her mind in signs of decadence.[79] In many case, she criticized Austro-Hungarian officers as incompetent disciplinarians, especially in comparison to German officers, and thought they had significant problems bridging national lines. In Khabarovsk, Kinsky was mortified to discover that an orchestra from the local POW camp performed in concerts organized on the outside by the Russian Red Cross society. The fact that the concert's proceedings went to support wounded Russian soldiers meant in her mind that Austro-Hungarian POWs were not taking the distinction between friend and foe very seriously.[80] Visiting the camp of Peshchenka [Chita, east Siberia] she commented that "Magyar [POWs] want to Magyarize everybody, which causes problems now and then."[81] She also noticed how Czech POWs kept to themselves, but were always overjoyed, in her view, to meet her and chat in Czech. Kinsky's account displays extraordinary sensitivity to various signs of disintegration among the POW population along rank or national lines or on a personal level. Like Revertera she advocated strict maintenance of hierarchy as a solution, though her attitude to the prisoners was much warmer and less confrontational.

Six weeks into her inspection tour, Kinsky ran out of funds. Money that was supposed to be transferred from Petrograd via telegraph by the Danes did not arrive, and the delegation had to visit camps empty-handed: "So much trouble and effort were made to reach these areas and now nothing can be done to help these unhappy people. This is so stupid. Curse these Danish institutions in Petrograd!"[82] Kinsky's exasperation grew sharper upon encountering logistical problems, bureaucratic annoyances, and unpleasant individuals. Caustic remarks and portrayals increasingly peppered her account; after meeting the Cossack Ataman of the Transbaikalia she commented: "he is a small, black, horrible man; I believe [he is] a completely evil individual."[83] Regarding various Russians who monitored her actions, Kinsky complained: "we are constantly surrounded by spies, male and often also female. These latter are even dumber and more incompetent than their colleagues."[84]

She also found it humiliating that some POWs would rather talk to the Russian member of the delegation, Prince Boris Kochakidze, than, presumably, confide in a woman, and she declined an invitation to dinner with an American delegate because she did not want stories circulating that she ran around with crowds of men.[85] Thus, endemic organizational problems, a growing sense of fatigue, and the various limitations emanating from her gender frustrated Kinsky and contributed to her irritability. Four months into her Russian journey, she did not think it was progressing as well as it should and wrote in her diary: "I do not know what impression I made on the prisoners, but I hope that at least they noted my good will."[86]

The death of Francis Joseph on 21 November 1916 seems to have changed the tone of Kinsky's account. Hearing the news first from the Danish member of the delegation, she refused to believe it until receiving confirmation from home. Kinsky immediately submitted a petition to the Russian governor requesting to hold a requiem for Francis Joseph "with as many POWs as possible." [87] The request was approved on 7 December 1916, and the requiem was held the following day in a big church in the town of Chita: "It was very solemn . . . the soldiers sang somewhat off-key but with enthusiasm."[88]

Following the requiem and approaching the final part of her mission, Kinsky's narrative increasingly shifted to her brother and her fiancé, whom she revealingly called "the brothers," and the chances of seeing them in the camp of Omsk. Relying on her contacts, including an audience with the governor of Siberia, Kinsky was granted permission to be with "the brothers" in Omsk for five emotional days. Consequently, she decided to seek permission to stay in Russia as a simple nurse and be close to the two, wherever they might be interned.[89]

Waiting in Petrograd for authorization, Kinsky experienced firsthand the

March 1917 revolution and the Tsarist regime's downfall. Eating chocolate in her room in the Hotel Regina, she described the noise of cannon and machine-gun fire and evaded a stray bullet that entered through the window. She had a brief confrontation with five drunken revolutionaries who barged into her room, but won them over by her feistiness. Although the Danes wanted her to transfer to the embassy for protection, she returned to her hotel room, noting in her diary that being in Russia was much more interesting than staying at home in Chlumec. On 20 March 1917 Kinsky received the notification that her request had been approved by the Provisional Government and that she could now go to Astrakhan, where her brother and fiancé had been sent. No longer a k.u.k. delegate, Kinsky worked as a nurse in Astrakhan until March 1918, experiencing immense material and health problems while simultaneously describing the revolutionary upheavals from her vantage point in southern Russia.[90]

The Austro-Hungarian POW relief effort officially continued until May 1918. In addition to material relief distributed by the Swedish Red Cross throughout Russia, a permanent Austro-Hungarian delegation was established in August 1917 in Moscow, headed by Andorine von Huszár. However, following the Bolshevik revolution in November 1917, her ability to operate became increasingly limited, and she found herself under arrest following the German Army's advances in the early months of 1918. By then Russia had collapsed into anarchy, the opportunity for visitation and inspection had ceased to exist, and the repatriation of POWs had already begun.

During World War I upper-class women often stood at the forefront of relief organization and distribution. In this sense POW relief was no different from other endeavors such as relief for the poor, refugee relief, or a host of other important causes that needed dedicated champions. Although the contours of the welfare state gradually began to appear during the war, the efforts of numerous women volunteers were still required to tackle the multitude of grave problems created by four years of warfare.

This kind of relief work had much in common with traditional upper-class involvement in charity and philanthropy but was in many cases a great deal more; under the socially acceptable label of "nursing," women such as Elsa Brändström or Anna Revertera were asked to perform complex assignments and were given the official sponsorship of their states. These diplomatic and political missions bestowed on women delegates considerable power and granted them formal and informal authority over millions of men. The fact that they came from aristocratic backgrounds and had access to influential officials strengthened their authority even further. Still, at the end of the day they had to find a way to appear caring, warm, and nurturing, even when this did not suit their personal temperament.

Although appreciated by their government and by top officials at the War Ministry, the Austro-Hungarian nurses received only a lukewarm reception from the prisoners. The fact that the Habsburg Monarchy was not generous in its relief allocations, especially in comparison to Germany, had much to do with this reception. As Kinsky observed, the lack of sufficient funds jeopardized the whole mission.[91] However, this reception had to do also with the tremendous social gulf between POWs and nurses, as well as the supervisory and disciplinary nature of their task. Von Mihalotzy may have been half joking when she wrote that she reminded herself of a "female general," but for many prisoners these women were indeed intimidating figures who could cause great harm. It is therefore no coincidence that, after the war, ex-POWs preferred to honor and remember those women who best fitted the traditional mold of a compassionate and caring nurse.

Notes

1. For a full discussion on the number of Austro-Hungarian POWs, see Alon Rachamimov, "Becoming Prisoners of War," in *POWs and the Great War: Captivity on the Eastern Front* (Oxford: Berg, 2002), 31–66. The figure 2.77 million is from Hans Weiland and Leopold Kern, eds., *In Feindeshand: Die Gefangenschaft im Weltkriege in Einzeldarstellungen*, 2 vols. (Vienna: Bundesvereinigung der ehemaligen österreichischen Kriegsgefangenen, 1931). Statistical appendix at the end of the second volume.

2. Russia also lost a tremendous number of men to captivity. Evgenii Sergeev claims that roughly one of every five Russians mobilized during the war became a prisoner of war: "Russkie voennoplenye v Germanii i Avstro-Vengerii v gody pervoi mirovoi voiny," *Novaia i noveishaia istoriia* 4 (1996): 66.

3. On the link between charity and control, see Deborah Cohen, *The War Come Home: Disabled Veterans in Britain and Germany, 1914–1939* (Berkeley: University of California Press, 2001); John Hutchinson, *Champions of Charity: War and the Rise of the Red Cross* (Boulder, Colo.: Westview Press, 1996).

4. For example, a collection of first-rate essays on World War I from Oxford University Press contained twenty-three contributions from some of the best-known scholars in the field, none of them on POWs and refugees: Hew Strachan, ed., *World War I: A History* (Oxford: Oxford University Press, 1998). Fortunately, this lacuna has gradually been filled in recent years. On refugees, see Marsha L. Rozenblit, *Reconstructing a National Identity: The Jews of Habsburg Austria during World War I* (New York: Oxford University Press, 2001); David Rechter, *The Jews of Vienna and the First World War*, The Littman Library of Jewish Civilization (Oxford: Littman, 2000); Peter Gatrell, *A Whole Empire Walking: Refugees in Russia during World War I* (Bloomington: Indiana University Press, 1999); on POWs see Verena Moritz and Hannes Leidinger, *Gefangenschaft, Revolution und Heimkehr* (Vienna: Böhlau Verlag, 2003); Rachamimov, *POWs and the Great War;* Reinhard Nachtigal, *Die Murmanbahn: Die Verkehrsanbindung eines kriegswichtigen Hafens und das Arbeitspotential der Kriegsgefangenen 1915 bis 1918* (Grunbach: Greiner, 2001). Recent studies on POWs in Russia owe much to the pioneering work of Gerald H. Davis, in particular his groundbreaking essay, "The Life of Prisoners of War in Russia, 1914-1921," in Samuel Williamson and Peter Pastor, eds., *Essays on World War I: Origins and Prisoners of War* (Boulder, Colo.: East European Monographs/War and Society in East Central Europe, 1983), 162–96. Also Gerald H. Davis, "National Red Cross

Societies and the Prisoners of War in Russia, 1914-1918," *Journal of Contemporary History* 28, no. 1 (January 1993): 31-52.

5. The expression is from Käthe von Mihalotzy, "Eine Reise durch Kriegsgefangenenlager in Rußland und Turkestan. Aus dem Tagebuch einer delegierten des österreichischen Roten Kreuzes," in *In Feindeshand*, 2:255.

6. On POW perceptions of the Austro-Hungarian relief effort see Rachamimov, "Imperial Identities and Personal Concerns: The Perspective of the Prisoners," in *POWs and the Great War*, 191-220; and Rachamimov, "Imperial Loyalties and Private Concerns: Nation, Class and State in the Correspondence of Austro-Hungarian POWs in Russia, 1916-1918," *Austrian History Yearbook* 31 (2000): 87-105.

7. Hague Convention IV with Respect to the Laws and Customs of War on Land, ch. II. Article 4. A copy of the POW section of the Hague Convention can be found in Jonathan Vance, ed., *Encyclopedia of Prisoners of War and Internment* (Santa Barbara: ABC Clio, 2000), 362-64.

8. Davis, "National Red Cross Societies," 31-33.

9. Regarding the "mood of 1914" there is still no definitive study on Austria-Hungary comparable to Jean-Jacques Becker's work about France. Still, most historians agree that the failures of 1914 coupled with the growing dependence on Germany shattered the hopes for a short and decisive war. Norman Stone, *The Eastern Front 1914–1917* (New York: Charles Scribner's Sons, 1975); Manfried Rauchensteiner, *Der Tod des Doppeladlers: Österreich-Ungarn und der erste Weltkrieg* (Vienna: Böhlau Verlag, 1993); István Deák, *Beyond Nationalism: A Social and Political History of the Habsburg Officer Corps 1848–1918* (New York: Oxford University Press, 1990).

10. Although postwar memoirs tend to emphasize that both conditions and treatment in captivity were bad from the very beginning, POW letters from the first months of the war paint a very different picture. For an extensive discussion of living conditions in captivity, see Rachamimov, *POWs and the Great War*, chs. 1, 3, 4.

11. According to Elsa Brändström, 4,500 of 8,600 POWs brought to Novo-Nikolaevsk in the winter of 1914-1915 died from typhus and other diseases. See Brändström, *Among Prisoners of War in Russia and Siberia* (London: Hutchinson Publishers, 1929).

12. Ibid., 73.

13. Heinrich Freiherr von Raabl-Werner, "Österreich-Ungarns offizielle Kriegsgefangenenfürsorge," in *In Feindeshand*, 2:324-31.

14. Ibid., 326-27; Magdalene von Walsleben, *Die deutschen Schwestern in Sibirien*, (Berlin: Furche Verlag, 1919), 6; and Alexandrine von Üxküll, *Aus einem Schwesterleben*, 2nd ed. (Stuttgart: Kohlhammer, 1957).

15. Reinhard Nachtigal, "Kriegsgefangene der Habsburgermonarchie in Russland," *Österreich in Geschichte und Literatur* 40, no. 4-5a (July 1996): 255.

16. Roger Chickering, *Imperial Germany and the Great War, 1914–1918* (Cambridge: Cambridge University Press, 1998), 117.

17. On the checkered track of the welfare state, see Cohen, *The War Come Home.*

18. Erwin Jesser, "Käthe von Mihalotzy," in *In Feindeshand*, 2:335.

19. Von Raabl-Werner, "Österreich-Ungarns offizielle Kriegsgefangenenfürsorge," 325-26.

20. Nora Gräfin Kinsky, *Russisches Tagebuch 1916–1918* (Stuttgart: Seewald Verlag, 1976).

21. To a lesser extent it also included independent neutral inspections by delegates of the American State Department and the Swedish Red Cross organization. American

delegates inspected camps in their capacity as official representative of Austria-Hungary and Germany in Russia until April 1917.

22. Rachamimov, "Imperial Indentities and Personal Concerns," in *POWs and the Great War,* 191–220.

23. This is based on Elsa Brändström's data in *Among Prisoners of War,* 173.

24. There is significant discrepancy in the sums Brändström provided in *Among Prisoners of War,* 173–74, and those in his article "Das Rote Kreuz in Rußland" in *In Feindeshand,* 2:286–87. The former lists 85,572,990 Austrian crowns while the latter lists 361,306,300 crowns. Since the latter article also discusses monies sent to cover the costs of neutral delegations, I interpret the discrepancy to mean the difference between net transfers to POWs and total costs of the relief operation as a whole. Thus, according to this calculation, only 23 percent of the funds actually reached the POWs.

25. Von Raabl-Werner, "Österreich-Ungarns offizielle Kriegsgefangenenfürsorge," 326.

26. Figures from Holger Herwig, *The First World War: Germany and Austria-Hungary 1914–1918* (New York: Arnold, 1997), 230–31.

27. Johann von der Wülbecke, "Meine Erlebnisse in russischer Kriegsgefangenschaft," Bundesarchiv Militärarchiv, Freiburg im Breisgau, Msg 200/932, 15–17.

28. Hans Weiland, "Elsa Brändström: Caritas inter arma," in *In Feindeshand,* 2:238.

29. J. Viktor Kowaleski, *Vergewaltigte Menschen: Blätter aus dem Felde und der Kriegsgefangenschaft* (Vienna: Amon Franz Göth Verlag, 1926).

30. Elsa von Hanneken, "Die Tientsiner Hilfsaktion: Eine Hilfsaktion für Kriegs- und Zivilgefangene in Tientsin," in *In Feindeshand,* 2:267. According to Davis, "National Red Cross Societies," 47–48n7, von Hanneken's partial cooperation with the American Red Cross Society ended in acrimony.

31. Von Hanneken, "Die Tientsiner Hilfsaktion," 267.

32. Reinhard Nachtigal, "Die dänisch-österreichisch-ungarischen Rotkreuzdelegierten in Rußland 1915–1918: Die Visitation der Kriegsgefangenen der Mittelmächte durch Fürsorgeschwestern des österreichischen und ungarischen Roten Kreuzes," *Zeitgeschichte* 25, no. 11–12 (1998): 367–68.

33. Käthe von Mihalotzy, "Eine Reise durch Kriegsgefangenenlager," 251.

34. Ibid.

35. Gräfin Anna Revertera, "Als österreichische Rotkreuzschwester in Rußland," *Süddeutsche Monatshefte* 20, no. 12 (Sept. 1923): 271.

36. Von Mihalotzy, "Eine Reise durch Kriegsgefangenenlager," 251.

37. Ibid., 252.

38. Ibid.

39. Rotkreuzschwester Gräfin Anna Revertera, "Als Rotkreuzschwester in Rußland und Sibirien," in *In Feindeshand,* 2:245; von Mihalotzy, "Eine Reise durch Kriegsgefangenenlager," 252; Nachtigal, "Die dänisch-österreichisch-ungarischen Rotkreuzdelegierten," 368.

40. Revertera, "Als Rotkreuzschwester in Rußland und Sibirien," 245.

41. Ibid.

42. Brändström, *Among Prisoners of War,* 166.

43. Von Mihalotzy, "Eine Reise durch Kriegsgefangenenlager," 255.

44. Ibid.

45. Ibid.; on Totskoe see Rachamimov, *POWs and the Great War,* 95; for an in-depth analysis of the typhus epidemic in Totskoe, see Reinhard Nachtigal, "Seuchen unter militärischer Aufsicht in Rußland: Das Lager Tockoe als Beispiel für die Behandlung der Kriegsgefangenen 1915/16," *Jahrbücher für Geschichte Osteuropas* 48 (2000): 363–87.

46. Von Mihalotzy, "Eine Reise durch Kriegsgefangenenlager," 255.

47. "Ladislaus Baczy an Emerich Diossy, Reichstagabgeordneter in Szent mihalyiur," Behandlung der österr. Kgf. in Antipicha bei Tschita (Russland), Österreichisches Staatsarchiv (hereafter ÖstA)/Kriegsarchiv (hereafter KA)/AOK (1916)/GZNB:Karton 3740, Akt 3511.

48. Von Raabl-Werner, "Österreich-Ungarns offizielle Kriegsgefangenenfürsorge," 327.

49. Brändström, *Among Prisoners of War,* 167.

50. Von Mihalotzy, "Eine Reise durch Kriegsgefangenenlager," 256.

51. For an analysis of POW response to nurses' visits, as expressed in their letters, see Rachamimov, "Imperial Indentities and Personal Concerns," in *POWs and the Great War,* 191–220, and Rachamimov, "Imperial Loyalties and Private Concerns."

52. Von Mihalotzy, "Eine Reise durch Kriegsgefangenenlager," 255.

53. Ibid., 256.

54. Revertera, "Als österreichische Rotkreuzschwester in Rußland," 258.

55. Nachtigal, "Die dänisch-österreichisch-ungarischen Rotkreuzdelegierten," 369.

56. "Brief von Anna Gräfin Revertera an Sr. Exz. Frh. v. Spiegelfeld," ÖstA/KA Nachlaß Raabl-Werner B:141:4/2, 3.

57. Regarding the Austro-Hungarian POW censors' habit of constructing lists of "suspect" soldiers from specific nationalities see Rachamimov, "In Search of the 'Good and Loyal prisoner': The Austro-Hungarian Censorship and the POWs," in *POWs and the Great War,* 133–59.

58. Revertera, "Als österreichische Rotkreuzschwester in Rußland," 261.

59. Ibid., 267.

60. Ibid., 260–61.

61. Ibid., 276.

62. Ibid., 280; Francis Joseph however relented and promised to reconsider this request.

63. Ibid., 281.

64. On the living conditions of officers and men, see Rachamimov, "The Treatment of POWs in Russia," in *POWs and the Great War,* 133–59.

65. Von Raabl-Werner, "Österreich-Ungarns offizielle Kriegsgefangenenfürsorge," 327.

66. Brändström, *Among Prisoners of War,* 165; Nachtigal, "Die dänisch-österreichisch-ungarischen Rotkreuzdelegierten," 369.

67. Nachtigal, "Die dänisch-österreichisch-ungarischen Rotkreuzdelegierten," 369.

68. Ibid.

69. Her posthumously published diary, *Russisches Tagebuch,* written during what became a two-year stay in Russia, remains to a large extent a hidden jewel among World War I personal journals. The published portions of the diary do not encompass its entirety. The complete original is in Liechtenstein in the possession of the ducal family.

70. This time the German and Austro-Hungarian nurses traveled together.

71. Kinsky, *Russisches Tagebuch,* 23.

72. Brändström, *Among Prisoners of War,* 169.

73. Kinsky, *Russisches Tagebuch,* 29.

74. Ibid., 30; it seems unlikely that a captain in the Hungarian National Guard (*Honvéd*) did not know at least some Hungarian and German. Notwithstanding, Kinsky's point was that she managed to reach prisoners emotionally by employing their mother language. The form "Rumanian"—and not "Romanian"—was the spelling chosen by Kinsky and commonly used at the time. To avoid anachronism it is also employed in the translation.

75. She spoke German, French, English, Italian, Czech, Hungarian, Romanian, Croat, and Polish. During her two-year sojourn in Russia she also acquired Russian and some Turkish. See Heinrich von Raabl-Werner, "Schwester Nora Kinsky, eine Heldin der Pflicht," in *In Feindeshand,* 2:243; and Kinsky, *Russisches Tagebuch,* Introduction.

76. Kinsky, *Russisches Tagebuch,* 44.

77. Ibid., 45.

78. Ibid., 47.

79. Ibid., entries for 22 September 1916 and 11 October 1916. Kinsky thought that sloth on the part of k.u.k. officers resulted in nervousness and an inclination to complain.

80. Ibid., 51.

81. Ibid., 63.

82. Ibid., 62.

83. Ibid., 64.

84. Ibid., 56.

85. Ibid., 55, 62.

86. Ibid., 112–13.

87. He was the same Cossack ataman she characterized as "an evil person" and a "total bastard." Ibid, 64.

88. Ibid., 64–65.

89. Her decision to stay in Russia was strongly opposed in Vienna; see Davis, "National Red Cross Societies," 48n16.

90. Returning home considerably weakened, she spent most of the next two years attempting to recuperate. Kinsky married her fiancé in January 1921, gave birth to a daughter (the future Princess Gina von Liechtenstein), and died on 26 March 1923. She had apparently been preoccupied during the last months of her life with translating her diary into French and preparing a typed manuscript.

91. Kinsky, *Russisches Tagebuch,* entry for 1 December 1916.

3 Civilizing the Soldier in Postwar Austria

Maureen Healy

Among ads for prosthetic limbs, gravestone engraving services, training courses for returning soldiers, and artificial glass eyes ("indistinguishable from the real thing"), we find an ad in an Austrian newspaper from 1919 that reads: "Civilize yourselves."[1] *Der Invalide,* the newspaper running the ad, carried many articles and announcements of interest to Austria's returning soldiers, the "war-damaged" in particular. Except for the relatively small number of officers and soldiers drawn into the *Volkswehr,* the Republic of German-Austria's new army, most Austrian men who fought in the Habsburg armed forces would be making a transition back to civilian life.[2] Did the injunction "civilize yourselves" imply that a return from battle might require some sort of civilizing process? Was the ad suggesting that soldiers had become uncivilized while away? Were becoming civilized and becoming a civilian synonymous? In this case, the "civilizing process" was imagined as a fairly superficial one. The ad came from a dry cleaner in Vienna's II. district who offered to convert military uniforms into civilian clothing. The cleaning and tailoring was called *Umarbeitung* (adaptation) and would prove important for soldiers who otherwise had no clothes. Austria-Hungary had experienced extreme shortages of wool, cotton, and other fabrics during the war, and many men would still be wearing their "adapted" shirts and trousers into the 1920s.

A much larger kind of adaptation was under way in Austria in the years following the war. This essay considers the *Umarbeitung* not simply of uniforms but of men themselves—the work of cleansing the war out of the warrior. Demobilization did not take place at the instant when a man was discharged from the armed forces; rather, it was a gradual process by which men made the transformation from soldier to civilian in their everyday lives. This process began with homecoming, the initial encounters with family members and the home front community. The *Umarbeitung* also involved the practical step of finding civilian work; the emotional process of reestablishing one's place in the family; and the psychological work of shedding, hiding, forgetting, ignoring, repressing, or in some other unspecified way coping with the violence one had seen and committed. The Austrian men in the following pages seem to have undergone an incomplete or unsuccessful *Umarbeitung,* and their stories comprise a partial history of defeat from below. They provide glimpses of what it meant, in everyday terms, to lose World War I.

In recent years historians have examined Europeans' efforts to reestablish normalcy and "order" following the Great War. These efforts invariably focused on gender. Restoring relations between men and women, grappling with women's new public visibility, and mending the bodies and minds of broken men were seen as fundamental to the restoration of order—even civilization—in postwar Europe. Several historians have framed postwar debates about gender as metaphoric "reconstruction" projects. In France, postwar fears that "this civilization . . . no longer has sexes" contributed to a profound cultural despair. According to Mary Louise Roberts, the discourse of French reconstruction focused on female identity and the figures of the "modern woman," the "mother" and the "single woman."[3] Similarly, in her study of postwar Britain, Susan Kingsley Kent maintains that many saw "in a reestablishment of sexual difference the means to re-create a semblance of order." Lasting peace, Britons thought, required a gender peace, "a relationship of male-female complementarity in which women did not compete with men in the public sphere."[4] In addition, Seth Koven has argued that restoring British men "to their masculine roles as heads of households, independent wage earners, and fathers was a major task of the postwar reconstructions of men's bodies, gender relations, the economy and the nation."[5] Class also figured in these reconstruction efforts. Jon Lawrence notes that in debates about "brutalization" in postwar Britain, it was often assumed that working-class men were most affected, "those for whom 'civilization' had always been held to run only skin deep."[6] As difficult as these social concerns were in France and Britain, it should be remembered that they played out against the backdrop of *victory.*

In the defeated countries, fears about loss of "order" in gender relations were woven into explanations for the loss of the war itself. Historians have described a general collapse of patriarchal order that accompanied defeat in Germany and Austria. On an individual level, a crisis of masculinity developed when soldiering men returned to their families. Reinhard Sieder describes demobilization as the return of the "disabled patriarchs." Men were wounded psychically, like Klaus Theweleit's angry Freikorps members, or physically, like Robert Whalen's invalid veterans. Helga Embacher describes emasculated soldiers, "who had to return as losers, hungry, louse-ridden or even as invalids." Elisabeth Domansky paints a similar picture, stating, "On the one hand, there was a large number of fatherless families; and on the other, fatherly authority seems to have changed in those families to which men returned." At the societal level, the collapse of empires, abdication of emperors, demise of prewar military and bureaucratic structures, and rising revolutionary spirit in central Europe entailed a patriarchal crisis for society as a whole. "[T]he collapse of the Austro-Hungarian Monarchy," Sieder suggests, "was in fact the collapse of a male society."[7] In these accounts, historians have usefully delineated a crisis of masculinity or collapse of patriarchal order that occurred on two levels: it happened to actual men within their real families, and it happened to the family writ large as the paternal pillars of prewar society crumbled.

Rebuilding individual men and rebuilding authority within the family were interdependent necessities for restoring order to a defeated society. The civilizing process—transforming soldiers into civilians—would begin within the family; at the same time, "disorder" within the wartime family (marked by wayward women and delinquent youth) would be corrected by men's return. In postwar Austrian politics, the family emerged as the institution central to the transition from war to peace. Not surprisingly, each political party had a different conception of what a family would look like and how its individual members would contribute to the building of a new state, but they were in agreement that becoming a *civilian* was synonymous with becoming a *family man* again.

A socialist pamphlet told returning POWs of the important place they would occupy in family and society:

> Your return from the lonely prison of captivity signals a turning point in your lives. You have been granted freedom . . . and with that the energy to be active and to produce for yourselves, for your families, for your class, for the living generation.[8]

A pastoral letter read aloud in Catholic churches across German-Austria in 1919 similarly addressed itself to the homecomers. It admonished them not to despair over defeat because they had new, pressing duties to fulfill:

> You, dear homecomers, are to begin again the sacred, serious duties within the family, of which you are the head. The children, who for too long have been deprived of the strong hand of the father in their upbringing, must again be strictly disciplined. We ask you to lead a true, Christian family life and your home will become paradise.[9]

This Austrian recipe for social reconstruction, which posited the reciprocal restoration of the man and his family, contained a number of assumptions. First, contemporaries assumed (and soldiers expected) that defeated soldiers would be welcomed home. Second, they assumed that men *wanted* to give up soldiering and return to family life. Angered, however, by what they considered a less than receptive homecoming, and feeling betrayed by civilian "weakness" during the war, some veterans' associations urged members to continue soldiering. These martial men had no intention of reclaiming authority as family fathers; rather, they based claims to authority on their perpetual soldiering. Third, employment, or "productivity" more generally, was seen as a defining characteristic of a family man. However, economic conditions in postwar Austria made it impossible for many men to perform the "useful labor" constitutive of civilian manhood. Finally, it was assumed that the disordered family would benefit from the man's return. Strict, but not violent, the family man would restore discipline that had disappeared during wartime. However, some returning men displayed violence in the streets and within their families. If civilizing oneself meant adopting a relationship to violence suitable to the civilian, then these men had failed to undergo a successful *Umarbeitung.* In public and in private, the truly civilized man exercised physical self-restraint and recognized that violence was sanctioned in some realms but not in others; in this context, becoming civilized and becoming civilian were nearly synonymous.

The "Fatherless Society"

When the war ended and the first defeated Habsburg soldiers came home to German-Austria, intense public discussion about the demise of the Austrian family had already been under way for several years. In prewar society, one of the defining attributes of a man had been the possession of authority, defined as the (perceived) power to make and enforce rules. Within families, the enforcer had been the father; within society at large it had been city fathers, policemen, military and civil servants, topped by the paternal figure of the emperor. Max Weber's traditional but still useful definition of "patriarchalism" held that the authority of "the father, the husband, the senior of the house" over wife and children resembled the authority of the "prince (*Landesvater*) over the 'subjects.'"[10] During the war, as millions of men were removed from family life and conscripted into military service, Austrians had blamed the absence of male authority for wartime social phenomena such as youth delinquency, rising crime, women's "sexual depravity," food riots, vandalism, and even reckless driving.

The motif of the "lost father" operated at different levels. In concrete terms, many actual Austrian fathers had become war casualties. The Habsburg Monarchy as a whole suffered a loss of approximately 1,200,000 war dead, nearly 650,000 of whom were Austrian.[11] About 70 percent of the Viennese men who died in service between 1914 and 1918 were married and 55 percent left behind orphans.[12] In a more general sense, the dissolution of social order on the home front aroused fears that traditional male authority had become a casualty of war, and that Austria had become, in the words of contemporary psychoanalyst Paul Federn, a "fatherless society."[13] In reality, the home front had never been solely a realm of women and children. For a variety of reasons, millions of men had spent all or part of the war on the home front. As holders of authority, however, they seem to have been invisible. In countless instances, Austrians voiced the opinion that order and authority would return to society only when the soldiers returned from battle. By war's end the stage was set and expectations were high that returning men could begin to repair four and a half years of social and familial disorder. But those who arrived to carry out this reconstruction were indelibly marked by defeat.

Welcome Home?

Men returning in late 1918 and 1919 from Austria-Hungary's various battle fronts and POW camps in Italy and the Balkans—and much later from

POW camps in Russia—were called *Heimkehrer* (homecomers). The term is more specific than the English equivalents "returning soldier" or "veteran" in that it signals a specific destination: home. Habsburg schoolbooks had spelled out only two possible outcomes for Austrian soldiers: "win or die."[14] The homecomers had done neither. Slavic and Italian soldiers returning to their successor states might have been received as national heroes, but the German-speakers among them were losers.[15] Some complained bitterly that the other successor states "received their troops with joy and full honor," while German-Austria "greeted its heroes with insults and heaped filth upon them."[16] One state commission acknowledged the awkwardness of receiving the losers: The men could not be greeted "as we had hoped and wished, and as would have been the case had we been the victors." Rather, "despite unending pain in our hearts, we reach out to them as brothers to lead them into the new, unhappy, fatherland."[17]

The soldier's return from battle had been a popular theme in European literature long before 1918. W. Splettstösser's 1899 book, *Der heimkehrende Gatte und sein Weib in der Weltliteratur,* charted common tropes of the encounter between returning men and their women dating back to the ancient Greeks.[18] Various scenarios included a woman not recognizing her man; children not recognizing their father; a man finding his woman in the arms of another; a woman being frightened at the sight of a man she'd thought to be dead; and a man being unable to locate his family. In one 1918 Austrian variation on the homecoming theme, the man returned to a family that was intact but a home that was "broken." Figure 3.1, entitled "A German-Austrian's return home," appeared in a Viennese newspaper in November 1918. The drawing depicts a demoralized soldier who has returned after the war to his poor wife and children, who are huddled in an apartment. In this scene, the individual family suffers the fate of the defeated collective. The wife equates the poverty of her family's home with the poverty of Austria, noting that the Slavs have taken all the good "rooms." She says, gesturing around her, "Well, the Tschecho-Slovak took the sitting room, the Southslav the bedroom, the Hungarian took the kitchen, and this is all that's left over for us." The economic consequences of the Empire's collapse and the redrawing of state boundaries in Central Europe had rendered this family man helpless to begin reconstruction. Instead of saving the family, he joins them in their misery.

The arrival of a returning soldier on the family doorstep played out in millions of individual scenes across Austria. Three themes emerge as central in these initial, sometimes awkward, encounters between fighting front and home front: some at home had developed a fear of the returning man; many homecomers felt they had not been welcomed properly by their families and communities; and from this, they quickly concluded that their sacrifices were not being remembered properly.

The *Arbeiterzeitung* published an article in May 1918 entitled "Broken Marriages." It spelled out some of the fears that family members had about the return of their men from battle. "It is to be expected that the end of the war will bring with it an increase in cases in which the presumed dead reappear, in which

Deutschösterreichers Heimkehr.

.... Alsdern, dös schöne Zimmer hat sich der Tschecho-Slowak genommen, dös Schlafzimmer der Südslav, dö Speis der Ungar, für uns is nix als dös Übrig blieb'n.
Alsdern, schön schau'n m'r aus, Alte!

Figure 3.1. A German-Austrian's Return Home. Source: *Der Morgen* (11 November 1918), 8.

persons who had been written out of the family circle will want to take their places again, places which are occupied by others." The article continued, "Although it sounds terrible, one hears it almost everyday: I am afraid of the return of my man."[19] While most families undoubtedly hoped and prayed for the safe return of husbands, fathers, and brothers, the article suggests that their return would also disrupt family relations that had been realigned during war.[20]

Beyond fears about what the return of an individual man might entail for his family were wider societal concerns about the homecomers as a group.[21] Contemporaries worried that soldiers—in particular those returning from the east—would bring with them criminality, political instability, social deviance, and infectious diseases. In 1918, censors summarized the complaints about the returnees they found in citizens' letters: "The nuisance of begging is frequently felt to be a true plague of the land. Soldiers and prisoners of war are said to make up the main contingent here."[22] Even before the war ended, impoverished POWs returning from Russia were held for a period in "Bolshevik quarantine" within Austria to prevent the spread of ideological contagions.[23] A woman warned a returning family member, "Here you are considered Bolshevik poison that people want to stamp out with drills and [discipline]."[24] More literal contagions were equally feared; homecomers in fetid, lice-ridden clothing were steered away from civilian population centers to limit the spread of typhus.[25] In addition, medical authorities in the east warned government officials in Vienna about the mental health of the homecomers, including a sizable contingent of "psychopaths"—men suffering from "oversensitivity, excitability, impulsiveness, alcoholism, lack of ethical feelings, mendacity, hallucinations, violent and criminal tendencies [and] sexual aberrations." War had not caused but triggered these "inborn" tendencies in men who now threatened the general public and posed "a great danger for the state."[26] These fears, in which the returnees appear as social pathogens, contrasted with hopes that returning soldiers would repair and replenish the "fatherless society." What if the men brought with them the very ills they were supposed to remedy?

Knowing of these widespread apprehensions, authorities in the new republican government encouraged civilians to give the homecomers a warm welcome. It was the postwar duty of civilians, they wrote, to perform a great "work of love" [*Liebeswerk*] on behalf of soldiers, so that the latter could "never once say that they had given their great sacrifice to the fatherland in vain."[27] Officials wanted to ensure "that the homecomers in all regions will be received by the population with extra special love."[28] This did not happen. Homecomers from across the political spectrum echoed one refrain: they felt they had not been properly welcomed home. At a meeting of German nationalist homecomers in January 1919, a speaker noted spitefully, "We imagined the return to our fatherland, the entrance into the *Heimat*, very, very differently." The *Heimat* was a warm, familiar place that predated the war, whereas the military term *Hinterland* connoted the civilian realm behind the lines:

> The *Heimat* did not receive her sons. [In one sense] it was still the old *Heimat*—the same people—but [in another sense] it wasn't the old *Heimat*. It was the *Hinterland*.

"Where," he wondered, "was the welcome, the thanks of the fatherland?"[29] The same month, a poorly attended rally for homecomers and war victims caused the leftist Free Union of Demobilized German-Austrian Soldiers to complain about the population's "lack of interest" in the homecomers' plight.[30] Christian homecomers railed against the "humiliating treatment" they received upon return, and others wondered what had become of all the home front patriots of 1914. The fine ladies bearing refreshments at the train stations had disappeared and the hurrah-gentlemen had crawled into their corners:

> After more than four years of war, depressed and worn by terrible sorrow and privation, the soldiers returned with sick, infirm, wounded bodies, [and] hearts filled with bitterness. "Our brave *Feldgrauen*" as one liked to call them in July and August 1914, had to make their way home hungry and begging, under the most terrible toil, abandoned by their leaders, deprived of bare necessities.[31]

Austrian homecomers did not believe losing the war explained this poor reception. They imagined that their German brothers-in-arms (and fellow losers) had been welcomed home with honor, parades, and ceremonies. Only in Austria did the homecomers' return elicit "not the slightest public reaction."[32]

The ignominy of not being *welcomed* quickly fed into the homecomers' conviction that their sacrifices would not be *remembered.* Here, too, they pointed to remembrance ceremonies being held "in all of Germany," while in Austria such fanfare was missing. Historian George Mosse notes, "The cult of the fallen soldier became a centerpiece of the religion of nationalism after the war, having its greatest political impact in nations like Germany which had lost the war and had been brought to the edge of chaos by the transition from war to peace."[33] If it came to Austria at all, the cult of the fallen soldier came too late to satisfy the demands of the newly returned. Although war memorials were built in most small towns and villages in the early 1920s, the capital city Vienna did not erect a monument to World War I sacrifice until 1934.[34] A monument built in 1925 in Vienna's central cemetery depicted a grieving mother and bore the inscription "Never Again War!" but did not address what the homecomers wanted memorialized: their own sacrifices.

In January 1919, while millions of Habsburg soldiers were still in transit or detained in enemy POW camps, the myth of the forgotten soldier (an Austrian variation on the cult of the fallen soldier) was taking shape at home. "The fatherland has forgotten its warriors and their sacrifices," read a poster advertising a memorial rally.[35] Proof of this forgetting could be found in the local cemetery. The corpses of soldiers who had recently died of wounds or disease were being transported to the city cemetery in carts, stacked in hastily constructed coffins, covered with tattered black cloths. A Viennese city councilman claimed to have observed coffins with ill-fitting lids and bodies stuffed into coffins too small to hold them, and noted, "It makes an especially painful impression to see how the next-of-kin have to run behind the cart."[36] The burial sites were no more dignified. Another city councilman complained in 1920 that soldiers' graves "offer the most wretched sight." Despite a provisional monument bearing the words "The Thankful City of Vienna," the graves "are not cared for, the burial mounds are disordered, the grass isn't even mowed. The grounds resemble a wasteland."[37] Throughout the 1920s, such routine examples of neglect reinforced homecomers' bitterness about the ungrateful welcome they had received. Homecomers themselves cultivated Austria's cult of the forgotten soldier, and this cult provided a discursive underpinning for their organized political actions.

Perpetual Soldiers

Dozens of veterans and war-invalid associations formed in Austria in the years following World War I. For homecomers, the transition from fighting front to home front entailed leaving behind the all-male society of the front and led to postwar nostalgia for comradeship.[38] Such nostalgia permeated the writings of the veterans associations. Although some groups strove for cross-political appeal, no single veteran's group could claim to represent all men who had served in the Habsburg armed forces.[39] At a rally sponsored by the Association of Austrian War-Wounded in 1919, speakers from the Pan-German People's Party, the Social Democrats, and the Communists all spoke in favor of better invalid care, and tried to "leave all party politics behind."[40] But other partisan associations offered refuge for displaced men who did not *want* to give up soldiering. The most bitter among them found their true homes in German nationalist veterans' organizations. *Neues Leben*, a newspaper for German Christian homecomers, urged its readers not to surrender their "brotherhood of blood and arms" just because they were "now at home among [their] loved ones." War had "ripened [them] into serious, far-sighted, worldly men" whose collective strength must be put to use for the economic betterment of those who had been cheated by war profiteers (implicitly, non-Christians). The brothers would have to prepare themselves "for this battle just as we mobilized for war." And for this they would be "thanked by the coming generation even more than for our deeds in battle."[41] A right-wing group calling itself the Protective Association of German War Combatants asserted that nobody was more qualified to educate the *Volk* and to lead German youth than the brave front soldiers who had proven themselves in battle.[42] Such claims to authority were based not on men's status as family fathers, but on their strength as perpetual soldiers. Sacrifices in battle prepared the martial man to *lead*, rather than to *father*.

Historian Elisabeth Domansky argues that in Germany a significant gender rupture occurred following World War I: "Male supremacy . . . was no longer rooted in men's/fathers' role in the family."[43] This claim would need to be modified for Austria. Here, some veterans *wanted* male supremacy to be based on soldiering rather than fathering, but these fighters who felt themselves entitled to lead did not necessarily find themselves in positions of leadership. Many German nationalist homecomers in Austria complained that the one institution that could best utilize their talents—the army—was closed to them on political grounds. Because the postwar *Volkswehr*, under the direction of socialist Defense Minister Julius Deutsch, was indeed closely affiliated with the left, fighters joined anti-republican paramilitary organizations. They addressed each other as "comrade," and even in 1920 vowed to "stand dutifully at our posts."[44] Where their "posts" were meant to be in postwar civilian society was not always clear, but one venue homecomers vowed to infiltrate was electoral politics. "The voices of the Front must be heard in the new ordering of the state," the Protective Association declared. Traditional politicians would not find fighters "especially pleasant, because we are not comfortable party cogs. We want to be a new element, a kind of fermentation in public life." Public life could only be rejuvenated by "new men and new leaders."[45] We see in the category of "new men" that some returning soldiers had come to see front service as the defining feature of postwar Austrian manhood.

The grueling work men performed at the front (fighting, killing, attacking, defending) changed cultural perceptions of labor in Austria in ways that devalued other male contributions to the economy and society. The newspaper *Der Invalide* proposed that a tax be levied on all men who had "not performed war service in the strictest sense of the word."[46] Not included among the post-war "new men" were millions of men who had performed their war service (*Kriegsdienst*) in industrial and administrative positions behind the lines. The masculinity of the factory worker, the policeman, the bureaucrat, the railroad worker—precisely the jobs that soldiers would return to after war—was devalued by the wartime elevation of soldiering as the only pursuit of a true man.

Homecomers' insistence that front soldiers had the only legitimate claim to authority challenged the conventional patriarchal logic underlying Austrian society. Authority—the vaguely defined but highly prized social glue thought to be missing in the "moral chaos" after 1918—had long been established in Austrian family law as a *male* attribute, but the war taught that not all men possessed it.[47] Declaring that power "belongs after the war only to the front soldiers,"[48] homecomers saw themselves fit to rule not only over women and children (the traditional position of men) but over non-fighting men as well. The criterion for determining whether a man was a hero or merely a piece of *Hinterlandsbagage* was sacrifice. In its most extreme form, this position—what we'll call sacrificialism—called for a new hierarchy of power within society. It was not class, nation, or gender that determined one's place in the social and political order, but level of sacrifice. Returning soldier Robert Weishut articulated this new sacrificialist worldview: no one who had sacrificed less could stand above one who had sacrificed more. After demobilization, "no recruit, whether he was previously a farmer, a worker, a businessman, an academic, or nothing at all, is to be economically worse off" than his peers who had not served.[49] These perpetual soldiers would be Austria's new über-citizens, occupying all positions of political and economic power, enjoying special voting privileges, and subordinated to none. While this new arrangement of society never came to pass, we see in homecomers' expressions of entitlement that the war had fractured the category of "men" into fighters and non-fighters.

Work and Manhood

For Weishut and other sacrificialists, the cowardice of non-fighters had "made of us a privileged caste." One of the things fuelling their postwar rage was the fact that members of the new caste had to compete with "these pigs" for jobs.[50] Mass unemployment among demobilized soldiers was one of the most challenging problems facing the coalition government that came to power in November 1918. In mid-December the mayor of Vienna warned that action was needed "to prevent the economic collapse of our heretofore thriving city and the pauperization of its population."[51] The new republican government quickly instituted a large system of unemployment benefits, but the payments did not create jobs and did not keep pace with wild inflation.[52] December's concern that the number of persons laid off from the war industries could reach 25,000 seemed almost quaint by May 1919, when the number of unemployed in Vienna alone reached 131,000. During those months, homecomers continued to stream into the city. The Christian Social *Reichspost* estimated that 920,000 homecomers had passed through Vienna in the first three weeks of November.[53] Some were transient, but many stayed, expecting to find work but finding themselves *brotlos* instead. That "breadless" had become synonymous with "jobless" reveals how closely hunger and unemployment were linked in the chaos of the postwar economy.

Historians have identified *female* labor as a key component of the unemployment crisis facing Austria after the war. Soldiers and prisoners of war returned home, angry to find "emancipated" women working in traditionally male roles. As Sigrid Augeneder and Gabriella Hauch explain, legally removing women from traditionally male jobs constituted one facet of the return to a "healthy order" [*gesunde Ordnung*] in the postwar period.[54] A 1919 Austrian law required women to leave certain jobs in order to make room for the returning men. This pleased homecomers who saw in female labor the seeds of the postwar "battle of the sexes."[55] Using terminology borrowed from the battle front, one anonymous homecomer railed against women who had used war as an opportunity to "conquer" jobs previously closed to them. Complaining that men's jobs were now "occupied" by this insidious force, he asked: "Should young men, who really gave their lifeblood for our state, now be denied their entire right to exist on account of the woman? No, I say, no!" The letter-writer linked employment with a man's very "right to exist," and believed this right could only be secured by crushing the "women's economy" (*Weiberwirtschaft*).

But even removing female "opportunists" and "double-earners" (working women whose husbands also had a wage) from the labor market did not create enough jobs for homecomers. Unemployment, "one of the most characteristic features of the Austrian economic structure" in the postwar period,[56] resulted from a breakdown of economic relations among the Habsburg successor states. Trade had been severely disrupted by war and postwar transportation stoppages within the Central European rail network. Czechoslovakia all but refused to ship essential coal to German-Austria, reflecting what foreign relief advisers called the "war spirit" and "system of mutual isolation" that plagued relations among the new states in Central Europe.[57] Because of the coal shortage, industry was operating at only 20–25 percent capacity two years after the war's end.[58] A foreign technical adviser summarized the general postwar economic scenario: "As yet, after two years, nothing has been done to rehabilitate the country industrially or financially . . . Bear in mind that many people have had no work for two years and they cannot work until there is coal for the factories and they cannot buy things with their worthless money."[59] These advisers were discussing unemployment in the context of *economic* reconstruction. Because of the close link between manhood and productivity, however, unemployment also impeded the postwar *gender* reconstruction. Work was central to the civilizing process of turning soldiers into civilians. A job was a prerequisite for a successful *Umarbeitung* because it allowed a man to resume the role of family provider.

The importance of productive work to manhood can be seen most clearly in discussions of employment for invalid soldiers. Like other Europeans, Austrians believed that a "war-damaged" man's masculinity could be restored through productivity. Hard work was the cure for the self-pity that a man might succumb to on account of his missing body parts. An organization for war invalids told its members that doctors "often had to remove parts of your bodies," but they tried their best "to preserve as much of the body part as possible so that the arm stump would be capable of work." Through hard work, one could forget one's suffering: "Work heals you!"[60] Such sentiments guided postwar Austrian benefits schemes. Invalid pensions were determined according to percentage of *Erwerbsunfähigkeit,* the inability to work. In search of productive potential, doctors performed close readings of invalid bodies. They composed detailed charts to calculate how much a particular body part was "worth" in productive terms. Loss of a whole arm was thought to cost a man 70–80 percent of his productivity; the thumb (at 25–35 percent) was more valued than the rest of the fingers (valued at only 0–15 percent); loss of half a leg reduced a man's productive capacity by 50–60 percent, while loss of both legs from the thigh might render a man 100 percent unproductive if he had poor quality stumps.[61] A man reaching this maximum was placed in the category of "helplessness" and received a "helpless pension." Severe facial wounds might also limit a man's productive capacities. "It is clear," wrote Viennese surgeon Ernst Eitner, "that in many professions, a disfiguring facial defect can be as detrimental to one's advancement as the loss of a limb or the like."[62] He argued on employment grounds that homecomers who had lost their "human appearance" required reconstructive surgery.

To be found 100 percent fit for work did not, of course, guarantee that a man could *find* work. This was a problem confronting Austria's able-bodied homecomers. For these men, the problem was not reduced physical capacity for work, but the economy's inability to make use of their labor. In painful letters to state and city authorities, able-bodied homecomers recounted their failure to provide for their families, despite having served long and arduous years at the front. In March 1919, thirty-five-year-old Wilhelm Schürer, a Viennese bookkeeper who had served three years at the front, wrote to the State Office of Social Welfare pleading for a job. His unemployment payments had been eaten away by his sick daughter's operation, "so that almost nothing is left over just for living." He was ashamed to even consider asking his elderly parents for money, "because they too are destitute, and considering their advanced age could rightly make a claim to support from their children." Humiliated, he concluded, "In my hopeless situation . . . I ask for work."[63] Fellow unemployed homecomer Ernst Bürger was convinced that his soiled clothing had prevented him from finding a job. Twice he had applied for bookkeeping positions, "but my appearance, my tattered clothing, is always the reason I [am] turned away." With an elderly mother to support, he wrote to the State Office of Social Welfare requesting a subsidy to have his clothing cleaned and repaired, something he could not afford on his unemployment payments.[64] Bürger portrayed himself as a good man who had served his country and was eager to find work. He believed that one sort of *Umarbeitung*—the repair of a suit—would help him make the more difficult transition back to productivity. Schürer, Bürger, and tens of thousands of able-bodied, unemployed homecomers could not fulfill the primary duty of a family man—to provide.

While these letter-writers made individual requests, many returning men sought dignity in numbers and appealed for work through their organized veterans associations. The communist-oriented Free Union of Demobilized German-Austrian Soldiers held a rally on 15 June 1919 to protest living conditions for homecomers. Its call to comrades mixed Soviet-style revolutionary rhetoric with the woes of the family man:

> For four and a half years we waded in blood up to the knees in the interests of the robber-baron capitalists and suffered indescribable tortures. Now we stand with our families, unemployed, hungry, worn. . . . We demand 5,000 crowns [for every homecomer] so that we can save our families from starvation and mend our tattered clothing.[65]

This rally of destitute communist family fathers ended in bloody clashes in the streets of Vienna that left eleven people dead and more than eighty seriously wounded.

Members of the anti-Semitic, German nationalist *Frontkämpfervereinigung* were no strangers to rallies that became shoot-outs or protests that dissolved into violence.[66] But in some cases they took a different approach to restoring the dignity of the impoverished family man: self-help. In the pages of their newspaper, *Die neue Front,* readers called on one another to protect the dignity of their fellow brothers in arms. Karl R. from Vienna wrote to the paper requesting help from his "better-situated comrades." "Presently I live together with my wife and child in a [2×2] bathroom." He had no furniture, and asked if any fellow comrades out there had "dishes, clothing, linens, shoes, and above all an oven," for which he could pay in installments.[67] J.P., a fellow sufferer and former officer, supplied a detailed inventory of the destitute homecomer's impoverished home:

> I am an Aryan, married with three children. As a result of the collapse I have lost my furniture, clothing, and so on, and since my return to Vienna I have been living in the most unthinkable conditions. We have no pillows and bedding so that we use our items of clothing as pillows and blankets . . . Now I ask if my war comrades can be of any kind of help to me in my need, whether by giving me old linens, bedding . . . or other things such as a pram [baby carriage] and also a civilian hat.[68]

These domesticated men, publicly soliciting dishes, bedding, and other housewares, do not conform to our image of the postwar *Frontkämpfer.* Perhaps the experience of failing as husbands and fathers reinforced the attachment men like Karl R. and J.P. felt for their "other" families—their "eternal brothers in arms."

The inability of unemployed men to resume traditional positions as household providers had ramifications beyond the individual family. Restoring order in the family was seen as the first step in restoring order in Austrian society at large. To cure postwar social ills, wayward individuals (delinquent youths and "fallen" women) needed to be reined in and placed under the guidance of strong family authority. Nowhere was this more urgent than in the struggle to combat rising prostitution. During the war, many wives of conscripted soldiers had been accused of supplementing their meager state subsidies by resorting to an "immoral way of life." "Since this time," the State Health Department noted in 1919, "the vice squad in Vienna has lost its control over prostitution." As women were released from their wartime jobs (many of them were ineligible for unemployment benefits of their own), they entered lives of "depravity." Officials estimated that the number of officially registered prostitutes in the capital stood at 1,100, while the number of unregistered "could well surpass ten thousand."[69] More alarming than the numbers were the class origins of the women entering prostitution. "How many of these women and girls would, under normal conditions, have become respectable housewives and daughters!" lamented a women's newspaper. While their men were away at the front, women and girls with incomes had gotten used to "entertainment and free spending":

> And then came the backlash. The earnings disappeared, but the taste for pleasure remained . . . We understand, from authoritative sources, that it is primarily the wives of homecomers who have lost the state subsidy [paid during wartime] and whose men still haven't found work [. . .] who are prime perpetrators of secret vice.[70]

This "poisonous herd" of women, whose unemployed men could not support newly acquired tastes, threatened the well-being "of the entire population."[71] Men were implicated in the prostitution scandal not because they were *frequenting* prostitutes, but because they could not keep their female family members from *becoming* prostitutes.

Postwar Violence

Austrians attributed a second social ill—rising violent crime—to the homecomers' inability to make the psychological transition to peacetime. The transition from soldier to civilian would require men to leave their violence at the front. They were ostensibly moving from a realm in which violence and killing were sanctioned and expected, to a realm where such behavior was considered uncivilized. This adaptation was made difficult by the fact that postwar Austrian society was saturated with the weapons of war. Quite simply, large numbers of homecomers were never disarmed. In the chaotic conditions of the fall of 1918, the Habsburg armed forces collapsed, and no authority was in place to gather weapons and prevent their proliferation in civilian society. In unsystematic fashion, millions of troops crisscrossed Central Europe, making their way home in overcrowded trains and along roads clogged by military hardware.[72] Returning soldiers traveling alone or in small bands plundered their way home, stealing supplies at gunpoint or trading weapons for food. Seeing danger, in early November the new republic's political leaders ordered that homecomers be disarmed. Attempts to do so, however, led to bloody clashes with returning troop units; in the end the policy of disarming was abandoned.[73]

The arrival of an armed homecomer could be terrifying for family members. Viennese cook Agathe Stekowicz and her employer Isabella Theiller did not live to recount their experience with a front fighter. Stekowicz's nephew, Josef Tschampa, murdered the women with "bestial ferocity" using "a so-called trench knife," stabbing each thirty to forty times. Tschampa, a homeless homecomer, had returned to Vienna with his front mentality unchecked. Police found among his belongings two Russian guns, two bayonets, a dagger, a gas mask, and an Italian infantry cap—a collection that suggested he had brought his front home.[74] Other families had less gruesome but no less deadly encounters with homecomers and their weapons of war. The *Arbeiterzeitung* reported that "homecoming soldiers playing with weapons they brought with have already claimed many victims . . . one homecomer shot his sister, another his mother."[75] The War Office reported to the Viennese police in February 1919 that there had recently been an increase in the number of accidents involving shells, hand grenades, cartridges, detonators, and the like, artifacts that soldiers had brought back from the field as souvenirs in the belief that these objects were not dangerous.[76]

Journalists and police statisticians interpreted rising crime rates as another sign that the war had come home. The *Wiener Montagsblatt* recounted the Viennese "blood chronicle" for the first week of January 1919 that included a "double murder-robbery, a murder-robbery, an aggravated murder, a dozen manslaughters, and around a hundred stabbings."[77] A police retrospective summarized the situation in 1922: "As a result of the long-lasting war, there appeared a rise in criminality understandably very unsettling to the population."[78] While many of the crimes were economic in nature—petty theft increased fourfold between 1915 and 1922—violent crimes of murder and manslaughter filled postwar newspapers. Stories of hacked body parts found in suitcases, women and children walking unsuspectingly into the line of fire of rival gangs, and armed attacks against the police force itself were everyday fare. As Table 1 indicates, the number of persons convicted of murder rose as soldiers returned home. Of course, the number of murderers *convicted* is not the same as the number of murders *committed*, a statistic that is not available. These figures tell us as much about perceptions of crime as they do about incidents of crime. The popular perception that murder was on the rise was repeated in police circles as well. "The number of murders," a police publication noted, "increased dramatically especially after the collapse [of the Habsburg state]."[79] While women were widely blamed for a decline in sexual morality and figured prominently among the thieves and petty criminals, violent crime was attributed to the "unchecked brutality of men."[80]

Less dramatic than the headline-splashing murders, but more damaging for the prospects of a return to "ordered" family life, was a topic rarely discussed in print: domestic violence. Domestic violence is difficult to reconstruct from sources because male head-of-household physical and verbal abuse of family

Table 3.1. Persons Convicted of Murder in Austria by Year.
Source: *Zahlenmäßige Darstellung der Rechtspflege* 2, no. 1 (1925), 49–57.

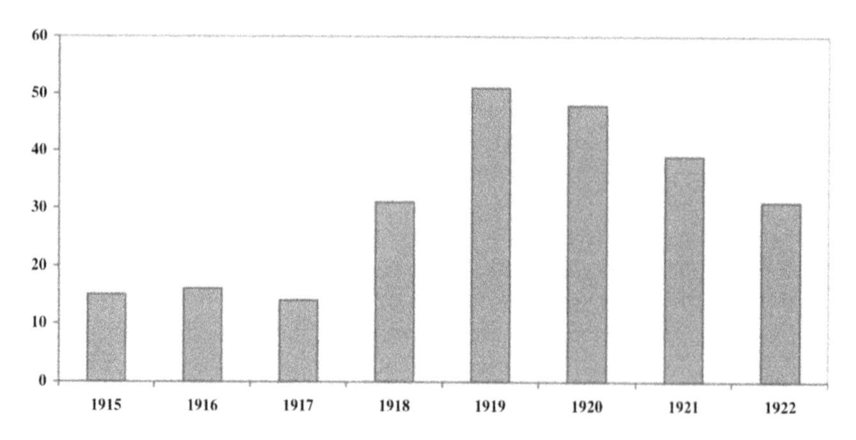

members could fall into the legal category of "discipline" (*Zucht*) and go unrecorded. And as in the case of the Catholic sermon for homecomers noted above, many felt that strict discipline was precisely the thing needed in the postwar family. Austrian law granted a husband the right to "discipline" his wife and children and threatened only a light penalty for those who disciplined too forcefully.[81]

A scene from *Die freudlose Gasse,* Hugo Bettauer's well-known 1924 novel about murder and moral corruption in Vienna, suggests that homecomers had learned some new disciplinary practices in wartime, and that being beaten was a topic for commiseration among women. In this scene, a thin, careworn woman stands weeping in a doorway while several other women comfort her. One of the women says, "Her husband has hit her in the face and made it bleed, the dirty beast!" An older woman assures the crowd, "They're a rough, brutal lot, all of them," and another concurs, "Oh yes; when my old man found anything not just as he liked it, he laid into me right away." The victim's husband, a drunk homecomer who spent the war in Siberia, shouts to the women in a thick voice, "Don't worry yourself about it . . . in Siberia the women cry if their husbands don't knock them about because then they think they don't love them anymore."[82] Bettauer, who was himself murdered in Vienna in 1925, presents domestic violence as something that predates the war; the women's reactions suggest that such behavior was to be expected of a husband. But the war also provides new justifications for domestic violence. From observations made while soldiering abroad, the husband is reassured that his actions are perfectly normal.

This fictional episode echoes what we learn from the contemporary Austrian women's newspaper *Die Unzufriedene:* wife beating was a concern of many women, and husbands' increased brutality could be linked to their war experiences. The newspaper published drawings of men beating their families (see figs. 3.2 and 3.3). Precisely how often this happened we do not know; violence within families is not counted in any crime statistics from the period. But one reader lamented, "If only there were an organization that could help us poor, trampled women with our rights. There are hundreds of us, maybe thousands."[83]

Domestic violence was not a new phenomenon of the postwar period, but letters written to *Die Unzufriedene*'s advice column underscore that women understood the violence directed against them as a legacy of the war. One reader complained of her husband's rage. The man was a construction worker who "earn[ed] a good wage," but who drank and terrorized his wife and daughters:

> What should I do? I fear a coming catastrophe. I am thirty-five years old [and] he is too. From the rough handling and punches I look as white as an old lady. Since the year 1919, since he came home from the war, we have been subjected to terrible brutality. He still believes that I had it so good at home during the war, and now he wants to make me pay for that . . . [84]

The advice columnist responded, "Above all, the man appears to be a war victim [*Kriegsopfer*]." His brutality and violence were evidence of a "war mentality that clearly has a strong hold on him." She suggested that the reader consider a separation. In 1924, another reader described family life with her abusive homecomer husband as "hell on earth." Her husband of sixteen years subjected her to "brutality and vile insults," and she blamed the war:

> There is one thing I have to say and that speaks for my husband, he is a war victim. He spent years at the front and all the brutality of the war, noticeable in him immediately, still sticks to him today, as if he had just come back from the front yesterday. That is perhaps the only excuse for him . . . [85]

Still bearing "noticeable" signs of the war, this family man had failed in one of the key tasks of re-civilizing. He had been unable to shed, hide, forget, ignore, or repress his war experiences. He had failed to undergo the necessary "adaptation." His ferocity might have once made him a good soldier, but in the context of 1924 he was not a good man.

These incidents of domestic violence can be linked to larger questions about Austria's transition from war to peace. Austria is said to have undergone a "bloodless" revolution in early November 1918. By bloodless, historians mean that a multiparty coalition took the reins of state power from the dynasty and declared a republic with little of the violence that accompanied such transitions elsewhere.[86] While the immediate transfer of state authority may have been bloodless, the longer-term reordering of familial authority was not. The new Austrian state was not borne of violence, but violence permeated its public and domestic life in the postwar decade.

In the early years of the Austrian First Republic, parties across the political spectrum identified the family as the institution that would regenerate Austria.

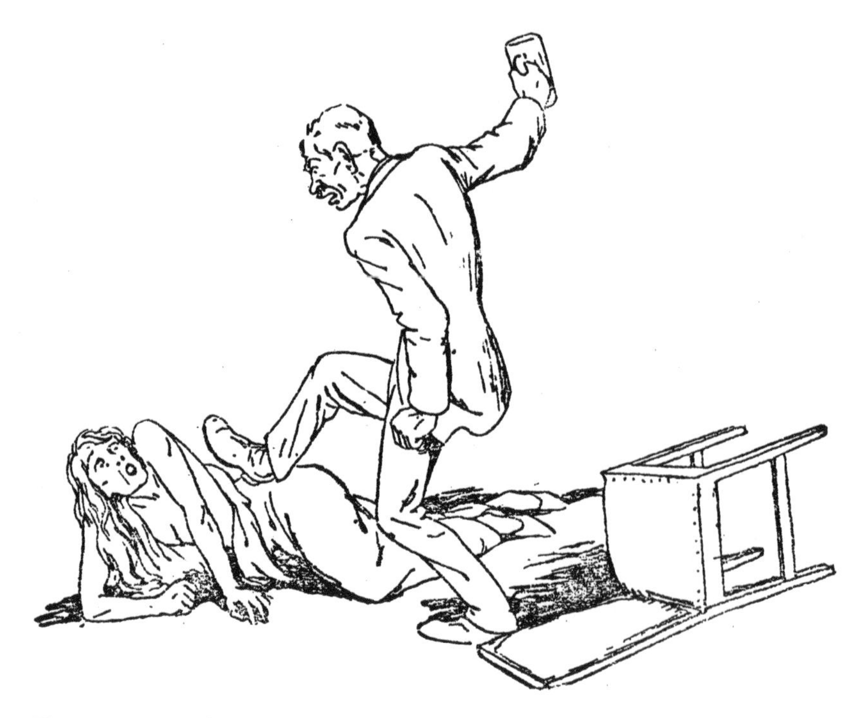

Figure 3.2. Scene of Postwar Domestic Violence. Source: *Die Unzufriedene* (1923).

Figure 3.3. Scene of Postwar Domestic Violence. Source: *Die Unzufriedene* (1923).

But Austrians' hopes for the regenerative powers of family rested on a model of paternal authority upset by the war. Before it could be regenerated, the family first had to perform a cleansing function. In ways unspecified, the post–World War I family was expected to absorb and neutralize a soldier, producing from him a civilized man. Through unexplained means, the family would perform an *Umarbeitung*, analogous to the dry cleaner who transformed old uniforms into wearable civilian clothing. To help with the transition back to family life, state authorities offered men a preliminary cleansing. The government established cost-free delousing stations. It warned families that the lice in homecomers' uniforms and underclothes were a danger to family health. Homecomers were to visit a station to be freed of their lice before setting foot in the family apartment.[87] Once the soldier was inside, however, a more difficult, and in many cases incomplete, civilizing process began.

Notes

1. "Zivilisiert euch," *Der Invalide* (15 May 1919), 6.

2. By February 1919, the Volkswehr, the army of the new Republic of German-Austria, had absorbed 2,679 officers and about 60,000 soldiers. The numbers were then cut in half by the Treaty of St. Germain. Peter Melichar, "Die Kämpfe merkwürdig Untoter: K.u.K. Offiziere in der Ersten Republik," *Österreichische Zeitschrift für Geschichtswissenschaften* 9, no. 1 (1998): 51–84.

3. Mary Louise Roberts, *Civilization Without Sexes: Reconstructing Gender in Postwar France, 1917–1927* (Chicago: University of Chicago Press, 1994), 9–11.

4. Susan Kingsley Kent, *Making Peace: The Reconstruction of Gender in Interwar Britain* (Princeton: Princeton University Press, 1993), 99, 113.

5. Seth Koven, "Remembering and Dismemberment: Crippled Children, Wounded Soldiers and the Great War in Great Britain," *American Historical Review* 99, no. 4 (October 1994): 1167–1202, 1188.

6. Jon Lawrence, "Forging a Peaceable Kingdom: War, Violence, and Fear of Brutalization in Post–First World War Britain," *Journal of Modern History* 75 (September 2003): 557–589, 559.

7. Reinhard Seider, "Behind the Lines: Working-Class Family Life in Wartime Vienna," in Richard Wall and Jay Winter, eds., *The Upheaval of War: Family, Work and Welfare in Europe, 1914–1918* (Cambridge: Cambridge University Press, 1988), 109–38, 109; Klaus Theweleit, *Male Fantasies*, 2 vols., trans. Stephen Conway (Minneapolis: University of Minnesota Press, 1987); Robert Whalen, *Bitter Wounds: German Victims of the Great War, 1914–1939* (Ithaca: Cornell University Press, 1984); Helga Embacher, "Der Krieg hat die 'göttliche Ordnung' zerstört! Konzepte und Familienmodelle zur Lösung von Alltagsproblemen, Versuche zur Rettung der Moral, Familie und patriarchalen Gesellschaft nach dem Ersten Weltkrieg," *Zeitgeschichte* 15, no. 9–10 (1988): 347–63, 350; Elisabeth Domansky, "Militarization and Reproduction in World War I Germany," in Geoff Eley, ed., *Society, Culture and the State in Germany, 1870–1930* (Ann Arbor: University of Michigan Press, 1996), 427–63, 459. See also Eric J. Leed, *No Man's Land: Combat and Identity in World War I* (New York: Cambridge University Press, 1979).

8. *An die Heimkehrer und Soldaten* (Vienna: Wiener Volksbuchhandlung, 1919), 2.

9. "Hirtenbrief," *Wiener Diözesanblatt* 57, no. 21–22 (24 November 1919): 65–69, 66–67.

10. Max Weber, *From Max Weber: Essays in Sociology*, ed. and trans. H. H. Gerth and C. Wright Mills (New York: Galaxy, 1958), 296.

11. Wilhelm Winkler, *Die Totenverluste der öst.-ung. Monarchie nach Nationalitäten* (Vienna: L. W. Seidl & Sohn, 1919), 37, approximate total as of 31 December 1917. Others give a lower monarchy-wide figure of 780,000 dead, but this does not include men who died in POW captivity. Richard Plaschka et al., eds., *Innere Front: Militärassistenz, Widerstand und Umsturz in der Donaumonarchie 1918*, 2 vols. (Munich: R. Oldenbourg Verlag, 1974), 1:44.

12. *Amtsblatt der Stadt Wien* (1 January 1919), 17–21.

13. Paul Federn, *Die Vaterlose Gesellschaft: Zur Psychologie der Revolution* (Leipzig and Vienna: Anzengruber-Verlag Brüder Suschitzky, 1919).

14. Cited in Ernst Hanisch, "Die Männlichkeit des Kriegers: Das österreichische Militärstrafrecht im Ersten Weltkrieg," in Thomas Angerer et al., eds, *Geschichte und Recht: Festschrift für Gerald Stourzh zum 70. Geburtstag* (Vienna: Böhlau, 1999): 313–38, 318.

15. Edmund Glaise von Horstenau et al., eds., *Österreich-Ungarns letzter Krieg*, 7 vols. (Vienna: Verlag der Militärwissenschaftlichen Mitteilungen, 1930–1938), 7:41–42. The Habsburg Armed Forces had mobilized a total of 8,420,000 men by the end of 1917. About 1,200,000 were killed in battle or otherwise died in service. The Habsburg soldiers heading home to German-Austria and the other successor states numbered about 4,410,000; another 2,000,000 were in POW camps by the end of the war.

16. Military newspaper, 1 January 1919. Cited in Wolfgang Doppelbauer, *Zum Elend noch die Schande: Das altösterreichische Offizierscorps am Beginn der Republik* (Vienna: Österreichischer Bundesverlag, 1988), 19.

17. *Mitteilungen der Staatskommission für Kriegsgefangenen und Zivilinterniertenangelegenheiten* 1, no. 9–10 (14 August 1919), 1.

18. W. Splettstösser, *Der heimkehrende Gatte und sein Weib in der Weltliteratur* (Berlin, 1899).

19. Hoover Institution Archives, Alfred Hermann Fried, box 4, Dokumente zur "grossen Zeit," *Arbeiterzeitung* (19 May 1918).

20. This is borne out by Sieder's study of the wartime family. Oral interviewees recall older siblings taking on family authority in the absence of the father.

21. For the predicament of the returnees, see Plaschka et al., *Innere Front*, I: 283.

22. Österreichisches Staatsarchiv (ÖStA), Kriegsarchiv (KA), Armeeoberkommando-Gemeinsames Zentralnachweisbüro (AOK GZNB) 1918, 3759 #5123. Censor's report May 1918.

23. *Stunde der Rache. Ein Wort an die Soldaten* (Vienna: Verlag der Wiener Volksbuchhandlung, 1919), 15.

24. ÖStA, KA, AOK GZNB 1918, 3758 #5054. Censor's report April 1918.

25. ÖStA, Archiv der Republik (AdR), Staatsamt für soziale (St.A. F. soz.) Verwaltung, Volksgesundheit, carton 1605, #6357–19. Report signed by Max Winter, 5 February 1919; carton 15, #6357, memo received by deutsch-österreichisches Staatsamt für Verkehrswesen, early 1919.

26. ÖStA, AdR, kk Min. u. St.A. f. soz. Verwaltung, Volksgesundheit 1918, 1592 #287. Letter from medical faculty in Cracow to Minsterium für soziale Verwaltung, 7 May

1918. On mental illness among Austrian soldiers, see Georg Hofer, "Nerven-Korrekturen: Ärzte, Soldaten und die 'Kriegsneurosen' im Ersten Weltkrieg," *Zeitgeschichte* 27, no. 1 (2000): 249–68.

27. *Mitteilungen der Staatskommission für Kriegsgefangenen und Zivilinterniertenangelegenheiten* 1, no. 3 (28 June 1919), 1.

28. Ibid., 1, no. 1 (15 June 1919), 1.

29. "Heimkehrer und Heimat," *Die nationale Frau* 1, no. 2 (18 January 1919), 1–2.

30. ÖStA, AdR, Bundeskunzleramt (BKA) Inneres 22/nö carton 5067, #39800.

31. *Stunde der Rache,* 3.

32. Doppelbauer, *Zum Elend noch die Schande,* 5.

33. George L. Mosse, *Fallen Soldiers: Reshaping the Memory of the World Wars* (New York: Oxford University Press, 1990), 7.

34. On memorials in Austria, see Ernst Hanisch, "Die Rückkehr des Kriegers: Mänlichkeitsbilder und Remilitarisierung im Österreich der Zwischenkriegszeit," *Transit/ Europäische Revue* 16 (Winter 1998/99), 108–24, 114.

35. ÖStA, AdR, BKA Inneres, 15/3 carton 2435, #1076–19. Flier for "Dank-und Gedächnisfeier für die gefallenen Krieger," January 1919.

36. *Amtsblatt der Stadt Wien* 20 (8 March 1919), 548. Inquiry from municipal councilor GR Simon, 27 February 1919.

37. Stenographische Protokolle der Gemeinderats-Sitzungen, Wien 1920, 1 June 1920, 3.

38. See Thomas Kühne, "'. . . aus diesem Krieg werden nicht nur harte Männer heimkehren,' Kriegskameradschaft und Männlichkeit im 20. Jahrhundert," in Kühne, ed., *Männergeschichte–Geschlechtergeschichte: Männlichkeit im Wandel der Moderne* (Frankfurt/New York: Campus, 1996), 174–92; Jürgen Reulecke, "Männerbund versus the family: Middle-class youth movements and the family in Germany in the period of the First World War," in Wall and Winter, *The Upheaval of War,* 439–52, 444.

39. Associations included the Zentralverband der deutsch-österreichischen Kriegsbeschädigten, Witwen und Waisen, which advocated for "war-damaged" men, widows, and orphans. The Sozialwirtschaftlicher Reichsbund der deutsch-österreichischen Kriegsinvaliden broke away from the ostensibly nonpartisan Zentralverband, citing discrimination against social democrats and Jews. Among the groups attracting former officers were the Österreichisches Offiziersbund, the Wirtschaftsbund der Berufsmilitärgagisten, and the antiparliamentary, paramilitary Heimwehren, founded in 1919 to head off left-wing revolutionary threats. The anti-Semitic Frontkämpfervereinigung catered to German nationalists. Socialists joined the Zentralverband der Landesorganisationen der Kriegsinvaliden und Kriegshinterbliebenen Österreichs, which had links to the Geneva-based "Invalid Internationale," and other left-leaning veterans joined the Freie Vereinigung deutschösterreichischer abgerüsteter Soldaten und Heimkehrer. Jewish veterans formed the Jüdischer Heimkehrer und Kriegsbeschädigten, and the small Bundes jüdischer Frontsoldaten, founded in 1932, represented Jewish veterans whose sacrifices were negated by German nationalist organizations.

40. ÖStA, AdR BKA Inneres, Polizei-DirektionWien, Berichte 1919–1920, #2840/1. Police report, 21 March 1919.

41. *Neues Leben* 3, no. 2 (15 January 1920), 1.

42. "Heimkehrer auf Heimat," *Die nationale Frau* 1, no. 2 (18 January 1919), 1–2.

43. Domansky, "Militarization and Reproduction," 428.

44. *Die neue Front* 2, no. 1 (1 January 1920), 5. This right-wing veterans' newspa-

per later changed its subtitle from "Unabhängige Zeitung zur Vertretung der Interessen aller bodenständigen Kriegsteilnehmer Deutschösterreichs und ihrer Angehörigen" to "Deutsch-antisemitische Zeitung."

45. "Heimkehrer auf Heimat," *Die nationale Frau* 1, no. 2 (18 January 1919), 1–2.

46. *Der Invalide* 2, no. 16 (15 August 1919), 4–5.

47. For the subordination of women and children to men in Austrian family law, see Oskar Lehner, *Familie—Recht—Politik: Die Entwicklung des österreichischen Familienrechte im 19. und 20. Jahrhundert* (Vienna: Springer Verlag, 1987).

48. Robert Weishut, *Vademecum für Heimkehrer* (Alt-Aussee, 1919), 11.

49. Ibid., 6.

50. Ibid., 3–4.

51. ÖStA, AdR, StA f. soz. Verwaltung, Sozialpolitik, 1918, carton 21, #4152. Mayor Weiskirchner to Staatsamt für soziale Fürsorge, 16 December 1918.

52. ÖStA, AdR, StA f. soz. Verwaltung, Sozialpolitik, 1919, carton 26, #10758. Memo, May 1919. The Arbeitslosenfürsorge was instituted between November 1918 and February 1919, and repeatedly extended in three-month intervals thereafter. Eligibility hinged on one's proof of having been enrolled in sickness insurance before the war. The initial payment was around six crowns per day, and this was increased piecemeal by the state and city as inflation continued to rise in 1919 and beyond.

53. *Reichspost*, 22 November 1918, 4. Cited in David F. Strong, *Austria (October 1918–March 1919): Transition from Empire to Republic* (New York: Octagon, 1974), 146.

54. Sigrid Augeneder, *Arbeiterinnen im Ersten Weltkrieg: Lebens- und Arbeitsbedingungen proletarischer Frauen in Österreich* (Vienna: Europaverlag, 1987), 215; Gabriella Hauch, *Vom Frauenstandpunkt aus: Frauen im Parlament 1919–1933* (Vienna: Verlag für Gesellschaftskritik, 1995), 27. Hauch discusses the somewhat comical League for Men's Rights founded in the 1920s to "protect the endangered existence of men," 11–14.

55. ÖStA, AdR, StA f. soz. Verwaltung, Sozialpolitik, carton 21, 1918, #3242. Letter signed "Im Namen meiner gleichgesinnten Heimkehrer" to Staatsratdirektorium, December 1918.

56. Charles A. Gulick, *Austria from Habsburg to Hitler*, 2 Vols. (Berkeley and Los Angeles: University of California Press, 1948), 1:190.

57. *Reconstruction* 4 (1 September 1920), 3.

58. Ibid., 2.

59. Hoover Institution Archives, European Technical Advisers, box 2, general conditions, "Extract from a letter home," 29 December 1920.

60. *Der Invalide* 2, no. 3 (1 February 1919), 1.

61. Adolf Deutsch, *Anleitung zur Feststellung der Erwerbseinbusse bei Kriegsbeschädigte* (Vienna: Staatsamt für Volksgesundheit, 1919), 9; see also *Handbuch für jeden Kriegsinvaliden und Kriegshinterbliebenen* (Vienna, 1921).

62. "Gesichtsplastiken an Kriegsverletzten," *Wiener medizinische Wochenschrift* 5 (1919), 245–53.

63. ÖStA, AdR, StA f. soz. Verwaltung, Sozialpolitik, 1919, carton 25, #6733. Letter from Wilhelm Schürer, 10 March 1919.

64. ÖStA, AdR, StA f. soz. Verwaltung, Sozialpolitik, 1919, carton 27, #11922. Letter from Ernst Bürger, April 1919.

65. ÖStA, AdR, BKA Inneres, Polizei-Direktion Wien, Berichte 1919–1920, no doc. number.

66. Gerhard Botz, *Gewalt in der Politik: Attentate, Zusammenstösse, Putschversuche, und Unruhen in Österreich 1918 bis 1938* (München: Wilhelm Fink Verlag, 1983), 304,

counts 215 deaths and 640 seriously wounded from "political violence" between 1918 and 1933.

67. *Die neue Front* 2, no. 12 (18 March 1920), 6.

68. Ibid.

69. *Mitteilungen des Volksgesundheitsamts* 1 (11 April 1919), 23–24.

70. "Unsittlichkeit?" *Die Frau* (5 February 1919), 3.

71. Ibid.

72. On demobilization, see Wolfgang Etschmann, "Theorie, Praxis und Probleme der Demobilisierung, 1915–1921," (Ph.D. dissertation, University of Vienna, 1979).

73. *Die Gemeindeverwaltung der Bundeshauptstadt Wien in der Zeit vom 1. Juli 1919 bis 31. Dezember 1922 unter dem Bürgermeister Jakob Reumann* (Vienna: Magistrat der Stadt Wien, 1927), 858.

74. *Arbeiterzeitung* (2 January 1919), 5.

75. *Arbeiterzeitung* (23 January 1919), 5.

76. *Arbeiterzeitung* (2 February 1919), 8.

77. *Der Morgen. Wiener Montagsblatt* (6 January 1919), 6.

78. *Öffentliche Sicherheit* 2, no. 2–3 (25 January 1922), 1.

79. Ibid.

80. *Öffentliche Sicherheit* 2, no. 7–8 (20 April 1922), 1.

81. "Das Züchtigungsrecht des Gatten," *Die Unzufriedene* (1 December 1923), 1.

82. Hugo Bettauer, *Viennese Love*, trans. F. H. Lyon (New York: Macaulay, 1929 [1924]), 62–63.

83. *Die Unzufriedene* (22 December 1923), 4. There are no statistics on domestic violence from the period.

84. *Die Unzufriedene* (22 March 1922), 4–6.

85. *Die Unzufriedene* (7 June 1924), 3.

86. For in-depth review of the Austrian revolution of 1918, see John W. Boyer, "Silent War and Bitter Peace: The Revolution of 1918 in Austria," *Austrian History Yearbook* 34 (2003): 1–56.

87. *Mitteilungen des dö. Staatsamtes für Volksgesundheit* 1 (30 November 1918), 20–21.

4 Between Red Army and White Guard: Women in Budapest, 1919

Eliza Ablovatski

"It was like a plague of locusts had devastated the place. Consumed and exhausted, the town lay on the rubbish heap," wrote Dezső Kosztolányi of the Hungarian capital Budapest in the late summer of 1919.[1] Since the end of the World War in October, the city had indeed suffered a great deal: two revolutions (one democratic, the other soviet), a flu epidemic, Romanian occupation, a flood of refugees, and the armed gangs of the White Terror. The physical exhaustion he described, as well as the personal stories of hunger and suffering retold after both revolutions, were informed by the language of politics. In the postrevolutionary chaos that summer, Hungary's political and social elite began to reassert itself and its values, although, as Kosztolányi noted, "Trams which had been painted under Communist rule were still to be seen in their revolutionary scarlet with revolutionary slogans daubed across them, dashing suicidally through town like refugees from a mental institution."[2] Political slogans and political calculations were behind even the most ordinary personal interactions, from forms of address and greeting to interactions on public transit. In Kosztolányi's novel, *Anna Édes,* the upper-class Kornel Vizy observed the city that summer, noting that, "there were also encouraging signs of improvement. Middle-class passengers on the tram were no longer afraid to stand up to the bullying conductress who addressed them rudely. They took pleasure in reminding her that this was no longer a Bolshevist state. Men once again began to give up their seats to ladies. It was a new and glorious flowering of the age of chivalry."[3]

The old elites reasserted social and political power through the affirmation of class (the conductress should use proper honorific forms of address) and gender roles (chivalry of the upper classes). The front line in the perceived struggle of cultures in 1919 Hungary moved from the world of armies and politics to the personal lives of Budapest residents, and the reestablishment of traditional gender roles played an important part in the postrevolutionary "Christian and National" consolidation of power. The disordered world of revolution had shocked conservative intellectuals:

> It was as though the city had for years devoured countless Galician immigrants and now vomited them forth in sickness. How sick it was! Syrian faces and bodies,

red posters and red hammers whirled around in it. And Freemasons, feminists, editorial offices . . . night cafes came to the surface—and the ghetto sported cockades of national colors and chrysanthemums.[4]

For an observer like this nationalist woman, political restoration after 1919 was inextricably tied up with and dependent upon the restoration of the social, racial, and gender order that the revolutions had threatened.

In the expanding field of the cultural history of World War I, the role of gender in the experience and memory of those years has often been summarized in the fighting front–home front dichotomy. The experience of war on the fighting front and the soldiers' masculine world are contrasted with the realm of the home front, where women experienced the war through a variety of domestic hardships. There were, however, many men on the home front: older men, government officials, and skilled workers in the war industries among them. In addition, a limited number of women experienced the fighting front, mainly through the medical services, although also as civilians in the direct line of battle. Yet the division stands. A gendered division of experience of the war was something that contemporaries emphasized, and this gender dichotomy has inspired an impressive body of scholarly work on the cultural history of World War I and its aftermath.[5]

But what of revolution and civil war, where the generalized dichotomy of fighting front–home front does not hold? How do participants and witnesses experience and remember such events? Do the same gender differences apply? How does the presence of women in revolutionary movements and crowds affect the archetypes of the war experience: the myths of soldier's honor and bravery, the images of the enemy, the images of battle? Events in the Hungarian capital, Budapest, afford us the opportunity to consider some of these questions.

This essay examines the importance of gender within the two main cultures of remembrance that developed in postrevolutionary Hungary: a dominant right wing and an exiled and/or underground left wing. Both the left and the right wanted the events of 1918–1919 remembered as real revolutions not merely riots or upheavals. The events of 1919 became a founding myth, the basis for a collective identity. For those on the right, emphasis on the revolutionaries' violence and bloodthirstiness provided the justification for the excesses of the White brigades, as well as for continuing the legal state of emergency from World War I throughout the interwar period based on the law for the maintenance of order (Law III of 1921). This law permitted preemptive imprisonment for political crimes and prevented public meetings and rallies. Stressing the danger of revolution gave license for drastic countermeasures in the name of the nation.

While many on the left suffered as a result of these countermeasures, for them remembering the revolutions as real, as potentially effective, was a way to justify the martyrdom of the many who had been arrested or executed. It was also important for arousing the sympathy of radicals around the world. Although part of a defeated minority at home, they had not suffered in vain, nor made a revolution only in Budapest, but were participants in an international struggle, a potentially powerful collective.

On both sides of the political divide, women were symbolic representations of their community: either the nation or the workers' movement. The right was concerned with the dangerous women of the revolution, but left and right considered women to be their most vulnerable members. Both employed the rape and sexual mistreatment of women (or the danger of it) as the highest example of the immorality and barbarism of the other side.

In the aftermath of war and revolution in Hungary, many bourgeois city dwellers were in a state of agitation. Although shocked by their experience of violence, they were willing to tolerate further violence in the name of law and order. They felt the need to lose themselves in a larger purpose, a greater identity, but were terrified of the masses, the crowds. Fear of revolution and demonstrations of extreme nationalism were often expressed through highly gendered and sexual imagery, and often equally graphic anti-Semitism. This essay employs the portrayals of women in Hungary's 1919 revolution and the treatment of suspected female participants to highlight the violent anti-Semitism and gender stereotypes that were part of the political atmosphere of Christian and National Hungary during the early part of Admiral Miklós Horthy's regency.

The Revolutionary Context

Allied with Germany, Austria-Hungary had been one of the main belligerents in World War I. The monarchy's mobilization of over 8 million soldiers during the war threw millions of citizens and their families into the crucible of world events. The Austro-Hungarian Army's losses in World War I were devastating: by one estimate there were 1,200,000 dead; 3,620,000 wounded; and 2,200,000 missing or prisoners of war at the war's end, or almost 90 percent casualties.[6] The suffering caused by these losses was compounded by shortages and inflated prices for foodstuffs throughout the monarchy. Because of the wartime requisitioning of agricultural produce, Hungarian farmers were forced to sell to the government at controlled prices so that the costs of war were disproportionate. These controls, intended to keep the price of rations low for the military and urban war-industry workers, caused resentment among Hungarian farmers who believed that they alone were compelled to support the Habsburg war effort. They were giving their sons and their produce to the Habsburg imperial war cause, and they considered their sacrifice to be greater than that of the monarchy's other peoples.[7] Civil violence in Hungary after the Great War enhanced this national sense of unusual and unrequited sacrifice between 1914 and 1918. The notion of a special national burden—a "Hungarian Calvary," later popularized as a metaphor for the revolution and peace treaty—began developing during the war.

In the final year of the war, the battle front moved home and included the streets of the capital and the countryside. There were general strikes in Hungary during January and July 1918, each mobilizing some one-half million workers throughout the country. These strikes brought masses of ordinary disenfranchised workers onto the political stage. Many observers, citing the example of the revolution in Russia, thought the message was clear: "The front has taught our people to think, has awakened them, and they will no longer endure the domination of county pashas and city profiteers."[8] On the streets of the capital by late 1918 it certainly seemed that this was true.

Even before its armies signed the Armistice of 11 November 1918, revolution had begun in Austria-Hungary. The multinational Habsburg Monarchy dissolved into numerous successor states, which began fighting along their respective borders to secure the territories each considered integral to their new independent existence. In the twin capitals of Vienna and Budapest, democratic—or at least parliamentary—revolutions dethroned the Habsburgs. Mass demonstrations in Budapest—the so-called *őszirózsa* or "Chrysanthemum Revolution" in October (named after the flowers worn by demonstrators)—led King Charles to turn over power to a democratic government under Count Mihály Károlyi, who declared the First Hungarian Republic on 16 November.

The Károlyi government, like the Provisional Government in Russia in 1917, came under immediate attack from both the left and the right. Many conservative Hungarians, like their contemporaries in Weimar Germany, associated their country's new parliamentary government only with defeat in the World War and the demands of the Entente leaders in Paris. For Hungarian nationalists, even the long-awaited independence from Austria was only bittersweet when it resulted from military collapse and revolution. The leaders also found themselves confronted with the looming, extremely disadvantageous peace settlements. Economic collapse followed the military collapse, and the chaotic end of the war meant that tens of thousands of soldiers—many still carrying army-issued weapons—suddenly arrived in the cities, unemployed and suffering from the so-called front syndrome. In Hungary the situation was exacerbated by the arrival of hundreds of thousands of refugees from the territories of old Hungary that had been occupied by the neighboring successor states.[9] This proved a volatile political mix.

With the delivery on 20 March 1919 of the so-called Vix note from the Entente, the situation became too precarious for Károlyi to govern. This note delineated Hungary's new borders, making clear the extent of territory that Hungary would be forced to cede to its neighbors. The announcement of the terms of the peace treaty and these territorial losses led Károlyi's National Council to hand over power to a coalition of socialists and communists.[10] This new, united socialist party, led by Béla Kun, promised to fight against the terms of the "imperialist peace" and declared the Soviet Republic on 21 March. This government of councils (*Tanácsköztársaság*) lasted 133 days before collapsing under military and popular pressure. Even many officers of the old Habsburg Army and Hungarian nationalists supported the new regime initially—out of anger at the Entente and in the hopes of retrieving the lost territories. Only after the Red Army's first military losses in the late spring did the tables start to turn, and the organizers of the counterrevolution gained overriding support.

By the end of the summer of 1919, Hungary had slipped into anarchy, with remnants of the Red Army fighting Romanian forces and the Szeged-organized counterrevolutionary National Army, loosely under Horthy's command, wreaking revenge and terror in the countryside. These White Forces were responsible for a great deal of wild counterrevolutionary justice, executing many purported revolutionaries on the spot or after summary courts-martial under their own officers. These forces also instigated widespread anti-Jewish violence and pogroms.[11] International concern about the violent retribution that the White forces might take against socialists and Jews in Budapest led the Entente to forbid Horthy to enter the capital with his forces until he had provided assurances that his soldiers would not "punish" the city with violence. Instead, Romanian troops under Entente control secured order in the capital when the soviet government fled in August. Only in November did the Entente permit Horthy to enter the capital with his army. This he did with great pomp, astride a white horse and wearing his ceremonial Habsburg admiral's uniform. A period of restoration followed in the next two years with the Hungarian parliament naming Horthy regent for the Habsburg king. The initial diversity of political parties consolidated into the governing bloc of Christian and National parties and the (barely) tolerated Social Democratic opposition.[12]

Gender and Counterrevolution

The evolving myth of Hungarian national martyrdom—in the World War, the revolution, and the territorial losses of the Trianon Peace Treaty—was reflected in contemporary perceptions of women's roles in both revolution and counterrevolution. The tropes of the pure "white" woman and the dangerous "red" woman helped contemporaries to understand and react to the violent events around them, and often played an important role in shaping memories and narratives of the revolution, serving as symbolic guideposts in chaotic times.

The important role of gender in understanding the White Terror has been investigated for the case of post–World War I Germany, and there are certainly important similarities in the situations of the two countries. In addition to the lost war and its large-scale casualties, both had experienced many of the same social pressures and upheavals in the years before the war. The traditional elites felt their political and social influence doubly threatened: by the emergence of socialism and mass politics, and by a vast upwardly mobile, educated (and what disturbed many, often Jewish) middle class in the cities. Another similarity with important psychological consequences for nationalists in both countries was the phenomenon of lost territories and the refugees coming from these.

Klaus Theweleit's pathbreaking research on Germany recognized and analyzed the particular set of gendered literary tropes in the soldiers' memoirs published during the Weimar Republic. His research outlined a specific masculine psychology, recognizable in the way women appeared in the counterrevolutionary memoirs, which he called the "soldier male," who feared women and the crowd, and which expressed itself in violence.[13] However, Joan Scott has criticized such psychoanalytical approaches to gender history for perpetuating an "ahistorical, almost essentialist notion of woman" and man.[14] Historians like Theweleit assume the "timeless quality" of "the problem of sexual antagonism," to use Scott's phrasing. Scott argues that the work of historians has to be to critique these sorts of categories and to produce "a genuine historicization and deconstruction of the terms of sexual difference."[15] In the 1970s Theweleit sought to uncover the reason for the "soldier male's" dysfunctional socialization.[16] But Scott's advisory is well warranted, and by examining similar stereotypes and themes in the writing of a Hungarian female memoirist, we recognize that the tropes of the pure "white" woman and the dangerous "red" woman were not the product of the male soldier's front experience, but were the gender assumptions all across the political right in interwar central Europe. These were stereotypes and tropes that were used by both sexes and not only in the younger generations. By historicizing the White Terror and using a transnational comparative context, we can use some of Theweleit's insights to help us better understand Hungarian interwar society while avoiding his essentializing tendencies.

Cecile Tormay, author of the antirevolutionary memoir *An Outlaw's Diary*, was an important figure in the Hungarian nationalist women's movement. One of a small number of female authors in Hungary at the time, Tormay was well respected, especially in conservative and nationalist literary circles, as the author of a series of novels with romantic-national themes.[17] She served as the first editor of the literary journal, *Napkelet* (Orient), founded in 1923 as a nationalist counterpoint to the famous literary journal, *Nyugat* (West).[18] During the revolution, Tormay helped to found and served as president of the right-wing National Association of Hungarian Women. As the representative of this association, Tormay participated in the ceremonies welcoming Horthy as liberator of Budapest in November 1919, presenting him with a "splendidly embroidered banner" at a ceremony on the steps of the Parliament.[19] Upon his arrival Horthy famously condemned the capital, calling Budapest "the sinful city" for having "dragged the Holy Crown and the national colors in the dust" and "clothed herself in red rags."[20] Horthy asked Hungarians to join him on a "holy cause," and called for the "nation's soul" to be purged of all "poisonous elements."[21] Hungary should follow the new Christian and National political course.

Tormay's memoirs gave vivid literary imagery to this Christian and National program and its version of recent history. Like the memoirs examined by Theweleit of former *Freikorps* soldiers, Tormay's *Outlaw's Diary* does not represent a memoir in the traditional sense of an autobiographical work, but is a *political* book written for *political* purposes, while following the form of a diary and therefore of eyewitness testimony. The book is neither a diary nor a memoir with the goal of self-explication, but rather an explication of contemporary events written with the authority of the witness. Her work is a vivid example of the combination of nationalist politics with the perhaps eternal moral dichotomy of women as either angels or whores. Tormay and other nationalists perceived the women participating in the revolution (either in the rare cases where they took an active political role, or as part of the masses in demonstrations) not only as politically dangerous, but also as sexually dangerous and physically degenerate, unwomanly. Nationalists like Tormay depoliticized women on the right; the supposed political naiveté of these women, though making them morally irreproachable, also made them weak and susceptible to the influences of others. In this sense women were both the saviors of the nation and needed desperately to be protected by it. In Tormay's *Outlaw's Diary,* all of these ideas about gender roles and explanatory models were paired with an explicitly anti-Semitic message.

Early in her memoir, Tormay described how she and some fellow Red Cross members were sent away from their stand at the Budapest train station after the revolution. She contrasted the noble nature of her colleagues—the Red Cross nurses as the epitome of the national feminine ideal, helping and ministering to the soldiers—with the physically and politically dangerous women who replaced them. She described her discovery of the revolutionary takeover of the first aid stations: "We who had for many years worked there with the Red Cross, offered our services in vain." Tormay then criticized the new workers as Jews and represented their help for the soldiers—the distribution of bread and meat—as luxuriant bribes to go along with the overt political message that was contained in brochures they also handed out: "White bread, which we had not seen for a long time, and sausages, were distributed to the soldiers by Jewesses who wore neither hat nor cap and looked unkempt and untidy. They had been sent by the Social Democratic party, and care for the soldiers was only a secondary part of their duty: they distributed handbills and talked propaganda to the returning men."[22] Here the danger emanating from the women described by Tormay is political and, while not explicitly sexual, is a moral and even physical danger, through the luxurious foods (decadence in the face of rationing) and their unclean appearance.

Elsewhere in the *Diary* Tormay decried the desecration of Hungarian culture, again using the idea of unclean [Jewish] women and unclean food to dramatize her point. She pointed to the changes in the capital city since the revolution, "A new kind of public invades the restaurants, the theatres, and the places of amusement." Tormay considered this new public unappealing in terms of both class and ethnicity. She wrote, "People in gabardines occupy the stalls, while in the boxes Orthodox Jewish women in wigs chatter in Yiddish, and in the interval eat garlic-scented sausages in the beautiful, noble foyer of the Royal Opera, and throw greasy paper bags around."[23] This scene represented a disturbing revolutionary inversion of hierarchy and social order. Although Tormay also raged against the supposed orgies and "evenings of mixed company" which took place in the hotel taken over as the socialist headquarters, she more often focused on such images of filth and gluttony to represent the physical dangers posed by revolutionary women.

Tormay also vented her anger at another type of dangerous woman, the seductress or coquette, whom she condemned on two levels: for being immoral and insincere and, perhaps more importantly, for distracting the men of the nation from the important tasks at hand. She considered Countess Károlyi, the wife of Mihály Károlyi, to be one such coquette. Like her husband, the countess hailed from one of Hungary's most important political families—the Andrássys—and thus could not be criticized as foreign or coarse. However, Tormay believed this young woman did not take the responsibility of her heritage seriously. Her insincerity compounded what Tormay described as the physical and mental degeneracy of her husband. Though he was not a Jew, Tormay described Károlyi in ways that recalled Jewish stereotypes.

As much as she scorned the "ugly" Károlyi, Tormay seemed almost more affronted by his attractive wife, whom she saw driving in Budapest in the car of the former king, "rouged in a doll-like fashion, and her beautiful big eyes sparkled. Her voluptuous young mouth smiled in rapture, and she seemed to be drinking her success from the air greedily."[24] The perceived danger to the nation from such a vain and seductive woman caused Tormay to reflect, "The car had long disappeared but it seemed to me as if the smile of those painted lips had left a trail of corruption over the suffering, harassed people. It spread and spread . . . " According to Tormay, the results of that "trail of corruption" were that, "The frontiers of the country are bleeding. The enemy is victorious without having vanquished us. The army goes to pieces; the throne has fallen. St. Stephen's crown has lost Croatia and Slavonia. The rabble robs and pilfers. A Serbian army has crossed the frontier. And the painted lips smile, smile . . . "[25] Here Tormay laid the blame for all the country's suffering—territorial losses, revolution, even looting—at the feet of the coquettish young first lady.

The antithesis of the dangerous revolutionary woman and seductive coquette was the White angel of the nation, a component of Tormay's self-image and self-description. Despite Tormay's prominence in conservative political circles even before the war and her active role in organizing the counterrevolution, in her *Diary* she described her organization, The National Association of Hungarian Women, as nonpolitical, and called herself "a stranger in the world of politics."[26] Speaking to fellow female conspirators, Tormay delineated the battlefronts for women during the revolution: "our fortress is a triangle, the three advanced outworks being our country, our faith, and our family. These three outworks are threatened by Jewish socialist communism."[27] Although using a military metaphor of a bulwark, Tormay portrayed women's role as one of support: "Before the foe can storm the fort we must strengthen the souls of the defenders," the men.[28]

Unlike the women of the left, "red" women who made real politics, gave speeches, and distributed pamphlets, Tormay and her followers would strive for a behind-the-scenes political influence. For them these were not merely traditional, or conservative, female roles in a universal sense; they were highly national, part of Hungarian national character. Tormay tied these behaviors to Hungarian ethnic traditions and Hungarian history; the national character of Hungary's women particularly suited them to the sort of counterrevolutionary work she was organizing. Comparing the present danger of Bolshevism with the Turkish invasions, Tormay wrote:

> Our country has never suffered greater distress than now . . . we all knew that the women would respond to our call and would sow the seed of the counter-revolution. Not at meetings, not in the market-place, but in their homes, in the souls of their men exhausted by the hardships of war, men who are down-hearted to-day but who, to-morrow, will not dare to give the lie to the women who believe in their courage.[29]

Emancipation or the "Nationalization of Women"?

Women in Tormay's description were both the nation's bulwark and its most endangered members. In her speeches to the National Association, Tormay portrayed the particular danger posed to women by revolution. She referred to the myth that under communism there would be "free love" or the "nationalization of women." According to Tormay, "Of all humanity, women will be the heaviest losers if the war is lost and the communists win, for women are to be common property once the home is broken up, and God and country have been denied. . . . We who fight on the soil of dismembered, trampled Hungary do not fight for ourselves alone, but for every Christian woman in the world."[30] Just as in the wars against the Turks, the current battle of Hungarian counterrevolution would, in Tormay's view, be fought symbolically on behalf of all Europe.

The myth of the nationalization of women under communism was one of the most widespread horrific images held up to inspire fear of revolution. It was used as a rallying cry for counterrevolutionary troops. The German anarchist writer Erich Mühsam, one of the leaders of the contemporary revolutionary government in Munich, later reflected on the effects of this myth in the "Republic of Councils and Sexual Revolution," writing: "The terrible murder of Gustav Landauer [who was lynched by soldiers after his arrest] . . . can only be put down to the fact that the soldiers on those blacklists were convinced that Landauer and Mühsam had wanted to nationalize the women."[31] Mühsam recognized the danger of this myth that the communists would "nationalize the women" and break up the family; the myth was a source of much of the counterrevolutionaries' rage and violence against the revolution.

Even if women weren't "nationalized," it was clear that the revolutionaries intended to shake up traditional patterns of family and authority. Revolution threatened paternal authority over children as well as the authority of husbands over their wives. These perceived threats were terrifying to conservatives. Grace Hunter, an American reporter for the New York socialist *Call*, wrote from Budapest in 1919 trying to counteract rumors that the revolutionary government would destroy the family. Quite the opposite, she claimed; the soviet regime actually promoted marriage. Hunter reassured her American audience that "thanks to increased wages and sundry governmental provisions relative to housing, people in Budapest can now marry with impunity."[32] She quoted Dezső Somló, the People's Commissar for Housing, that "ten thousand couples have married in Budapest within the last two weeks and come to me for furniture and rooms . . . now that the working man and woman get a living wage with a surplus, they seem to get married very fast."[33]

Hunter, who was sympathetic to the Hungarian soviet regime, considered this information proof of improvements in the lives of proletarians, who now were free to pursue romantic happiness. Emancipation did not mean moral degeneration. To emphasize her point, Hunter quoted Somló's description of the decisive actions of the revolutionary government against prostitution and "houses of ill-repute." Hunter defended the regime against its critics. Did this encouragement of marriage and attack on prostitution, she asked rhetorically, "look like communism would abolish the home and encourage free love?"[34]

For conservatives, it looked exactly as if the abolition of home and family was, if not communism's conscious goal, then at least its logical result. In the report *The Dictatorship of the Proletariat in Hungary: A Faithful Portrait of the Bolshevik Reign of Terror* in 1920, the counterrevolutionary mayor of Budapest, Tivadar Bódy, portrayed the same wave of marriages that Hunter had found so reassuring as the disintegration of traditional family roles in society. Bódy complained that during the revolution the age of majority was lowered to 18, and as a result, "Many people who were not yet 24 years old married without the permission of parents, guardians or the juvenile authorities. It happened that many foolish, careless marriages were entered into."[35] Included in this publication organized by Károlyi Huszár, the prime minister of the first postrevolutionary Christian National government, to document the "Bolshevik reign of terror," this entry seems surprising; but conservatives took very seriously the challenge posed to the social order by lowering the majority and loosening marriage laws. The revolution threatened to emancipate women not only politically, but also socially.

Her fear of women's emancipation constituted a dilemma for an active, conservative woman like Tormay. An unmarried, financially independent writer, a well-known, politically connected literary figure, and a nationalist, she was, by most definitions, politically and socially emancipated. Yet her nationalist politics were anti-emancipatory. She took great pains to portray the realm of women's activity within traditional feminine roles but often described her frustration watching male contemporaries fail to stem the revolutionary tide. She wrote, "I realized that my own inactivity was part of the great culpable inactivity of the nation. I too was guilty of lethargy. No longer must I content myself with accusing others, no longer expect action from them alone."[36] To fight her lethargy, Tormay walked the city, describing how the revolutionary soldiers and "rabble" had besmirched its architectural monuments. At the end of her wanderings, however, Tormay came to a conclusion that seemed to belie her earlier determination not to "expect action" from others. She wanted a strong man to take charge and to rescue her and her country:

> I reached home tired out. Why had I gone out at all? What did I want? . . . I wanted to hear the sound of a name, the name of a man who was brave and strong, who

knew how to organize and how to give orders, who could lay his hand on destiny at the brink of the abyss.[37]

For Tormay, as for many Hungarians, Miklós Horthy was just the man to steer the nation away from the abyss. *Hungary's Admiral on Horseback*, as a recent biography of Horthy is called, seems almost a comic figure today: an admiral in a country with no navy and no outlet to the sea, regent in a kingdom which could never again have a king.[38] In 1919, however, Horthy's clout as one of the Habsburg Monarchy's few war heroes and the image of this hero in his admiral's uniform on a white horse were powerfully reassuring symbols of social order and masculine authority. This combination of symbols was powerfully advertised by one of the most widely reproduced posters for Horthy in 1919–1920 that showed only a powerful hand firmly grasping the helm of a ship (fig. 4.1). The message was clear: Horthy would steer the nation to safety like a ship in a stormy sea.

Gender, Anti-Semitism and Terror

The realm of the question of gender and revolution may be found in the blurred and contested line between the political and the personal. This is not only in the sense of a masculine public and political realm and a feminine private or personal domestic realm, but also in the realm of memory and how the events in one person's life are formed by them (and by others) into a narrative.[39] Within that narrative the political and the personal are interwoven and reconciled with one another. This reconciliation occurs within the dominant cultural values of the society in which the narrative is created, but the narratives created also influence society. The elemental vocabulary and symbols of gender descriptions are particularly important in the way that violent or traumatic events such as revolution and civil war are processed and understood.

Richard Bessel examined the process of reconciliation with dominant values for memories of the German demobilization after World War I.[40] He argued that the return to dominance of traditional values of discipline, authority, and honor in Weimar Germany caused a problem for many veterans, who, at the time of the chaotic demobilization in defeat and revolution, had in fact behaved quite differently than they should have; they overstayed their leave, shirked front duty, or did not follow demobilization orders. Bessel reported that in contrast with later memories of "ungrateful" citizenry, there were parades held in honor of returning soldiers all over Germany, but in many cases the veterans had already skipped out of their units. These embarrassing facts were later conflated in the minds of soldiers with the memories of officers who were humiliated in public by having their stripes cut off, even though it was their own soldiers who had done this. By the end of Weimar, the collective myth of honorable veterans returning to a society that scorned them was omnipresent in the press and memoirs. Despite its obvious lack of correspondence to the facts of the demobiliza-

Figure 4.1. Horthy's Guiding Hand at the Helm. Poster by Miltiades Manno, 1919.

tion, it was a better and psychologically easier way for the veterans to remember the immediate postwar conflicts.[41]

A similar distortion or rewriting in order to reconcile the subjective personal experiences and emotions felt at the time with the objective narrative of the political events was widespread for many aspects of the revolutions of 1919 in Budapest. Vilmos Böhm, the Károlyi government war minister and a Red Army lieutenant, invoked this when he wrote sarcastically about the so-called battles of the counterrevolution in his memoirs. He emphasized that the "'Army of Heroes' never fought an enemy force on the battlefield."[42] Horthy and his forces crossed the Danube into a region without Romanian troops, one from which the remnants of the Red Army had already fled. There, wrote Böhm, Horthy's National Army "battled only against the peaceful, unarmed population."[43] Under this "dictatorship of horrors," Böhm described, "Unarmed people were shot to death, hanged, castrated, mutilated, blinded; innocent, defenseless women were raped, unsuspecting children murdered,—these were the combat methods of the victorious Horthy army . . . parents executed in front of their children, husbands in front of their wives, brides before their grooms, all with refined, inhumane tortures."[44]

The actions of the White Terror—violence of armed soldiers and militiamen against a largely unarmed population—were difficult to reconcile with traditional notions of soldiers' honor or warfare. Therefore it was important that the citizenry be demonized in ways that disqualified it from honorable treatment. If women were in the crowds or among the victims, they must not have been proper women, but were dangerous, defeminized women. If old men (mostly Jewish) were among the victims, then the Jews needed to be understood as collectively dangerous. In Hungary a similar transference occurred—Jews were the main victims of the counterrevolutionary violence, but they were remembered as its instigators. The far greater violence of the counterrevolution was understood as the result of the revolutionary violence. As one right-wing historian of the Horthy era cleverly put it, "It was the [Red] Terror Detachments, without which the Dictatorship of the Proletariat couldn't have existed, which generated the White Terror."[45] Examining the role of gender in narratives of the revolution permits a better understanding of the anti-Semitism that followed. It was not a direct reaction to the presence of Jews in the revolutionary governments, but was a product of the need to reconcile the dishonorable and criminal behavior of the White Terror with existing societal norms. One important way to do this was by portraying the revolutionaries, both male and female, as outside of society's gender order.

Rape and Counter-Memory on the Left

For the right, the stereotype of the dangerous and unfeminine "red" woman justified her exclusion from traditional chivalrous protection, just as the naïve and pure "white" woman became a symbol of the nation in need of protection. These tropes made sense of the counterrevolution with its attacks by armed men on civilians. As we have seen, this right-wing narrative was politically dominant in interwar Hungary. The counter-memory of the left, excluded from much of Hungarian civil society, found its voice predominantly in works published outside the country. In these works, the symbolic role of women also played an important part in establishing moral legitimacy for the left's narrative of events.

Reports of the sexual depravity of White Forces and the mistreatment of women by the White officers' brigades became part of a myth of martyrdom on the left. As in Böhm's memoirs, writers on the left went out of their way to demonstrate the White Forces' barbarity, grasping particularly at examples of rape and cruelty to women and children, where the Whites violated the very codes of gender order that they claimed to uphold. The heroic myth of the Christian National rescue of a country in danger was not only the official government version of events, but was affirmed in memoirs like Tormay's, giving their eyewitness credence to the story. Böhm and other leftist memoirists challenged this version of recent history, pointing out that Horthy's army had been almost entirely militarily unchallenged and demonstrating the barbarism and moral depravity of the White forces.[46] They were not merely fake heroes who hadn't really fought, but were unmanly, and had attacked the innocent, the women and children, those who should have expected the protection of heroic soldiers.

Böhm and the thousands of other political refugees from Horthy's Hungary garnered international support, and several delegations were sent to Hungary to investigate the crimes of the White Terror.[47] These groups investigated on behalf of fellow organized labor or of Jewish coreligionists, but their reports often focused on questions of gender in order to persuade their readers about the plight of Hungary. A commission sent to Hungary in April 1920 by the Joint Distribution Committee (JDC) to investigate anti-Semitic violence and activities reported in a letter to Felix Warburg that "even in Budapest, there was hardly a day when Jews were not beaten, maimed and killed . . . No Jew, however prominent he might be, ventured even at the time I was in Budapest on the streets after dark and I was warned not to go out in the evening unless by automobile."[48] The JDC delegation recommended that aid to the indigent Jews of Budapest be given in ways that would not cause embarrassment to "large numbers of professional men whom it would be humiliating to assist in the way others are assisted." They also underlined the tragic situation of the Jewish students who had been prevented from attending universities by anti-Semitic rioting. The JDC report emphasized the special problems of the male members of the "respectable classes" (professionals and students); support for the Jewish poor was organized around such patriotic causes as "war widow and orphans," categories that called up traditional gendered images of charity recipients. In this way the JDC distanced itself from the impression that Jewish interests lay with the revolutionary lower classes or potential political actors like the students. Right-wing writers like Tormay as well as the popular press had drawn an equation between Jewishness and complicity in the revolution. The JDC and the bourgeois Jewish organizations with which it worked in Budapest were at great pains to try to disentangle these associations in the popular consciousness. Part of this disentangling was the reestablishment of bourgeois masculine norms of financially self-sufficient professionals.

Following reports in the press and information from trade unions, the British Labour Party sent its own delegation to Hungary. They were dissatisfied with a British government White Paper issued in February 1920, in which Admiral Ernest Troubridge had reported that "life is as secure here [in Hungary] as in England," and called the Horthy regime, "a Christian government in a Christian country." Labour delegates noted "this conveys a false impression unless it is fully understood that in Hungary the word Christian has a definite political significance."[49] The "Report of the British Joint Labour Delegation to Hungary" from May 1920 describes many cases of intimidation, mishandling, and judicial murder reported to representatives of the Labour Party and Trades Union Congress who were sent to Hungary to investigate the "allegations of persecutions of the working classes in Hungary."[50] The delegation, including Member of Parliament Colonel J. C. Wedgwood, conducted interviews in Vienna and Budapest and sent two members to prison camps in Szolnok and Abony.

Two of the dozen cases presented in the British Labour Report involve women, and these offer an especially interesting perspective on the international perception of violence in Hungary, as well as on the important role that female victims played in the propaganda of both the left and the right. In this report on the White Terror, crimes against women were held up as proof of the White Forces' barbarous nature, and the possible political activities or convictions of the women were swept aside in favor of their symbolic role as the ultimate victims.

One of the women who testified to the British Labour delegation was a young Jewish woman from Putnok, in northeastern Hungary, who had been arrested in Budapest in October 1919. She was taken to the Mozsár street police prison, where she was questioned repeatedly "about being a Communist" before being released.[51] She was subsequently rearrested and released two more times; at one point she was beaten at police headquarters for refusing to admit that she was a communist. After Horthy's arrival in Budapest, she went into hiding but was "compelled to leave the house to sell some of her things in order to live."[52] She was recognized on the street by an officer and taken to a police station, where she was locked up and threatened if she refused to sign an admission of being a "Socialist agitator." One of the officers then refused to let her be fed unless she would have sex with him. After this denial of food, "he visited her cell at night and violated her. Two days later he violated her again."[53] After a guard left her cell open, the girl was able to flee to Vienna, where the British delegates interviewed her. They reported that "[s]he is enceinte through the officer who violated her."[54] At a time when pregnancy out of wedlock caused great social stigma, this rape case seems included in the Labour delegation report in order to shock its readers with the moral consequences of the violence in Hungary. The report described the more gruesome physical brutality male victims expe-

Figure 4.2. "Rape" by Mihály Biró. Courtesy of Graphic Witness.

rienced (including castration and disembowelment from kicking and stomping), but the case of the young woman from Putnok is the final one described in the report and at great length. Its inclusion and attention to detail offered an example of the supposedly Christian regime's moral cruelty and sexual depravity, to trump the "merely" physical cruelty of the other cases.

The British Labour Report offered international authentication for the suffering of the victims of the White Terror in Hungary. The cases described in the report served as the basis for a 1920 book of drawings made in exile in Vienna by the artist Mihály Biró, who had earlier drawn propaganda posters for the Hungarian soviet regime. The postcard-sized book, "The White Terror in Hungary under the Regime Horthy," was republished during the interwar period and the war years, angering the Hungarian government, which demanded that Austria extradite Biró to face charges.[55] The twenty images roughly correspond to the cases described in the British Labour Report. Figure 4.2, "Rape," is a graphic rendition of the story of the young woman from Putnok.

The other woman whose story was included in both the Labour report and Biró's illustrations was Mrs. Hamburger, "her husband's brother [Eugen Hamburger] a known Communist and an ex-Commissary." She was picked up by the military after receiving a message from her husband who had fled to Vienna with his brother. She and her companions were taken to the Kelenföld barracks where officers, including the infamous White Terrorist Lieutenant Héjjas, subjected them to bloody and humiliating torture. They were held for five weeks, during which time an old friend of hers, a Jew named Neumann, had all his teeth pulled and was castrated for refusing to rape Mrs. Hamburger after officers ordered him to do so. The state prosecutor, Dr. Albert Váry, admitted to the British delegation that "a body had been washed up by the Danube that was supposed to be Neumann's, and that . . . he had granted facilities to the relative for identification. . . . "[56]

Hamburger's story made a strong impression on the Labour representatives. They interviewed her twice and her case was discussed at far greater length than the others. Having described the sexual torture of Hamburger and her friend, the authors protested, "Mrs. H. is a quiet, unassuming and a highly respected woman, and we were informed by all who knew her that she possessed a moral character beyond reproach. No charge was ever made against her; there has been no semblance of a trial."[57] The Labour delegation's defense of Hamburger focused on her "moral character," as well as on the moral depravity of her captors and the White officers. The counterrevolutionary officials, when defending their own use of force, used similarly gendered moral justifications. The revolutionaries were morally depraved and therefore could only be met with force.

The official story given to the British Labour delegates about Mrs. Hamburger followed the general pattern of portraying female political prisoners as morally dangerous and uncontrollable. The Labour delegation petitioned the Horthy government for an explanation of the case,

> but failed to get it in writing. The Hungarian government admits, however, that Mrs. Hamburger was badly beaten, but alleges that she was placed in a cell in which there was one man, and that they were found misconducting themselves. She was removed to another cell in which there was another man, and again found misconducting herself and was consequently beaten disciplinarily.[58]

In other words, the abuse of Hamburger did not violate the social and gender norms of civilization; rather the woman's "sexual depravity" caused her to fall outside of the usual protection afforded to women (and prisoners) in government custody. To counter these claims, the report established a counter-memory of events, also reinforcing gender distinctions. As the report stressed, Hamburger was far from the sexually depraved and dangerous prisoner described by the government; rather, she was a paragon of bourgeois female virtue. After quoting the government explanation, the Labour Report authors reemphasized their portrait of Hamburger as a moral woman, claiming that "[a]part from the inherent improbabilities of the semi-official Government defense . . . Mrs. Hamburger appears to be a respectable woman of good education. . . . We are quite unable to accept the semi-official story."[59]

Conclusion: Memory, Narrative, and Political Repression

Both sides in the Hungarian civil war emphasized rapes committed by the enemy in their rhetoric to highlight his general sexual pathology, as Tormay often did in her *Outlaw's Diary.* This rhetorical trope of the morally depraved enemy also meshed with the legal distinction between "political crimes" and "common criminals." If political actors and revolutionaries could be shown to be pathological, "criminal types," then they did not require special treatment as political prisoners. The lawyer Oszkár Szőllősy, a member of the Hungarian Ministry of Justice under Horthy, explained this distinction in an article titled "The Criminals of the Dictatorship of the Proletariat," writing that "every revolution has its idealistic champions . . . themselves ready to endure all the suffering of Calvary in the service of the creed which they profess."[60] He asserted that one must admire certain of these idealists—like Camille Desmoulins of the French revolutionaries—for their "unselfish enthusiasm." He reminded his readers that "[i]n our moral judgment we distinguish between political and other criminals; a similar sharp judgment is made by the general conceptions of criminal law."[61] He then employed this distinction to construe the actual activities of revolutionaries as criminal rather than political, claiming, "in cases where only the tendency or motive is of such [political] character, while the means employed are base, as is true of most revolutionary offences—for without violence and dangerous threats there can be no revolution—we are confronted not with political, but with common crimes."[62] Szőllősy, like many other legal and social scholars of the revolution in Hungary, delineated the criminal motives and psychopathic personalities of the revolutionaries.

The courts of counterrevolutionary Budapest found no legal differentiation between word and deed in the case of revolutionary politics. A police decree of 1 November 1919 expressly stated that "it is a capital crime to violate the law by trying to restore the past bloody reign of terror by spoken or written word."[63] Many people were tried before the postrevolutionary courts for making disparaging statements about the government or the military, or for voicing support for the revolutionary regime. The verdicts in these cases announced that such utterances amounted to "taking active part in a movement aimed at upsetting the legal Hungarian government."[64]

This was the case in the verdict against Anna Rivészi, who was convicted for statements that she made to the other passengers in her compartment as she traveled from Szekszárd to Sárbogárd on 20 July 1919.[65] When the subject of counterrevolution arose, the forty-nine-year-old signalman's widow became "enraged," asserting that "every one of the rascals and traitors should be hung."[66] Hearing her remarks, one passenger asked the Catholic mother of nine children what she would say "as a mother, if in the pursuit of free love they 'communized' your daughters?" According to witnesses, Rivészi "retorted that if such times came, she wouldn't regret it." This shocking statement of Rivészi's willingness to support even this most unnatural and radical result of communist rule was taken as proof of her criminal participation in the regime. The court's verdict proclaimed that these statements not only "glorif[ied] criminal acts," they also demonstrated active support for the revolutionary movement. Thus Rivészi was sentenced to two and a half years in prison and the loss of civil and political rights for five years.[67] The conflation of word and deed in counterrevolutionary Hungary's legal code meant that rhetorical politics, and the gendered code of many revolutionary narratives, could have real legal consequences.

The chaos of 1919 in Budapest left its residents confused between their own personal memories, political propaganda from both sides, and the often wild rumors that circulated in the city. As they remembered and attempted to make sense of the recent past, both the left and the right wing depended on a store of preexisting stereotypes and tropes within society for their explanatory power. This examination of the portrayals of women's participation in the revolutions allows us to see how the revolutionary experience was instrumentalized in the service of a variety of nationalist and conservative and even leftist ideologies. Just as the polarization of remembering was a product of both recent struggles and deep chasms already existent within society in Hungary before war and revolution, images of women in the memories of 1919 were often the same as in earlier prerevolutionary years. These included images of women in crowds and food riots, of women as being naturally apolitical or domestic, of the stereotypical radical "Russian" female student, and of other anti-Semitic and class-based gender tropes.[68] On both sides of the political divide women were considered symbolic representations of their community: either the Christian National cause or the emancipatory revolutionary movement.

The reassertion of traditional gender roles played an integral part in reestablishing the social hierarchy and legal order in war-torn counterrevolutionary Hungary. The conservative forces in power throughout interwar Hungary produced a narrative of revolution that emphasized the dangerous results of upsetting traditional gender roles. For the left, women were also used to represent vulnerability and the brutal dangers of their opponents, the counterrevolutionaries. Both sides employed the rape and sexual mistreatment of women or the danger of it as the greatest example of the other's barbarism. Rumors of licentious behavior by female members of revolutionary organizations became part and parcel of the myth of the revolution that the right continued to describe throughout the interwar years. Similarly, reports of the sexual depravity and the mistreatment of women by the White officers' brigades became part of the myth of martyrdom on the left. The language of gender was a powerful tool in the battle for historical memory and moral ascendancy in the atmosphere of civil war and ideological confrontation of 1919 Hungary.

Notes

1. Dezső Kosztolányi, *Anna Édes,* trans. George Szirtes (New York: New Directions, 1993 [1926]), 74.
2. Ibid.
3. Ibid.
4. Cecile Tormay, *An Outlaw's Diary,* vol. 1, *Revolution* (London: Philip Allan, 1923), 1:9.

5. For example: Ute Daniel, *The War from Within: German Working-Class Women in World War I*, trans. Margaret Ries (Oxford: Berg, 1997); Belinda J. Davis, *Home Fires Burning: Food, Politics, and Everyday Life in World War I Berlin* (Chapel Hill: University of North Carolina Press, 2000); Jay Winter, *Sites of Memory, Sites of Mourning: The Great War in European Cultural History* (Cambridge: Cambridge University Press, 1995); Winter and Jean-Louis Robert, eds., *Capital Cities at War: London, Paris, Berlin, 1914–1919* (Cambridge: Cambridge University Press, 1997); and Winter and Emmanuel Sivan, eds., *War and Remembrance in the Twentieth Century* (New York: Cambridge University Press, 1999).

6. These casualty figures are from Martin Gilbert, *First World War* (London: Weidenfeld and Nicolson, 1994), who gives the total Austro-Hungarian mobilization at 7.8 million.

7. István Deák, "The Decline and Fall of the Habsburg Monarchy, 1914–18," in Iván Völgyes, ed., *Hungary in Revolution, 1918–1919: Nine Essays* (Lincoln: University of Nebraska Press, 1971), 18, gives a higher number of total men mobilized in the Habsburg armies, 8.3 million, of whom 3.8 million (45 percent) were Hungarian citizens. Of these numbers, at least 3.8 million of those mobilized, 660,000 of the dead, and 740,000 of the wounded came from the Hungarian crown lands. Deák points out that this is higher than the relative portion of the population of the Dual Monarchy, where Hungarian citizens made up 41 percent of the total population.

8. In October 1918 a self-described "group of anxious patriots," including Károlyi and Oszkár Jászi, sent a "warning" to King Charles, urging reforms; in Jászi, *Revolution and Counter-Revolution in Hungary* (New York: Howard Fertig, 1969), 5–14.

9. For the refugee crisis and its political implications for Hungary, see István Mócsy, *The Effects of World War I: The Uprooted* (Boulder, Colo.: East European Monographs, 1983). Mócsy (p. 10) estimates that "426,000 Hungarians left the [ceded] territories" between the end of the war and 1924: 197,035 from Romania; 106,841 from Czechoslovakia; 44,903 from Yugoslavia; and 1,221 from the new Austrian province of Burgenland." These figures, from the National Refugee Office, represent only the registered refugees.

10. Károlyi's role in this declaration has been much debated. For his own version of the transfer of power: Mihály Károlyi, *Fighting the World: The Struggle for Peace* (New York: Albert and Charles Boni, 1925) and *Memoirs of Michael Károlyi: Faith without Illusion* (New York: E. P. Dutton, 1957).

11. According to Gusztáv Gratz, a member of the Horthy government, of 97 death sentences after the revolution, 68 were carried out (many prisoners were traded to Russia or granted reprieve), *A forradalmak kora. Magyarorszag törtenete 1918–1920* (Budapest: Magyar Szemle, 1935). Gratz lists only 202 dead as a result of actions of the Whites *after* the fall of the revolution, whereas Vilmos Böhm gives the number of 5,000 in his memoirs. Historians now generally agree upon the number of 1,500–2,000 victims of the Whites.

12. Though Horthy used the title Regent and always proclaimed his loyalty to the Habsburgs, he rebuffed both attempts of King Charles to return to the throne.

13. Especially Klaus Theweleit's *Männerphantasien 1 & 2*, 2 vols. (Munich: Piper, 2000 [1977]).

14. Joan Wallach Scott, "Gender: A Useful Category of Historical Analysis," in *Gender and the Politics of History* (New York: Columbia University Press, 1999), 39–41.

15. Ibid.

16. Theweleit seemed to be offering a psychoanalytic version of the German *Sonder-*

weg argument by identifying the psychological origins of fascist violence in the authoritarian family structure of Imperial Germany; the comparison with Hungary here counters such explanations of national exceptionalism (for either country).

17. Such as the novel *The Stone Crop,* which idealizes the hard life of a Croatian peasant family that remains steadfastly loyal to the Hungarian lords (New York: R. M. McBride and Co., 1923).

18. Ágnes Kenyeres, ed., *Magyar Életrajzi Lexikon,* rev. ed. (Budapest: Akadémiai Kiadó, 1990).

19. Horthy's description of the welcoming ceremonies in chapter 9 of his *Memoirs* (New York: Robert Speller, 1957), 104–106; also Thomas Sakmyster, *Hungary's Admiral on Horseback: Miklós Horthy, 1918–1944* (Boulder, Colo.: East European Monographs, 1994), 41–43; Rolf Fischer, *Entwicklungsstufen des Antisemitismus in Ungarn, 1867–1939. Die Zerstörung der magyarisch-jüdischen Symbiose* (Munich: Oldenbourg, 1998).

20. *Pester Lloyd* (17 November 1919), 1.

21. Ibid. and Sakmyster, *Hungary's Admiral,* 42.

22. Tormay, *Outlaw's Diary* 1:173.

23. Ibid., 197.

24. Ibid., 72.

25. Ibid.

26. Ibid., 229.

27. Ibid., 197–98.

28. Ibid.

29. Ibid.

30. Ibid.

31. Mühsam quoted in Christiane Sternsdorf-Hauck, *Brotmarken und rote Fahnen. Frauen in der bayrischen Revolution und Räterepublik 1918/1919* (Frankfurt/Main: isp-Verlag, 1989), 31.

32. Untitled article from the *Call* reported in *Literary Digest* (30 August 1919), 102–103.

33. Ibid.

34. Ibid.

35. Theodor Body [Tivadar Bódy], "Bolschewistische Willkürherrschaft in der Landeshauptstadt Budapest," in Karl [Károly] Huszár, ed., *Die Proletarierdiktatur in Ungarn. Wahrheitsgetreue Darstellung der bolschewistischen Schreckensherrschaft* (Regensburg: 1920), 135.

36. Tormay, *Outlaw's Diary,* 1:89–90.

37. Ibid., 91–92.

38. Sakmyster, *Hungary's Admiral.*

39. For example: Karen Hagemann, "Men's Demonstrations and Women's Protests," *Gender and History* 5, no. 1 (1993): 101–109.

40. Richard Bessel, "The Great War in German Memory: The Soldier of the First World War, Demobilization and Weimar Political Culture," *German History* 6, no. 1 (1988): 20–34.

41. Jan Gross has noted a similar conflation of two memories in order to cover up one's own shameful behavior in his study of the 1941 pogrom at Jedwabne, Poland, *Neighbors: The Destruction of the Jewish Community in Jedwabne, Poland,* 2nd ed. (New York: Penguin, 2002). The effect of these conflated memories is like the Russian saying that "either he robbed someone or he was robbed," implying that it did not really matter either way; the man is now associated with a criminal act.

42. Vilmos Böhm, *Im Kreuzfeuer zweier Revolutionen* (Munich: Verlag für Kulturpolitik, 1924), 538.

43. Ibid.

44. Ibid.

45. Albert Kaas and Fedor de Lazarovics, *Bolshevism in Hungary: The Béla Kun Period* (London: Grant Richards, 1931), 315.

46. Also: Böhm's fellow commissar, Josef [József] Pogány, *Der Weiße Terror in Ungarn* (Vienna: Verlagsgenossenschaft Neue Welt, 1920); Josef Halmi, "Akten über die Pogrome in Ungarn," in Jakob Krausz, ed., *Martyrium: Ein jüdisches Jahrbuch* (Vienna: 1922), 59–66.

47. Böhm (539) claimed that 100,000 fled Hungary after Horthy's takeover of power. This, like his figure of 5,000 victims of the White Terror, is not based on specific evidence and may be just the impression of an informed observer. No more accurate figures exist, but thousands certainly passed through Vienna and Berlin.

48. Archive of the Joint Distribution Committee, New York, Letter of Dr. Julius Goldman to Felix Warburg, 13 April 1920.

49. British Joint Labour Delegation to Hungary, *The White Terror in Hungary. Report of the British Joint Labour Delegation to Hungary* (London: Trade Union Congress and The Labour Party, May 1920), 24.

50. Ibid.

51. Ibid., 16.

52. Ibid., 16.

53. Ibid., 16–17.

54. Ibid.

55. This illustration comes from a 1946 edition of "The White Terror in Hungary under the Regime Horthy," published in Argentina. Image courtesy of Graphic Witness, an online exhibition, "Visual Arts and Social Commentary," http://www.graphicwitness.org/contemp/biro.htm.

56. British Joint Labour, 10.

57. Ibid.

58. Ibid.

59. Ibid., 11.

60. Oszkár Szőllősy [Oscar Szollosy], "Bolschewistische Verbrechern," in Huszár, *Die Proletarierdiktatur*; in English as, "The Criminals of the Dictatorship of the Proletariat," reprinted in Tormay, *Outlaw's Diary*, vol. 2, *The Commune* (London: Phillip Allan, 1923), 2:217.

61. Ibid.

62. Ibid.

63. *Pesti Hírlap* (15 November 1919).

64. For example, Magyar Országos Levéltár (MOL)/K616, Igazságügyminisztériumi Levéltár/Koronaügyészség 1920/IVy, 3–114.

65. Ibid., 3–114, 42.

66. Ibid.

67. This sentence was reduced on appeal to three and a half months imprisonment.

68. For stereotypes of women during the Paris Commune and its aftermath, see Gay L. Gullickson, *Unruly Women of Paris: Images of the Commune* (Ithaca: Cornell University Press, 1996). On the radical Russian female student, see Aaron J. Cohen, "Revolution und Emanzipation: Bilder der russischen Frau in der deutschen Úffenlichkeit," in

Gerd Koenen and Lew Kopelew, eds., *Deutschland und die Russische Revolution, 1917–1924* (Munich: Wilhelm Fink Verlag, 1998), 527–33. Sander Gilman and others have demonstrated how Jews, the poor, and other marginalized groups are often both feminized, and conversely seen as sexually dangerous.

Part Two. *Gendered Collaborating and Resisting*

5 Dumplings and Domesticity: Women, Collaboration, and Resistance in the Protectorate of Bohemia and Moravia

Melissa Feinberg

This chapter examines the work of a Czech women's organization active during World War II, looking particularly at its efforts to show housewives how best to cook meals during a time of shortages and rationing. My analysis of these "kitchen politics" will show how living in an occupied territory changed the character of everyday tasks, bringing the moral choices of the war into the lives of ordinary citizens, women as well as men. Historians interested in the problem of collaboration and resistance tend to neglect places like kitchens, seeing the domestic world as somehow removed from the harsh realities of war and occupation.[1] Choices about whether to collaborate or resist are made on battlefields, in concentration camps, or perhaps government offices, with guns, or policies, and not with ladles. However, in occupied territories such as the Protectorate of Bohemia and Moravia, this was not the case. Here, the seemingly mundane world of the kitchen also became a site of struggle, a place that shows us the problems involved in thinking too narrowly about the concepts of collaboration and resistance. Examining what this group of Czech women hoped to accomplish as they wrote about food and cooking challenges our preconceptions of how and where wars take place, and also complicates common notions about how war experiences are gendered.

Recent scholarship on women and war has tended to view wars as moments that magnify gender difference. Taking inspiration from the model of the double helix proposed by Margaret and Patrice Higonnet, scholars have argued that violent conflicts create an atmosphere that maintains or even accentuates the boundaries between male and female worlds, even if these conflicts also push both men and women into new tasks and responsibilities. As the argument goes, wars may send women into better jobs and increase their independence, but these apparent gains are only an illusion; they do not reflect a similar increase in the social status of the men who have left to take part in the fighting. Once we correct for this variable, it becomes apparent that women as a group still lag behind men on the social ladder. The new jobs women have acquired are still being performed "at home," in private and behind the lines. Although they may have moved outside of their own homes and onto a larger home front, they were still operating in what amounts to the domestic sphere of war.[2] This double helix model has been very useful for thinking about why women's wartime "liberation" has often proved to be so ephemeral. However, its analysis of how war is gendered assumes that we are dealing with combatant nations. It breaks down if we think about the situation of occupied territories, which includes not only the Czech lands but also most of Europe during World War II. In these regions, both men and women generally remained at home, fighting together in a very different kind of war.

In the Czech lands few men spent the war in the military. The Germans wanted Czech men to work in factories, not fight in armies. Nor had Czech men seen fighting before they became attached to the Reich; the occupation of Czechoslovakia took place without a single battle. After German forces marched unopposed into Prague on 15 March 1939, Hitler split the country in two, transforming the Czech provinces of Bohemia and Moravia into a semi-autonomous "Protectorate." The representative branches of the Czechoslovak government were abolished and a German official, the Reich Protector, became the ultimate authority. However, the Czechs were allowed a measure of domestic self-rule. President Emil Hácha retained his post, and most government ministries continued to function. This Czech bureaucracy remained on the job throughout the war, although the office of the Reich Protector increasingly limited its autonomy.[3]

The impact of the invasion on the daily lives of ordinary Czechs was subtle but pervasive. These invaders did not drop bombs, but instead inserted themselves into the ordinary institutions that touched the material of daily life, exerting their influence from government offices, within factories and businesses, in the media, in the arts, and on the streets.[4] Nazi occupying forces demanded accommodation and acceptance from all Czechs, men and women alike, requiring that everyone publicly accept the legitimacy of their presence and assist with the German war effort. All individuals were faced with a host of complicated and personal choices over how or whether to submit to these demands. Any fighting or negotiation that took place occurred in the intimate spaces of those individual lives, as men and women alike wrestled with the numerous daily demands of defeat. Ordinary citizens were compelled to show their support for their new rulers in a variety of ways; they had to work for the new regime, conform to its ideas and values, and publicly accept their subordinate place in a German empire. To refuse to support the occupation regime could bring consequences; to actively resist might result in imprisonment or death.

How did civilians cope with this kind of attack, one that not only infiltrated their governments, but even wormed its way into their homes and offices? Historians have tended to describe the scope of responses to such an occupation under the rubric of collaboration and resistance, dividing occupied populations into those who accepted and those who rejected the occupier. This kind of analysis makes it easy for us now to write uncomplicated history; we can simply pick out the good from the bad, dividing the population into its heroes and villains. But, while it may be emotionally satisfying, this dichotomy is not analytically very helpful for examining the realities of the Czech situation. For many Czechs, the primary struggle during the occupation was not whether to collaborate with or resist the Germans. The battle that most concerned them was the struggle to protect the Czech nation and its interests. This meant that most never had a fixed answer to the question of whether to oppose or support Germany, but re-evaluated their response according to the specifics of any particular situation. Their answer was not based so much on an abstract moral code, but on practical concerns about what would best serve their nation.

The survival of the Czech nation had emerged as the dominant concern for Czech politicians and the Czech public following the debacle of the Munich conference in 1938. When the participants at the conference agreed to dismember Czechoslovakia and award control of the Sudetenland to Nazi Germany, the need to protect the very existence of the Czech nation took on a new urgency. However, the means to this end were a matter for debate. Different visions of what would best insure the nation's survival were bound up with competing versions of the "Czech nation" itself. Before Munich, the dominant view of the Czech nation was heavily influenced by the ideas of Tomáš G. Masaryk, Czechoslovakia's first president. Masaryk was an ardent democrat, and his conception of Czech nationhood was closely linked to his ideas about democracy and equality.[5] Following Masaryk, many Czechs had come to believe that the legacy of the distant Hussite past had given their nation a unique affinity for democracy. They saw democratic government and democratic values as national needs, crucial to Czech self-realization.[6] For those who held to this view, keeping the Czech nation alive meant protecting the democratic Czechoslovak state established in 1918, defending its egalitarian constitution, and resisting authoritarianism at all costs. But this view of Czech nationhood, so closely bound up with democratic ideology, had never been unconditionally accepted, and it had come under increasing attack in the 1930s, even before Munich.

Linking the Czech nation with the cause of democracy certainly contained an inherent potential for conflict. The need to protect the interests of one specific nation could easily rub uncomfortably against a democratic government's duty to protect the individual rights of all its citizens. Indeed, while the Czechoslovak Constitution of 1920 promised equal rights for all, regardless of ethnicity, religion, or gender, many Czechs did not really like the idea of having to share the freedoms of their democratic government with the members of other nations, most especially Czechoslovakia's German minority; nor did they particularly want such freedoms to be available to traditionally subordinate social groups, like women.[7] The demands of such groups for inclusion in Czechoslovak politics and society helped to create a conservative backlash against the link between democracy and the Czech nation, paralleling the rise of the right in countries such as France, Poland, or Germany. The Czech right did not embrace fascism and did not speak against democratic government as such, but it did begin to emphasize different essentials for Czech national survival, such as the protection of traditional family values or the celebration of a more exclusively Czech national culture.[8]

When the Czechoslovak government caved in at Munich and agreed to surrender the Sudetenland to Nazi Germany, it struck a powerful blow against the idea that there was a necessary connection between democracy and Czech national interests. To many Czechs, the debacle of Munich indicated that democratic values were simply not capable of protecting the Czech nation from its enemies, creating a profound spiritual crisis. And according to the right-leaning historian František Kutnar, the proper response to Munich was to create a "Second" Czechoslovakia, "new not only in its borders, but politically, economically, culturally and morally." This, he said, was "the only way out of the crisis, the only protection. The evil that came must change the soul of Czechoslovakia."[9] With the national legitimacy of the democratic regime completely destroyed, it was the conservative wing of the Czech right that seemed most able to effect such a transformation. This new regime, which dubbed itself the Second Czechoslovak Republic, would take national defense as its founding premise, realizing that goal via a political philosophy that the new prime minister, Rudolf Beran, dubbed "authoritarian democracy."[10] Although it was never exactly clear how this new regime would balance authoritarianism with democracy, it did plan to strengthen the coercive power of the state, segregate national enemies (which included foreigners, Jews, Communists, and independent women), limit free speech, and follow a conservative social agenda. Within a few weeks after its rise to power, the Beran government had passed laws that muzzled the press, banned the Czechoslovak Communist Party, prohibited both Jews and married women from working in the civil service, and allowed the possibility of rule by emergency decree. It began to "streamline" Czech politics and cultural life, forcing the merger of political parties and other independent associations into government-sponsored blocs.[11]

However, only a few months after the Second Republic came into existence, the Czech lands were occupied by Nazi Germany, forcing its leaders to rethink their plans for reorganizing Czech political and national life. Their bid to save the Czechoslovak state had failed, but the Czech nation remained. How could they best serve its needs? What course of action would insure the nation's survival and give rise to the kind of national society they had envisioned? On the one hand, these strong nationalists hated the loss of Czech national independence and strongly opposed being forced into the German Reich. As members of the conservative Czech right, they were also suspicious of fascism and looked askance at some aspects of the Nazi regime. However, in other respects, they found themselves ideologically in step with their new occupiers. A "New Order" that promoted strong family values, put women back into the home and men to work, strengthened the state, fought socialism, and tried to "purify" the national community by segregating outsiders was exactly what they had been trying to create on their own with the Second Republic. Thus, in some respects the Protectorate paradoxically represented an opportunity to realize some of those goals. Other than being inside a German empire, the kind of regime the Germans wanted in Prague was what many Czechs had been hoping for after Munich.[12] And for older Czechs who had grown up when the Czech lands were part of the Habsburg Monarchy, living within a state ruled by German speakers was at least familiar. Indeed, the decree creating the Protectorate had granted the Czechs cultural autonomy and jurisdiction over local affairs: exactly what many Czech nationalist leaders of the late nineteenth century had been seeking from Vienna. With this in mind, some Czechs could easily see it as their national duty to try to continue to work for their earlier program of national regeneration, even if that meant publicly accepting the occupation and working with the occupiers. Cooperating with German administrators and officials could become the means for continuing with their plans to rejuvenate and reorganize Czech national life.

The question of how to best serve their nation was faced by Czechs at all levels of society, from high-level government bureaucrats to factory workers, by women as well as men. While for a few this goal mandated active resistance and a total rejection of occupation, for most the answer was more complicated. They would accept and support the Protectorate regime but continue to struggle within it to maintain their national distinctiveness. In essence, they rejected defining the Czech nation in political terms (as a democracy) and concentrated on its cultural, social, and linguistic meanings, dedicating themselves to defending Czech culture, language, and values. In the battle to protect "Czechness" on this level, women as well as men could be effective soldiers, and they eagerly entered the fight.

This complicated response to the Nazi occupation of the Czech lands is particularly well exemplified by a prominent group of rightist Czech women—members of an organization called the Women's Center. An analysis of their beliefs and activities shows how Czechs could act in what might seem to be contradictory ways and with sets of conflicting motives, working with and even praising their German occupiers while at the same time fighting against them. The Women's Center itself had a wide-ranging collection of goals and interests. Its stated purpose was to work in the interests of the Czech nation, and specifically to promote the interests of Czech women in a newly invigorated Czech national community. Of course, the battle its members waged was fought in the service of their own particular conception of what was in the nation's interests and in the interests of Czech women. These women were working for a certain kind of Czech society, one in which they, not coincidentally, would have an influential place.

The Women's Center was an organization that came together during the tense months after the Munich agreement. It was composed of well-connected Czech women from the right, mostly professionals and politicians, who were supporters of the Second Republic and wanted to provide a voice for women in that regime.[13] With the assistance of prominent government leaders, they formed the Women's Center (*Ústředí žen*) within the auspices of a longstanding Czech cultural organization, the Czech National Council (*Česká Národní Rada*).

The Czech National Council had been an important player in the Czech nationalist movement of the nineteenth century, but it had lost its central role as a national/cultural institution after Czechoslovakia achieved independence in 1918. However, the leaders of the Second Republic gave it a new prominence, assigning it the task of "coordinating" Czech cultural and national life.[14] The founders of its new Women's Center also envisioned themselves becoming "coordinators," leading a "women's sphere" within Czech national life. Therefore, the group was not a mass organization, but a small group of leading female experts who pictured themselves working closely with the government to mold a new set of policies towards women and redefine women's place in the Czech lands.[15]

The Czech women who created this Women's Center shared many of the Second Republic's political leaders' ideals and priorities, including their emphasis on national survival, their authoritarian leanings, and their position on gender difference. Simply put, they wanted to see gender matter more in Czech society. They believed that each sex should have its own distinct social, economic, cultural, and political roles—its own "sphere" of activity that mimicked the division of responsibilities between husbands and wives, mothers and fathers. In the minds of the Women's Center's leaders, however, a more gendered world would not mean giving up the idea of equality between men and women. Its leaders were highly educated professional women, many of whom had extensive experience both in party politics and in the Czech women's movement. They did want to see women develop and pursue distinct social roles from men, but they believed that women should expect equivalent political, economic, and social status with their male counterparts in return. The Women's Center's mandate was to realize this goal of equality in difference, and they industriously began to sketch out programs to redesign women's education, to train women for careers appropriate to their womanly talents, to strengthen families, and to provide state assistance for motherhood.[16]

However, as it turned out, the new circumstances of occupation offered fewer possibilities than they had expected. While the occupation had curtailed the freedom of *all* Czech public actors, it had had an even more crushing effect on the field of possibilities open to Czech women. Since even at its inception the relationship of the Women's Center to the state and its policy makers had not been clearly defined, except in the minds of its founders, its ability to have any impact on policy was dependent on the willingness of administration officials to listen to the views of Women's Center activists and pursue their policy proposals. After March 1939, those officials were both less able and less willing to do that. In fact, arguing that politics had a new element of danger in an occupied land, Czech Protectorate leaders had used the invasion as an opportunity to impose new restrictions on women's ability to participate in public life—restrictions the Women's Center would protest, but ultimately had to accept.[17] Thus, while the Women's Center was close enough to the regime to remain in existence throughout the war, it was never able to exert much influence on the

Protectorate administration and remained essentially powerless in official political circles. Yet, while their efforts to represent women on the level of the state may have been thwarted, the women in this organization continued to work, shifting the focus of their efforts from a dialogue with the state to a dialogue with Czech women at home. Looking at the agendas of the Women's Center from March 1939 on, we see them occupied with a variety of projects designed to show Czech women just what they could do for the nation, and for themselves. These activities emphasized the value and meaning of women's domestic roles as wife, mother, and housekeeper, but the goal behind them was not simply to glorify domesticity as such. They wanted to show how women could and did use their feminine qualities to make a positive contribution to the Czech nation, whether this meant working in conjunction with Protectorate officials or subtly resisting them.[18] Like the Protectorate regime as a whole, they would openly support their German overlords, aping many of their ideals, while at the same time defending Czech national autonomy. But in addition, the Women's Center would set itself against the Czech Protectorate administration when it tried to curtail women's standing in public life or belittle their social roles.

This mixed message came out in a wide variety of cultural projects undertaken by the group during the early 1940s, ranging in venue from lecture series and concerts to published books and pamphlets to museum exhibitions, with topics as varied as "women in the national economy," "women's health," and "the mother in art."[19] These kinds of events would on the one hand reinforce the idea that women and men had very distinct roles to play in Czech society, but would on the other call for women's unique achievements to be recognized as equally important as men's, or urge the public to pay attention to women's special economic or medical needs. One of their first such endeavors was a lecture series held in April–May of 1940 on women's contributions to Czech history and culture, which included presentations by prominent Czech academics and writers, including Pavla Buzková, Albert Pražák, Josef Šusta, and Flora Kleinschnitzová. They later published this series as a book, which they tried to have placed in schools and public libraries throughout the Protectorate.[20]

The book's chapters celebrate the achievements of strong and talented Czech women, from the medieval Princess Libuše, who was transformed during the nationalist movement of the nineteenth century into a universal symbol of Czech independence and strength, to Eliška Krásnohorská, an activist from the late nineteenth century who fought for women's right to a secondary education. In the short introduction to the collection, the Women's Center was quite explicit about its reasons for reminding the Czech public about women's contributions to Czech national life. Recognizing women's special role as mothers and housewives, they wanted to remind their readers that this was never the sum of Czech women's contributions to their nation. "Even in the current times," they wrote, and even while remaining committed to their maternal and feminine tasks, "women are [also] capable of the tasks and functions which flow from the essence of humanity."[21] So, while the book did not take any stands against

Nazism or against the Protectorate regime, it was certainly a defense of Czech national culture in a newly German-dominated world, and also a defense of Czech women and their place within that culture.

Similarly, when the leaders of the Women's Center approached the Museum of Applied Arts in Prague about mounting a public exhibition that celebrated Czech motherhood, they did so with a rather complicated agenda. Their working plan for the exhibition, which would be entitled "Mother and Child," contained a very broad interpretation of that theme. At the most basic level, the motivation behind the exhibition was to glorify the place of Czech women in the national community by extolling their vital role as mothers and caregivers. A public display centered around the link between mothers and children would place women's reproductive role in the forefront of the public's attention, emphasizing the essential part women played in bearing new generations of Czechs. However, the leaders of the Women's Center did not want to reduce women to their wombs, but to portray mothers as productive and creative individuals. In the first place, this meant that the artistic portion of the installation would include not only images of mothers and children, but also art produced by mothers. But going even further, the exhibition would not just look at motherhood through art; it would contain an informational component that would focus the public's attention on the practical realities of motherhood. Sections were planned on how society should properly care for its mothers, on scientific advances in knowledge about childcare, and on details of current legislation that affected the lives of mothers and children.

Even more interestingly, there would be a section on the problems facing mothers who worked outside the home, including a look at prominent working mothers from the Czech past, such as Božena Němcová, the most famous woman in the Czech literary pantheon, best known for stories that glorified women's role in protecting and transmitting Czech culture. This attempt to use a figure so strongly associated with Czech nationalism to promote the idea of women working outside the home highlights the ways in which the Women's Center served conflicting goals. The leaders of the group believed strongly that women should be economically independent and had committed themselves to bettering women's economic opportunities, helping them to find suitable professions and the means to practice them.[22] Pointing out that a woman as universally admired as Božena Němcová was a working mother was certainly an effective way of urging the Czech public to support women in their drive for economic freedom. In addition, it was a way of urging Czech women to use all of their talents for the nation's benefit, not to limit their work to their maternal responsibilities. Němcová, after all, performed her invaluable work for the Czech nationalist movement as a writer, not as a mother. However, most Czech women would not work as novelists. Instead, they would labor in industries crucial to the Nazi war effort. The Women's Center certainly knew that their efforts to show Czechs why they should support working mothers were assisting Nazi economic planners, who were actively trying to entice more Czech women into the workforce. Their discussions about the exhibition coincided with discussions on how best to "reeducate" Czech girls to "calm them down" so that they would adjust to, and work in, the "new order."[23]

This interplay of motives comes through even more clearly in a series of menu planners written and published by the Women's Center in 1942. This project is a splendid illustration of the group's goals and how they fit into the troubled ideological landscape of the Protectorate; it was also probably the way their ideas reached the greatest number of women. The idea to write a guide that would show housewives how to make the best use of the new rationing system for scarce foods (meat, fats, eggs, etc.) actually did not come from within the Women's Center itself, but from the men high up in the Protectorate administration.[24] It was at the suggestion of Emanuel Moravec, the Protectorate Minister of National Enlightenment, that the Women's Center presidium decided to take up the issue of nutrition in a time of rationing and began working on a menu-planning guide for this purpose.[25] They published their first guide—which contained a detailed plan for creating a week's worth of meals for a family of four plus some general cooking advice—in May of 1942, in a run of 25,000 copies. A second came out a few months later, and 30,000 copies were printed. The guides were not free but were sold for 1 Kč (Czech crown) each. There was obviously a great interest in advice on how to make bread dumplings without eggs, entrees without meat, and cakes without white flour; almost all of both guides were sold within a few months.[26]

The realities of rationing and wartime shortages of consumer goods had certainly had a profound effect on the daily chores of shopping and cooking, both of which were almost always performed by women. A variety of basic foodstuffs, including meat, fats, milk, eggs, and bread, had been rationed in the Czech lands since October of 1939. By May of 1942, most foods had been incorporated into the rationing system, with the exception of cheese, sour milk products, fish, and vegetables (except potatoes, which were rationed).[27] As the war went on, the amount of food rationed to each consumer fell precipitously. The meat, fats, and eggs so essential to traditional Czech cuisine were in particularly short supply. For example, while in 1931–1932 Czechs had on average consumed 4.4 eggs per person per week, by 1943 that average had fallen to 1.23 eggs/week. The amount of meat consumed per person fell from an average of 849 grams/week in 1931–1932 to 481 grams/week in 1943, an amount equal to only roughly half the meat available per capita in Great Britain in the same year.[28] The consumption of fats (butter, lard, margarine, oil) went down even more, from a prewar average of 414 grams/week to a mere 220 grams/week in 1943. Hidden in this statistic is the fact that the fat most favored by Czechs, lard, had largely been replaced by the far less satisfying margarine; margarine consumption actually went up quite substantially during the war years, while the amount of lard eaten fell by about 75 percent between 1931 and 1943. In evaluating these numbers, we must also take into account that workers in heavy industry or on long-shift or night work received substantially larger rations of all foods, which skewed the averages for the Protectorate as a whole. For example, the weekly meat ration granted each "normal consumer" in 1939 was only 500 grams/week, which dropped significantly down to 300 grams/week in April 1942. However, those classified as heavy workers had an official ration of 1000 grams of meat each week in 1939 and 600 grams/week in 1942.[29]

This meant that middle-class office personnel, who would have enjoyed a more meaty diet than factory workers in the years before the war, now found the tables had turned on them in quite dramatic fashion. At the same time, while these statistics do paint a grim picture, it is important to remember that the Czechs were on average eating much better than many of their Central and East European neighbors during these years, and better than they had during the First World War.[30] Indeed, historian Detlev Brandes claims that rations in the Czech lands were quite comparable with those in Germany itself, except that the Czechs received a *higher* ration of sugar, combined with a lower ration of fats. While it is of course true that Czechs could not always actually either afford or find the meat technically granted to them in their ration books (prices were higher in the Protectorate than they were in the Reich), Brandes at least claims that workers especially were "relatively satisfied with their provisioning."[31]

In any case, rationing and food supply were quite serious issues in the Protectorate. Even so, one might wonder why a group composed of professional women—women who had once envisioned themselves creating and administering a wide range of policies at the national level—was now spending its time and energy over recipes for oat burgers. A closer look at how they approached their task, though, makes it clear that the leaders of the Women's Center had an agenda that stretched beyond the specific content of the menu project. First, the menu guides have a lesson to teach housewives about how to think about themselves and their cooking chores. The authors do not address housewives simply as women doing women's work, but speak to them as domestic professionals, charged with the essential task of maintaining national health and fitness. The guides portray domestic work as valuable and skilled labor, and their tone accordingly resembles that of a professional publication, not a frothy fashion magazine. The text is written in technical, scientific-sounding language and is filled with specialized information about which commonly available foods can provide which nutrients, how to make sure family members get the right amount of calories, how to best protect valuable food from spoilage, and so on. Some of the information, like noting that rosehip or strawberry leaf tea is a good form of vitamins, might merely be "scientific" endorsements of peasant custom, but other tips, like crumbling rather large amounts of yeast (*kvasnice*) into various dishes as an extra protein source seem to come from a test kitchen equipped with a working laboratory.[32] This kind of approach tells housewives their job preparing meals is not just a personal labor of love, it is a crucial economic task that can only be performed by appropriately trained and educated personnel.

By writing to housewives more as nutritionists than as mere cooks and extolling their importance for the national good, the guides seek to show women how society should properly value their work. However, with their emphasis on professionalism and skill, they also assume that these women need formal education and expert guidance in order to do their jobs well. It is the backing and knowledge of science that transforms an ordinary woman into a domestic professional. Thus, the highly educated women behind these menus were not just giving useful advice, they were setting themselves up as a source of intellectual authority, as arbiters of the domestic sphere. So, while the leaders of the Women's Center were trying to show society that housewives were necessary national personnel who should be respected for their work, they were also arguing that the only way women could achieve this respectable professional status was by submitting to the guidance of academic experts in the discipline of the domestic arts—in this case, the Women's Center. In fact, the menus were only one of the Women's Center's efforts to not only professionalize but also monitor and control domestic work. They also sponsored a number of formal courses in domestic science, wrote brochures on various aspects of housework, studied how best to fit domestic science into the public school curriculum for girls, conducted sociological research on rural women's lives, and so on. All of these activities rested on the assumption that housewives needed the kind of training that only university-educated professionals could provide.[33]

Aside from their goals of redefining and revaluing housework, the menu planners show the Women's Center putting forth a recipe for Czech women to serve their nation in its time of need. The text makes much of a housewife's duty and responsibility in such troubled times, locating her at the heart of national struggle. It is up to her to make sure that her family stays healthy and well nourished in times of scarcity, but even more crucially, to make her family feel as if their home life, at least, had not changed at all. Mitigating the psychological aspects of rationing was an explicit part of the Women's Center's agenda right from the start.[34] It was with this in mind that they struggled to come up with ways women could continue to prepare the same kinds of foods they had prepared in happier times, even if basic ingredients were lacking. The recipes they included in their guides did not encourage Czech women to explore new cuisines, or even to simply find tasty ways of using the foods now available to them. Instead, they generally taught women how to mold unfamiliar ingredients into old Czech culinary standards. So, for example, there were instructions on how to make the ubiquitous Czech dumplings out of uncommon starches (like millet mixed with potato starch), to prepare cream sauce without cream, or to cook a goulash of potatoes instead of meat.[35]

The recipes for soups are a good illustration of the underlying imperative to make meals seem as normal as possible. Soup was, and is, an indispensable part of a traditional Czech *oběd* (midday meal). Every proper dinner had to begin with some sort of soup. In a time of rationing and shortages, however, it did not make sense to use the little meat or vegetables a family got to make soup stock. Despite this, the Women's Center did not simply advise women to stop serving soup; in fact, every single menu they proposed for a midday meal included one. To make this possible, they came up with recipes that could be made from almost nothing. So, there were recipes for things like caraway soup (made with water, caraway seeds, onion, old bread, and flour) or soup made mostly from bits of old bread and water, or a tomato soup composed of water and tomato paste, thickened with a handful of millet and some cornstarch. From a nutritional standpoint, these dishes were a waste of the cook's time; they provided those who ate them with few calories or vitamins (one also must wonder how they tasted). But, from a psychological standpoint, they were worth the energy they took to make. Dinner would simply not have seemed right without a bowl of soup to start it. And, as the guides told their readers, cooks needed to think about appearances just as much as taste. So, a soup might be mostly water, or a "meat" loaf might be mostly dried vegetables, barley, and grated potatoes, but if they looked like familiar dishes, presented in familiar ways, they were worth the labor and artifice that went into them. Because if a woman could put what appeared to be a "real" meal on the table, no matter what was actually in it, she nourished her family in more ways than one. As she filled their stomachs, she lifted their spirits and lightened their hearts, preserving the essence of home, and providing an illusion of normality in uncertain times.

Promoting the mundane work of women as crucial work, work that was necessary not only for the comfort of their own families but also for the survival of the nation, was at the heart of the Women's Center's mission. Its leaders had dedicated themselves to showing how the "female element" was an important component of all national questions, and particularly the project of national defense.[36] In their eyes, their work was helping Czech women to keep the nation physically and spiritually healthy, protecting it from the ravages of war and occupation. In creating ways to mimic traditional foods, they believed they were assisting women in preserving the most basic elements of Czech culture. With *koláče* (cookies) made of barley flour they could find a means of keeping their national distinctiveness even in the worst of times. Of course, the appearance of normality that Czech housewives cooked up in their homes served masters other than the Czech nation. From the perspective of the Nazi occupying regime, it was quite advantageous to teach Czech women how to prepare healthy meals in spite of rationing. Good nutrition was necessary for a fit work force, and Czech workers were a crucial component of the German war economy. In addition to preserving some idea of "Czech-ness," an illusion of normality could keep people doing normal things, like going to work, helping to make the extraordinary fact of being part of the Nazi regime seem rather ordinary, perhaps even palatable. This is of course why the Women's Center was encouraged to embark on its nutrition project in the first place. But, as one of their members remarked, "it's all about two (different) kinds of activities: the short-term and the long-term. It can be that short-term activities are antithetical to long-term ones."[37] While working with the occupation regime may not have been in the long-term interest of the Czech nation, it certainly seemed to make sense in the immediate context of the war.

The very different messages swirling around something like these menu guides make it clear that the leaders of the Women's Center were not operating under the same analytic categories as today's historians. They were working for their own set of priorities, which do not fit well into the concepts of collaboration or resistance. Their goals—to protect Czech national autonomy while effecting a social transformation that did indeed take inspiration from some Nazi policies, to encourage women to embrace their differences from men and their roles as wives and mothers, but also to fight against male domination of the economic and political sphere—might seem contradictory to us, since they do not fit neatly into our ideas about how people should have behaved in World War II Europe. Indeed, in some ways they were. But the contradictions themselves show us that groups such as this defy the labels we would like to attach to them. Some might like to call the Women's Center a collaborationist organization because it operated under the direction of those who linked themselves explicitly to the Nazi regime and helped to serve Nazi interests, noting that its direct superiors were men (like Drachovský and Moravec) heavily associated with strongly pro-German groups like the League against Bolshevism, and that its own leaders quite often publicly expressed their sympathy for the idea of a Czech "New Order."[38] Others might argue that the Women's Center deserves to be labeled a resistance organization for its determination to fight the attempts of Czech Protectorate leaders to marginalize women in public and economic life, or for its desire to promote Czech nationalism in the face of German opposition, recalling that some members of the organization were themselves arrested for their work at the very end of the war.[39] But neither of these labels actually allows us to fully comprehend the group's motivations, each excludes some aspect of their work and beliefs. This does not mean we should try to whitewash the more troubling aspects of a group like the Women's Center, to valorize them or revise history's opinion of them, or that we can not judge their motives or their words, some of which may be reprehensible. But it does imply that understanding them, their actions, and the society in which they lived, requires something that gets beyond the familiar dichotomy of collaboration versus resistance. It requires that we realize that the everyday realities of the occupation experience simply do not fit easily into such admittedly convenient but ultimately restrictive and perhaps even misleading analytical boxes.

Notes

1. For example István Deák et al., eds., *The Politics of Retribution in Europe: World War II and its Aftermath* (Princeton: Princeton University Press, 2000) usefully complicates standard notions of collaboration and resistance, while at the same time virtually ignoring how women fit in to the picture. A few women's historians, such as Claudia Koonz in *Mothers in the Fatherland: Women, the Family, and Nazi Politics* (New York: St. Martin's, 1987), have tried to show how women contributed to Nazi violence. However, the debate among German women's historians over Koonz's charge that German women "collaborated" with Nazism remained mostly mired in the either/or dichotomy

of guilt and responsibility. On this debate, see Adelheit von Saldern, "Victims or Perpetrators: Controversies over the Role of Women in the Nazi State," in David F. Crew, ed., *Nazism and German Society* (New York: Routledge, 1994), 141-165.

2. Patrice and Margaret Higonnet, "The Double Helix," in Margaret Higonnet et al., eds., *Behind the Lines: Gender and the Two World Wars* (New Haven: Yale University Press, 1987), 31-47.

3. Vojtech Mastny, *The Czechs Under Nazi Rule* (Princeton: Princeton University Press, 1971); Detlev Brandes, *Češi pod německým protektorátem: okupační politika, kolaborace a odboj, 1939–1945*, trans. Petr Dvořáček (Prague: Prostor, 1999).

4. This is the kind of infiltration of "everyday" life described by Detlev Peukert in *Inside Nazi Germany: Conformity, Opposition and Racism in Everyday Life*, trans. Richard Deveson (New Haven: Yale University Press, 1987) and Jan Gross in *Polish Society Under German Occupation* (Princeton: Princeton University Press, 1979).

5. See Tomáš Masaryk, *Česká otázka* (Prague: Pokrok, 1908).

6. Melissa Feinberg, "Democracy and Its Limits: Gender and Rights in the Czech Lands, 1918-1938," *Nationalities Papers* 30, no. 4 (2002): 553-70.

7. For a post-Munich comment on these kinds of attitudes: V. Chab, "Od národnostího k národnímu," *Sobota* 9, no. 36 (1938): 427-28.

8. For a fuller discussion of this Czech turn to the right: Feinberg, "Gender and the Politics of Difference in the Czech Lands After Munich," *East European Politics and Societies* 17, no. 2 (2003): 203-30, or Jana Čechurová, *Česká politická pravice*, (Prague: Lidové Noviny, 1999).

9. František Kutnar, "Naše nynější krise," *Brázda* 1, no. 40-41 (1938): 630-32.

10. Rudolf Halík, "Jdeme k zjednodušení politických poměrů," *Venkov*, 22 October 1938.

11. Jan Rataj, *O autorativní národní stát* (Prague: Karolinium, 1997).

12. The agrarian party journal *Brázda*, for example, held up German efforts to combat unemployment (their system of work camps in particular), and numerous aspects of Nazi family and population policy as a model for the Czechs to follow in designing their own strong national state. Antonin Pelaček, "K novému nacionalismu," *Brázda* 1, no. 43 (1938): 666-67.

13. Feinberg, "Gender and the Politics of Difference."

14. Václav Černý, *Křik Koruny České* (Brno: Atlantis, 1992), 55-56.

15. Agendas and programs from the founding meetings of the Women's Center. Státní Ústřední Archiv (hereafter SÚA)/fond Národní Rada Česká (hereafter NRČ), box 288.

16. Programs of the social and cultural sections of the Women's Center and minutes from meeting of Women's Center Executive Committee 17 February 1939, SÚA/NRČ, box 288.

17. Since the occupation had meant the elimination of democratic institutions, there was nothing to prevent administration officials from forbidding women's participation in what passed for politics in the Protectorate. See Feinberg, "Gender and the Politics of Difference," 222-23.

18. "Outline of the program and goals of the Women's Center," 21 January 1940, SÚA/NRČ, box 288.

19. Minutes from the Women's Center presidium, 1941, SÚA/NRČ, box 290.

20. Minutes from the Women's Center Executive Committee, 1939-1943, SÚA/NRČ, boxes 288 and 290. The book that sprang from the lecture series was *Česká žena v dějinách národa* (Prague: Novina, 1940.) The Women's Center was only moderately successful in

its aims for the book. They initially hoped to have the Ministry of Education buy and distribute most of the copies, but, citing budget constraints, the ministry bought only one fifth of the books requested, leaving the Women's Center to market the books themselves.

21. "Introduction," *Česká žena v dějinách národa.*

22. As an example of their interest in women as economic actors, they planned a lecture series in 1940–41 to educate women on appropriate career and educational choices. Minutes from the Women's Center Executive Committee, July 1941, SÚA/NRČ, box 290.

23. Minutes from the Women's Center Executive Committee, 27 March 1941, SÚA/NRČ, box 290.

24. Minutes from the Women's Center presidium, 4 March 1942, SÚA/NRČ, box 290.

25. Moravec was one of the loudest supporters of the Nazi regime in the Protectorate. For his views on how Czechs had benefited by being part of German Reich, see Úřad Lidové Osvěty, *Tři roky v říše* (Prague: Orbis, 1942).

26. A few were given away rather than sold. Meeting of the Women's Center presidium from 2 March 1943, SÚA/NRČ, box 290.

27. For more on what was rationed and when, see Czechoslovak Research Institute, *The Food Situation in Bohemia and Moravia* (London: n.p., 1942); Dana Musilová, "Zásobování a výživa českého obyvatelstva v podminkách válečného řízeného hospodářství (1939–1945)," *Slezský Sborník* 89, no. 3–4 (1991): 255–66.

28. Ina Zweiniger-Bargeielowska, *Austerity in Britain: Rationing, Controls and Consumption, 1939–1955* (Oxford: Oxford University Press, 2000), 36.

29. Data from the Czechoslovak Research Institute, *The Food Situation in Bohemia and Moravia,* 4–10 and *Statistisches Jahrbuch für das Protektorat Böhmen und Mähren* (1944), 192. There is similar data in Václav Král, *Otázky hospodářského a sociálního vývoje v českých zemích v letech 1938–1945* vol. 3 (Prague: ČSAV, 1959), 195–210.

30. Musilová, "Zásobování a výživa," 65.

31. Brandes, *Češí pod německým protektorátem,* 378–79. According to official statistics, an average Czech working family in 1943 was operating on what was effectively 91 percent of the income it had enjoyed in March of 1939. *Statistisches Jahrbuch für das Protektorat Böhmen und Mähren* (1944), 178.

32. For example, a recipe for oat burgers (*karbanátky z vloček*) includes 20 dkg (decagrams) oats, 10 dkg dried vegetables, 3–4 dkg fat, 5 dkg yeast, a small onion, 2–3 cloves of garlic, bread crumbs, and an optional egg. They actually recommend each adult eat 2 dkg of yeast daily! For more, see the "Ukázkový jídelní lístek týdenní s podrobnými technicko-hospodyňskými návody," SÚA/NRČ, box 290.

33. Minutes from meetings of the Women's Center presidium, 1941–1943, SÚA/NRČ, box 290.

34. Report from meeting of the Women's Center's nutrition commission, 12 April 1942, SÚA/NRČ, box 290.

35. It is interesting to note that the recipes for meatless main dishes in particular are not very different from recipes published in periodicals directed at *working class* Czech women in the 1920s, such as *Ženské Noviny.* Now these same tactics are being appropriated for middle-class women as well.

36. "Nástin účelu a programu Ústředí žen při NRČ," SÚA/NRČ, box 290.

37. The remark was made in the context of discussing women's (re)education, not menus, but the circumstances were similar. Minutes from the Women's Center Executive Committee, 27 March 1941, SÚA/NRČ, box 290.

38. See for example, the panegyrics to the Reich in the 1942–43 edition of the year-

book published by the Women's Center: *Kalendář paní a dívek českých* (Prague: Ústředí žen při NRČ, 1943). These "calendars" were thick volumes of stories, poems, informational articles, and pictures by or about women published and sold by the Women's Center beginning in 1940. The 1942–43 edition was the first to have a separate "political" section; it continued, however, to mix its praise of Nazi Germany with articles about Czech women activists like Eliška Krásnohorská.

39. One of the founders of the Women's Center and the director of its project to research the lives of Czech peasant women, Růžena Bednáříková-Turnwaldová, was arrested (apparently in conjunction with her work on the project) along with other members of the Sociological Institute in March 1945 and held until 5 May 1945. Letter of 25 March 1946, SÚA/NRČ, box 526.

6 Denouncers and Fraternizers: Gender, Collaboration, and Retribution in Bohemia and Moravia during World War II and After

Benjamin Frommer

In the wake of World War II, Czechoslovakia sent investigators to occupied Germany in search of war criminals on the lam. Among the hundreds of suspects extradited over the next several years, one stood out not for her wartime crimes, but for her prewar fame. Along with SS and Gestapo officers, the captured included the femme fatale of interwar Czech film, Lída Baarová.[1] In September 1945, when Czechoslovak agents in American army uniforms surreptitiously brought the actress back to her homeland, Baarová returned to a country engulfed by the search for those who had allegedly aided the Nazis. Across Czechoslovakia, police and vigilantes threw thousands of suspected war criminals and collaborators into jails and makeshift prisons. While most of the detained were men, postwar justice-seekers and avengers did not exempt women from their hunt. Decades later Baarová recalled her fellow inmates in the women's ward of Prague's Pankrác prison:

> It was a very heterogeneous bunch. City women, who were guilty of marrying Germans. Gestapo denouncers, older ones but also quite younger ones, who were either dying from the horror of the gallows or reveling in gallows humor. Women who incessantly swore that they were innocent, that someone had denounced them out of revenge, and women who were silent.[2]

While Baarová's memory certainly faded over time, the scene she described in her memoirs was no anomaly. The two groups she mentions—fraternizers and denouncers—embody the stereotype of the Czech female collaborator. Baarová herself stood accused of both offenses. In addition to starring in German films during the 1930s, she had also allegedly denounced the prominent communist dramaturg E. F. Burian to the Gestapo. But it was most likely her prewar romantic affair with the infamous Nazi Minister of Propaganda Joseph Goebbels that made her the target of the Czechoslovak authorities in 1945.[3]

As an alleged denouncer Baarová faced the prospect of trial before one of the Extraordinary People's Courts, the revolutionary tribunals created by Czechoslovakia's postwar government to punish "Nazis, traitors, and their accomplices" in the provinces of Bohemia, Moravia, and Silesia (the territory of today's Czech Republic).[4] Of the approximately 33,000 defendants to go before the Czech People's Courts between June 1945 and May 1947, nearly one in six was a woman. According to official records, the twenty-four courts together tried 2,968 Czech women and 2,527 German women.[5] Sixty-nine women were executed, the vast majority for having committed the crime of denunciation.[6] Thanks to the intervention of the country's justice minister, Baarová was released from prison in December 1946 and never tried.[7] Alleged fraternizers who escaped conviction by the People's Court, however, still faced possible proceedings before local administrative tribunals empowered to punish "offenses against national honor." Baarová's friend and fellow actress, Adina Mandlová, answered charges before such a tribunal because she had starred in films produced by German studios and had engaged in "social relations" with a German man.[8] In total, these national honor commissions investigated nearly 180,000 persons, including considerable numbers of Czech women accused of having consorted with German men during the war.[9]

Despite the thousands of women prosecuted by postwar Czech retribution tribunals, the landmark texts on the Nazi occupation in Czech, English, and German all focus on male historical actors to the almost total exclusion of women. For example, in his compendium of *Czech Fascism (1922–1945) and Collaboration (1939–1945),* Tomáš Pasák barely mentions female collaborators.[10] The reasons for this oversight likely lie in the traditional focus of this scholarship on political and economic elites in the so-called Protectorate of Bohemia and Moravia.[11] In her analysis of the French underground, Pauline Schwartz notes, "Prevailing notions of resistance have tended to obscure women's contributions by orienting research away from participants who did not occupy leadership positions or distinguish themselves in some extraordinary way. . . . However, many resisters, especially women, rendered services without ever taking part in a group."[12] Similarly, collaboration in Bohemia and Moravia did not encompass only leaders and organized groups; women also "rendered services" to the occupiers individually. Through the use of postwar retribution tribunal records, this essay investigates denunciation and fraternization, two of the more ordinary and less visible means of wartime collaboration. In doing so, the following pages aim to challenge the gender assumptions that influenced the contemporary definition and prosecution of female collaborators.

Denunciation

In October 1945 the Czech journalist Jiří Hrbas penned a pseudoscientific analysis of denunciation for the communist daily, *Rudé právo* (Red Right).

To incarnate the typical denouncer, Hrbas chose Olga Trpišková, a schoolteacher who had betrayed thirty colleagues to her German secret police controller. Trpišková had repeatedly instigated anti-German conversations as a ruse to entrap her victims. One unfortunate student, who unwittingly showed her the Red Army's advance on a classroom map, paid for his knowledge with his life in a concentration camp. In his analysis Hrbas voyeuristically evoked Trpíšková for the reader: "She wasn't particularly beautiful . . . her erotic life was not balanced. She was strongly romantic, I'd say falsely romantic. She longed for distinguished acquaintances." If the typical denouncer was an unsatisfied woman, then all denouncers were effeminate deviants. They were "like peas in a pod," Hrbas explained, they were "cowards, criminals with inferiority complexes, sexual degenerates. . . . Take off their uniforms, take away their badge and you have before yourself wretched, mangy sorts of inhuman creatures, trembling from fear and terrible guilt."[13] When the Prague People's Court sentenced Trpišková to life imprisonment, the Czech press welcomed what it considered just punishment for a woman who was the "nastiest [sort of] provocateur."[14]

After her conviction Trpišková faded from public view, but the conflation of denouncer and woman has endured. In his analysis of the Ostrava People's Court (located in northeastern Moravia), historian Mečislav Borák concludes that women in that district were three times as likely as men to be tried for denunciation. He explains this gender gap by reference to "an apparent psychological connection" between the defendants' sex and their crimes.[15] Another scholar, Václav Jiřík, has similarly claimed, "it is evident that denunciation was to a certain degree the domain of the fairer sex."[16] But did women, in fact, denounce to the authorities more frequently than men? Phillipe Burrin cites reports from several areas in France that indicate that the majority of defendants tried there for denunciation were female. In both the Finistère and Eure departments the number equaled or exceeded two-thirds.[17] By contrast, several studies on Nazi Germany have indicated that the majority of German denouncers were male.[18] In the Czech case an analysis of retribution court records reveals a surprising picture that challenges the view expressed by Hrbas, Borák, and Jiřík. Contrary to the belief that denunciation is a particularly female act, the postwar Czech People's Courts were actually far more likely to punish men for denunciation. If denunciation was a feminine weapon, then it was one wielded more often by men than by women.

Czech People's Courts punished denunciation according to Paragraph Eleven of the June 1945 retribution decree, which declared criminal anyone who had "in the service or interest of the enemy, or by exploiting the situation created by the enemy occupation, denounced another for some real or invented activity." Penalties for the crime ranged from five years in prison to execution depending on the number of victims and their fates.[19] There are several drawbacks to using the postwar prosecution of denunciation as a means to determine its wartime frequency. First, the People's Courts tried an unknowable fraction of such crimes. Many denunciations were anonymous and their instigators were never identified, not to mention prosecuted. Second, Paragraph Eleven was only applied in cases where the instigator tried to contact the authorities. Perpetrators who simply threatened to denounce, but did not actually turn in their victims, were prosecuted under a different paragraph. Third, and perhaps most importantly, the public, police, and prosecutors were themselves embedded in contemporary gender assumptions. Thus, the courts' dockets were as much a reflection of the prevalent attitudes of their time as they are a window onto them today. Finally, the Justice Ministry's tabulations, as a whole, contain occasional errors and incomplete information.[20] Bearing in mind those caveats and the approximate nature of such statistics, the People's Courts records nonetheless reveal a remarkable "gender gap."

For purposes of analysis, let us consider the prosecution of Paragraph Eleven (denunciation) by all twenty-four People's Courts during the month of June 1946. That month roughly represented the approximate midpoint of postwar retribution, one year after the first official trial and eleven months before the last.[21] The blood lust of the early postwar months had subsided, but the courts still convicted more than two-thirds of defendants.[22] June 1946 was a fairly typical month in terms of defendant profile (34.1 percent Czech male, 9.5 percent Czech female, 46.4 percent German male, 8.8 percent German female, and 1.2 percent of other nationality), conviction rate (69 percent), and average prison sentence (7.5 years). It serves our purposes that this sample includes a slightly higher percentage of female defendants, both Czech and German, than the average for the entire period of postwar retribution (8.9 and 7.7 percent respectively). According to Justice Ministry records, in June 1946 the People's Courts tried 1,360 defendants including 251 women. In all, approximately 36 percent of defendants that month faced charges based on Paragraph Eleven.[23]

When we examine the figures for June 1946, we find that significantly more Czech men faced charges of denunciation than Czech women. In total 97 Czech women and 234 Czech men were tried that month for violations of Paragraph Eleven (sometimes in conjunction with other offenses). For Germans the gender gap was somewhat smaller, but men charged with denunciation still outnumbered women by the considerable margin of 101 to 55. In other words, in June 1946 the People's Courts tried more than twice as many men as women for crimes listed under Paragraph Eleven. How, then, did denunciation come to be associated primarily with women? The answer may lie in the frequency with which female defendants were prosecuted for denunciation (see table 6.1). Although the courts tried more men *absolutely*, those women who faced judgment were *proportionately* more likely to be charged with Paragraph Eleven. Of the 129 Czech females brought before the courts in June 1946, three-quarters faced charges involving denunciation. There were, by contrast, 464 Czech male defendants, but barely half were tried for denunciation. For Germans the gap between the sexes was even greater, though at considerably lower levels: while 45 percent of German women faced charges of denunciation, only 16 percent of German men did.

On closer examination, the figures cited by Borák for the entire operations

Table 6.1. Defendants Tried for Denunciation (§11) in June 1946

Nationality/Sex	Only §11[a]	Incl. §11[b]	Not §11[c]
Czech Female	67%	75%	25%
Czech Male	35%	50%	50%
German Female	30%	45%	55%
German Male	6%	16%	84%

a. Defendants tried for Paragraph 11 only.
b. Defendants tried for Paragraph 11 in conjunction with other offenses.
c. Defendants not tried for Paragraph 11.

Table 6.2. Conviction Rates for Denunciation (§11) for June 1946

Nationality/Sex	Only §11[a]	Incl. §11[b]
Czech Female	47%	48%
Czech Male	59%	63%
German Female	57%	62%
German Male	74%	84%

a. Defendants tried for Paragraph 11 only.
b. Defendants tried for Paragraph 11 in conjunction with other offenses.

of the court in Ostrava actually confirm this interpretation and challenge the idea that denunciation was a particularly female crime. He writes, "women were three times as likely as men to stand before courts for the crime of denunciation." But this statement only applies to female *defendants.* A female defendant in Ostrava was three times more likely than a male defendant to have been prosecuted for denunciation. But the Ostrava court tried more than nine times as many men as women. And of those men, 423 faced charges of denunciation, while only 182 women did.[24] If we assume that men and women were equally represented in the population as a whole, then the average man in the Ostrava district was actually 2.3 times more likely than the average woman to be tried for denunciation. In fact, the ratio was probably greater because of the contemporary population imbalance that resulted from male wartime military casualties, soldiers missing in action, and prisoners of war.

As table 6.2 indicates, the gender gap in denunciation cases only grew in the course of adjudication. On average, slightly more than two-thirds of all defendants were convicted in June 1946. But among Czech women tried for denunciation (alone or together with other offenses) fewer than half were convicted. For Czech men the corresponding rate was 63 percent. In other words, not only were more Czech men tried for Paragraph Eleven, but they were also substantially more likely to be convicted of the charge once brought before a court. That Germans were more likely to be convicted is hardly surprising considering the greater participation of Germans in Nazism and the virulent hatred of contemporary Czechs (including Czech judges) for all things German.[25] Even so, the gender gap for Germans as a whole was even greater than for Czechs: the courts convicted 84 percent of German men tried for denunciation, but only 62 percent of German women.

The strikingly different conviction rates could have stemmed from several causes. Prosecutors and judges might have treated women more leniently because they believed collaboration, like war, to be a male business. Courts might also have been particularly reluctant to imprison mothers for extended periods of time.[26] Although the retribution law did not permit judges to consider mitigating circumstances, such as the livelihood of minor children who might be deprived of a convicted parent, in practice this provision was routinely ignored.[27] Chauvinism, however, could cut both ways: while some courts might have assumed that members of the "weaker sex" were less responsible for their actions, other courts could have held women to a harsher, idealized standard of noble feminine behavior. Some judges apparently distrusted women as a rule. One verdict explained: "Taking into account the facts and circumstances, the Extraordinary People's Court was cognizant of the criminological principle that a matter in which there are women is very difficult because they do not concern themselves with their consciences and are capable of talking mendaciously about the simplest details."[28]

Had the judges treated women more leniently, this approach should have also been reflected in sentencing. In June 1946, however, Czech female defendants only received slightly shorter sentences on average than Czech male defendants. In cases where denunciation was the only crime, the sentences of Czech women averaged 5.4 years and Czech men 5.9 years. In cases where denunciation was charged along with other crimes, Czech females received an 8.7-year sentence on average and Czech males 9.6 years. The discrepancy, a matter of months in both cases, is markedly smaller than the vast gap in the rate of conviction. Different circumstances pertaining to each defendant, crime, and trial make it difficult to conclude with any confidence whether women received harsher punishment than men for similar offenses. Nonetheless, in the 22 cases in June 1946 where a male and a female defendant sharing the same last name were tried together (or in immediate succession), the sentences were remarkably consistent regardless of sex. These cases usually involved a husband and wife, who together faced charges for the same crime or set of crimes. In five instances the women received the harshest punishment and in seven the man was more severely sentenced. In the other ten cases the male and female defendants received exactly the same sentence.[29]

Ultimately, from the available evidence one cannot conclusively determine the effect of gender bias on the rate of conviction. Even if this were possible, then one would also have to consider the cumulative effect of the gender bias of the people who turned in alleged denouncers, the police who interrogated them, and the prosecutors who chose to indict them. Nevertheless, if we assume that the courts' verdicts were based largely on reasoned deliberation (or consistent bias) and not erratic whim, then the different conviction rates vividly illustrate a striking discrepancy in the merits of the cases tried. In other words, the public, police, and prosecution combined to put forward a considerable number of poorly grounded cases against women in general and Czech women in particular. The extraordinarily low conviction rate for Czech women may thus reveal a commensurately high incidence of false accusation against them after the war.[30] Lída Baarová herself claimed to be the victim of such a false accusation, one that in fact did not hold up under investigation.[31] In the frequent acquittals of female defendants we may thus see the consequence of a conflict between the stereotype of the denouncing woman and the actual prevalence of female wartime denunciation. The popular belief that most denouncers were female encouraged Czechs to turn in women and courts to try them. It also likely gave malicious individuals cover to carry out individual vendettas against specific women. Before the bench, however, the prosecutors could not prove the charges against the women to the satisfaction of the judges, even with their chauvinist biases. As a result, the judges acquitted women at a significantly higher rate than men.

Granting the likelihood that men denounced more in the aggregate than women, it still remains to be explained why male and female defendants (both Czech and German) were prosecuted for denunciation at such markedly different rates. If the conflation of woman and denouncer stemmed from the extraordinary frequency with which female defendants faced charges of denunciation, then what explains this frequency? The answer probably lies in the particularly gendered nature of collaboration in Nazi Europe; simply put, women (especially women of occupied nations) were structurally excluded from many types of open collaboration so they were proportionately more likely to commit secret acts of collaboration. In the Nazi Protectorate of Bohemia and Moravia, for example, Czech men had significantly greater opportunities than Czech women to serve the occupiers openly through work in local administration or membership in various collaborationist or fascist organizations. In response to the German occupation of March 1939 and the threat of a domestic fascist takeover, conservative Czech leaders organized National Solidarity (*Národní souručenství*), a movement devoted to defending national interests by working with the Nazis. In a burst of patriotism, 98.4 percent of eligible Czechs signed up for the new organization.[32] That impressive figure, however, still represented less than half of the total adult population. For, unlike prewar political parties, National Solidarity denied membership to women. Czech leaders allegedly excluded women to protect them, but they probably also believed, like Hitler, that politics was a masculine profession.[33] Later the organization relented slightly and permitted female membership, but it still limited women to the traditionally feminine spheres of culture and welfare.[34]

Not only were women excluded from National Solidarity, they were also absent from upper positions within the region's administration. Not a single government minister in the Protectorate was female. The bureaucracy and the police were male preserves as well. In Czech fascist organizations, from the Banner (*Vlajka*) movement to smaller groups, men filled out the leadership and membership. Thus, from the outset, Czech men had opportunities to collaborate afforded by political and occupational contact with the German authorities. Czech women, by contrast, existed within a circumscribed space, largely excluded from the means to collaborate in the public sphere. Women were additionally constrained by the assigned responsibility of caring for the nation's children, nursing and raising them. This traditionalist ideology was reflected in a 1941 collaborationist article, which explained that the new order was based "on unadulterated laws of nature, directing women above all to their basic function in national society: maternity and running the household."[35] For women, in sum, their sex limited their ability to aid the occupier—that is, collaboration was structurally gendered. Perhaps the clearest evidence of the structural nature of political collaboration comes from the docket of the Prague National Court, an institution created after the war to punish the most prominent Czech collaborators, who had been "duty-bound to be a patriotic example to their fellow citizens." Among the eighty-three defendants tried by the National Court there was not a single woman.[36]

Limited in their opportunities to openly aid the Nazis, women could still help the occupiers covertly through denunciation. For those without direct access to power, denunciation was, Burrin comments, a "weapon of the weak" that enabled them to utilize the police indirectly, for their own ends.[37] Unlike in James Scott's classic study of Malaysian peasantry, however, this "weapon of the weak" was far from a form of resistance. Denunciation aided the authorities by turning every subject into a potential spy. Jan Gross explains, "The principal mechanism for the penetration of the state into the private realm is the practice of denunciation."[38] In Germany, writes Claudia Koonz, "Nazi policy . . . aimed at the creation of a family unit that was not a defense against public invasion as much the gateway to intervention."[39] If the private realm, the home, belongs primarily to women, then a regime with totalitarian aspirations needs to enlist them to penetrate it.

After Czechoslovak agents (smuggled in from abroad) mortally wounded Nazi leader Rheinhard Heydrich on 27 May 1942, the Germans offered substantial rewards for information leading to the capture of the perpetrators. Refusing to denounce them entailed severe penalties. In response, one woman reported that a bloody man had left a bicycle in front of her shop on the day of the assassination and that a girl had later picked it up.[40] Another, Anežka Rožková, told her husband, Cyril, a member of the Banner movement, that she had seen a bleeding man hit a woman with his bicycle. Cyril encouraged her to inform the police, and Anežka later identified the body of one of the agents. The Nazis gave the couple a 150,000-crown reward.[41] Františka Kocinová, a Czech-turned-German, denounced a couple who had praised the assassination of Heydrich. They were arrested and executed.[42] Denouncers also helped to police the occupiers' anti-Semitic measures, for instance, by contributing to *Aryan Struggle*, a tabloid devoted to outing Jews and "Jew-lovers." Julie Mušková, to cite just one example, wrote numerous letters-to-the-editor in which she praised anti-Jewish measures and denounced contacts with Jews.[43]

In her analysis of the French underground, Schwartz notes that familial ties led many women into the resistance.[44] The same can be said of collaboration. The records of the Czech People's Courts demonstrate that husbands and wives not infrequently collaborated in their collaboration. In some cases, like that of the Rožková couple described above, a male fascist was aided by his wife, who herself had likely been structurally precluded from joining his collaborationist organization. In another such husband-and-wife case, a postwar court convicted Jiří and Vilemína Taufner for denouncing a man who (presciently) threatened them, "When it all breaks, you'll be the first to be jailed." Typically, Jiří faced multiple charges (membership in the SA and being a Gestapo agent) in addition to a single charge of denunciation. By contrast, Vilemína faced several counts of denunciation (only one of which was proved). Despite the husband's additional offenses, the two received the same punishment: five years in prison and the loss of all their property. Perhaps the discrepancy between Jiří's multiple convictions and the couple's identical sentences can be explained by the court's analysis of the family's internal power relations. According to the verdict, Vilemína was the instigator of the crime—Jiří had only "succumbed to the influence of his wife." She contributed to the stereotype of the domineering wife by testifying, "I regret my denunciation . . . it was all [done] out of jealously. I forced [my husband] to write the letter."[45]

Frequently, husbands and wives were not partners, but enemies. Marital strife and extramarital affairs, unpleasant enough in peacetime, could lead to denunciation, arrest, and death during the occupation. After a twenty-three-year marriage, Anežka Kupčíková's husband divorced her, threw her out of their apartment, refused to pay alimony, and invited another woman to live with him. Kupčíková got her revenge by denouncing him for listening to foreign radio, an act for which he paid with his life.[46] Others used denunciation as a means to rid themselves of spouses so that they could start up with new lovers.[47] Denunciation could also function as a form of divorce. In a February 1947 verdict, the Prague People's Court noted:

> Because divorce or separation costs money, sometimes takes quite a long time until the spouses are free, and there are other difficulties and scandals associated with it, during the occupation wives helped themselves to other, easier and quicker means: simply, they denounced their husbands themselves, through their acquaintances or anonymously to the Gestapo and the husband disappeared without a divorce trial.[48]

For some, denunciation provided the means to escape intolerable conditions. On 28 September 1943 Alžbeta Böhmová denounced her husband for listening to foreign radio, whereupon he was arrested and eventually sent to the Sachsenhausen concentration camp, at which point all trace of him disappeared. Böhmová was no Nazi; in fact, before the war both she and her husband had been members of the Communist Party. Her own brother and her two nephews had been arrested for being communists. Böhmová's motivation was personal, not political: as she admitted to a postwar court, she had acted to rid herself of her physically abusive husband. The judges gave little weight to Böhmová's marital suffering and sentenced her to twenty years in prison.[49] In a similar case, the Prague People's Court sentenced a woman to ten years in prison despite her claim that she had turned in her fiancé because he had threatened and tyrannized her.[50] The two trials well demonstrate Gross's theory that denunciation not only allows the private realm to be publicized; it also enables the "privatization of the public realm."[51] Despite Böhmová's antifascist beliefs, she effectively employed the punitive power of the state to resolve a private matter.

Contrary to the view that denunciation was a particularly female crime, men denounced for many of the same reasons as women. Like Olga Trpišková, Ladislav Kamberec used his pedagogical authority to aid the Nazi regime. He inculcated his pupils with pro-Nazi propaganda and betrayed one of his colleagues for not participating in mandatory snow shoveling.[52] Like women, some men also denounced to evade their tormentors. František Zeman, for example, turned in the brother who beat him.[53] Borák concludes that spousal denunciation "was interestingly almost exclusively the domain of women, insulted or calculating wives," but this is only true if one distinguishes between wives and ex-wives.[54] Vladimír Němeček, for example, found in denunciation a way to smite his ex-wife's new husband.[55] Karel Svoboda also "privatized the public realm" when he betrayed his ex-wife for calling him a "whoremonger like Hitler." Under oath he explained, "It's true that I informed on my former wife, but I only did it because she didn't want to till the field."[56] If women were more likely to denounce current spouses and men former ones, that discrepancy also resulted from structurally imbalanced gender relations. During the occupation men apparently found it easier to rid themselves of unwanted wives through divorce or abandonment, while some women may have seen denunciation as a simpler and surer means to a separation that kept their public honor and familial property intact.

To return to the June 1946 results of the People's Courts, the variant rates at which the sexes and nationalities were prosecuted for denunciation likely reflect the effect of collaboration's gender bias on the courts' dockets. German men had the greatest opportunities for collaboration during the war and, not coincidentally, had by far the lowest rate of prosecution for denunciation afterwards. Although a number of crimes make up the rest of charges against German men, by far the most common was leadership and membership in Nazi and fascist organizations. German women had fewer such opportunities than their male compatriots, but they too held leadership positions in some Nazi organizations and served as party cell leaders (*Blockleiterin*). As for Czech men, they were active in domestic fascist groups. For Czech women, by contrast, denunciation was one of the very few ways in which they could collaborate with the Nazis. As a result, People's Courts prosecuted Czech women overwhelmingly for Paragraph Eleven.

Fraternization

Like denunciation, fraternization was an offense embedded in the gendered conditions of the Nazi occupation. According to Alice Kaplan, the French perceived their occupation as an act of submission, as a form of rape.[57] But France fought Germany in 1940. The Czechs, one might argue, passively submitted to their "rape." After all, in September 1938 and again in March 1939 Czechs failed to defend their country against foreign demands and invasion. Employing a trope familiar throughout contemporary Europe, in 1939 renowned Czech film director Jiří Weiss produced a documentary on his country's destruction: *The Rape of Czechoslovakia.* In gendered terms, German occupation was a challenge to the Czech patrimony over Bohemia and Moravia. V. Spike Pederson explains, "Also implicit in the patriarchal metaphor is a tacit agreement that men who cannot defend their woman/nation against rape have lost their 'claim' to that body, that land."[58] Fabrice Virgili writes of a "crisis of masculinity" in France caused by the country's ignominious defeat.[59] The nature of Nazi rule over Bohemia and Moravia further emasculated the Czechs. When the Germans took control, they chose neither formal military occupation nor direct annexation. Instead, Hitler imposed a Protectorate headed by a Protector, who would allegedly take care of the Czechs and ensure their prosperity (and docility).[60] The Czechs had been forced to accept Germany *in locus parentis.* But if a German was to "protect" the nation, then what role remained for Czech men? That some Czech women fraternized with German men undoubtedly compounded frustration at the nation's impotence.

Fraternization could be professional and social, but the most detested form was sexual—what was known in France as *collaboration horizontale.* For the French, Virgili comments, "'Horizontal collaboration' became one of the most unbearable types of collaboration, not on account of its immediate effect, which was negligible, but because it represented the absolute defeat of France."[61] In the Protectorate, fraternization was seen to have another, far more pernicious dimension. For Czechs, such collaborators did more than just support the occupation; they aided a Nazi program of Germanization designed ultimately to annihilate the Czech nation, physically or culturally. In contemporary opinion, thus, Czechs who consorted with Germans not only stained their honor; they betrayed their nation. Only seen in this light can we understand the virulent hatred directed against Czech women who fraternized with Germans, irrespective of the sexism that may have demanded a higher standard of behavior of them than of Czech men.

According to Kaplan, liberation in France was "a state of desire."[62] Virgili describes a "rediscovery of a virile [French] identity that . . . [found] expression through a massive demonstration of sexual violence."[63] In spring 1945 Czechs unleashed an orgy of retributive violence directed against Germans and alleged collaborators. Thousands were murdered; many were viciously tortured.[64] In this postwar wave of vigilantism countless women were raped and otherwise brutalized.[65] To what extent misogynistic violence resulted from particular wartime gender relations is a matter of conjecture. The chaotic nature of the weeks after the war ended offered criminals and sadists the opportunity to act without fear of punishment. The Red Army's grievous misconduct likely encouraged others to carry out their own crimes. But the Czechoslovak government also contributed significantly to the violence by depriving Germans and alleged collaborators of nearly all rights and protections. In addition to decrees dispossessing and denaturalizing national minorities, numerous semiofficial pronouncements reinforced the common belief that Germans and collaborators were "free game." Law no. 115 of spring 1946 retroactively extended impunity to retributive acts against Germans and suspected collaborators perpetrated prior to 28 October 1945. No crimes were explicitly excluded from the law; even acts out of greed or "lust" could be covered if they had been committed as expressions of opposition to the enemies of the Czech and Slovak nations or their common state. In other words, any crime, even rape or murder, committed against a German or a person thought to be a collaborator, was potentially no crime at all.[66]

While most female victims of rape and sexual sadism were probably German, Czech women who had fraternized with Germans became targets, too. The designation of fraternization as collaboration, in particular, put many Czech women into a similarly lawless position as Sudeten Germans. In his memoirs, Jaroslav Drábek, the chief prosecutor of the Prague People's Court, recalled one such target: "On the ground floor of our building lived a prostitute . . . who everyone was gunning for after the war because only German soldiers visited her."[67] Much as in France, where women were paraded through crowds with their heads shaven, Czech females in the Moravian town of Frýdek were forced to sweep the streets for a month while wearing signs on their backs: "I consorted with Germans and am shirking work."[68] Like men, women were caught up in the indiscriminate dragnet that dumped thousands in jail without cause or even clear reason. Self-appointed security forces arrested women on the sole grounds that they had maintained "amorous relations" with collaborators and Germans. Once detained, women were at the mercy of their jailers. Investigators in Chrudim, for example, forced two women to strip naked for their interrogation.[69] Elsewhere incarcerated women were delivered to be raped by Red Army soldiers.[70]

In desperation one woman wrote the country's president to plead for her nineteen-year old sister, who had fraternized with a German man during the war. The letter explained,

> My sister has been in prison for ten weeks already. What she's suffered for such a small offense is so inhuman as to be incomprehensible. They have treated her from the very beginning as if she was the worst criminal. [Local officials] came into her cell drunk, ordered her to strip naked, thrashed her so roughly that her body was like a map, they cut her exquisite hair and after the beating they doused her in water. That was repeated several nights in a row.

The sister added with emphasis, "There are more such cases with girls in my parents' village near Prague." Not only were the Czech investigators cruel, they were, it seems, crueler to the female prisoners. According to the letter, male prisoners said they had not been treated so awfully. Unfortunately, the letter likely failed to ameliorate her sister's condition. Even if it found a sympathetic audience, its author was too afraid to sign her name or even mention the name of the village concerned.[71]

Even legally intermarried Czech women faced discrimination, intimidation, and sometimes outright terror. A teacher reported that intermarried women in the Jihlava region had been chased from their homes, robbed, and even raped. His own sixty-nine-year-old mother-in-law had a gun pulled on her "when, as a Czech, she hesitated to join a 'transport.'"[72] Local officials enforced anti-German sanctions against interethnic families. Self-appointed paramilitaries turned them out of their homes and confiscated or just plundered their property. Intermarried Czechs sometimes received smaller, "German" rations and had to wear armbands marking them as Germans. Many were interned as alleged collaborators and traitors. Intermarried Czech women and their children were even expelled from the country along with the Germans.[73]

In October 1945, concerned that the People's Courts were failing to try small-scale collaborators, the government authorized local authorities to punish "offenses against national honor." Over the next two years national honor tribunals investigated nearly 180,000 persons and punished more than 46,000 with penalties of up to one year's imprisonment and one million Czechoslovak crowns.[74] Since the tribunals were empowered to try transgressions of Czech national honor, nearly all of the defendants were Czech. "Offenses against national honor" included political, professional, economic, and social collaboration with Germans. According to a contemporary handbook for tribunal members, social collaboration "included not only attendance at German theaters and concerts, . . . hunting and drinking with Germans, but also frequent or regular visits to German families or inviting Germans into one's home."[75] As an official Ministry of Interior pamphlet stressed, "Amorous relations are in particular meant to be apprehended."[76]

Internal Interior Ministry records do not contain statistics broken down by sex, but archival evidence suggests that Czech women bore the brunt of the postwar punishment of wartime "amorous relations." Penalties ranged from public censure—a punishment normally carried out by posting the guilty verdict in a public place—to hefty fines and months in prison.[77] A few examples give some sense of how wartime fraternization was treated. Věra Nováková had to pay a 5,000-crown fine for her "intimate relations" with Germans and for hanging an anti-Soviet propaganda poster in her bathroom.[78] A commission punished Anna Sindlerová with four months in prison for her relations with two Germans soldiers and her meetings with a high-ranking officer stationed nearby.[79] Růžená Pokorná, who had cheated on her Czech fiancé with German soldiers, earned six months for the double betrayal of her nation and her engagement.[80] Marie Bartůňková received an eight-month sentence and public censure for relations with Germans, threatening Czechs, and testifying against them.[81] Marie Kavková was punished with a fine of 20,000 crowns for "intimate relations" with German officers. Apparently she had been caught in a locked room with one. Even the imminent demise of the Nazi empire failed to dissuade her: in April 1945 she brought a cake to a party celebrating FDR's death.[82]

Amidst widespread anger at Czech women who had fraternized with German men, there was also a sense of injustice that Czech men were not being held accountable for their own everyday collaboration. The liberal journal *Dnešek* noted that the state had not prosecuted Czech men who had voluntarily worked in Germany.[83] Male collaboration abroad also seems to have had its horizontal dimension. The sister's anonymous letter, cited above, complained:

> And what, Mister President, about our men? After all, they also took up intimate relations with German women. But only when they got to Germany. In Germany a Czech man wouldn't talk to one of our girls, but when he worked there he socialized with a *German one,* took her to cafes and movie theaters and so on. How many marriages were undermined because the man had a relationship with a German and never went home nor perhaps even wrote. That *isn't investigated,* not to mention punished. On the contrary, [Czech] workers from the Reich were favored when they returned home, it probably occurred to no one to measure men the same. Women always bear everything worse and always unjustly.[84]

In her memoirs, the actress Adina Mandlová also noted the sexist double standard that turned a blind eye to Czech men who had labored in the Reich and there consorted with German women.[85] After the war one such Czech worker, a barber's assistant named Josef Miřatský, pleaded with the authorities to exempt his female German partner from the expulsion. Miřatský had met her when he was quartered with her family in Germany. At the end of the war they fled to Bohemia with their three-month-old daughter, who soon died. In his letter Miřatský noted that his predicament was common: "I, like many other good Czech men, made this acquaintance in the belief that I was doing nothing bad." His plea clearly illustrates a double standard: the threat of punishment for an offense against national honor was so far from his mind that he felt safe presenting his case directly to the Interior Ministry in Prague. Instead of initiating national honor proceedings against him, the local police supported his request and the Interior Ministry approved it.[86]

Despite these examples, there was a limit to fraternization between Czech men and German women during the war. In addition to the social ostracism that each partner would face, the Nazis officially discouraged such liaisons.[87] In some cases they even prosecuted Czech men and their German partners.[88] During the war, liaisons between German men and Czech women were undoubtedly more frequent than those between Czech men and German women. For Czechs, male or female, there were significant advantages to building ties to Germans. A source in the Czech underground once commented: "the privileges for Germans are great in the allocation of wages, in shopping, in the rationing of goods, in travel, etc."[89] After Stalingrad these material benefits were increasingly outweighed by the likelihood of German defeat and Czech retribution. And with defeat, the Germans not only lost their privileges, they became underprivileged. In the immediate postwar years Germans received rations equivalent to those they themselves had given to the Jews. They were made to do forced labor, were subject to curfews, and were prohibited from using public transportation.[90] Amid the postwar wave of vigilante retribution German men were no longer a ticket to power, but rather a deadly liability to the women who had fraternized with them. A summer 1945 inventory of the jail in the eastern Bohemian town of Čáslav lists several Czech detainees whose only discernible cause for arrest was the German ethnicity of their spouses.[91] In May 1945, by contrast, Czech men became the new alpha males as they reestablished their dominance over public life.

Like their German counterparts during the occupation, after the war Czech male officials proved able (and willing) to attract women. In addition to the normal accoutrements of power, a Czech man now offered a German woman the possibility that their liaison might exempt her from the expulsion that threatened all Germans in the country. Postwar fraternization was frequent enough to raise the ire of the communist daily *Rudé právo,* which featured letters decrying the practice. For example, V. R. from Vilštejn complained that in the Cheb area (on Czechoslovakia's far western border) German women had attended many dances. F. Z. from Seletice similarly denounced a Mr. Procházka because he had allegedly brought a German woman—who had been assigned to him for work—to a dance. V. C. from Těšice wrote that there had been three dances during Lent and that Germans had attended them all. At two firemen's balls, the Germans had even received refreshments and stayed till four in the morning.[92]

Apparently, a considerable number of Czech men took the next step and married German women after the war. A petition to government ministers on behalf of intermarried Czech women complained of an unfair double standard. While intermarried Czech women faced official discrimination and open hostility, Czech men wed German women in peace and quiet. In particular, the petition decried the numerous postwar marriages between Czech men and German women—there had allegedly been 8,000 such unions. Even more scandalous were the nuptials of one current parliamentary deputy to a German woman after the Munich Pact and that of a "high state functionary" to another after 5 May 1945. The petition concluded bitterly: "Perhaps we will finally see the day when the leaders of our own state and nation will have as much understanding and good will for us as they do in cases of mixed marriage between Czech men and German women."[93]

Despite complaints of chauvinistic favoritism, some Czech men were punished for amatory offenses against national honor committed after liberation. On 3 May 1947 a Litoměřice tribunal separately tried and punished two Czech men for having "maintained amorous relations" with their German female partners even after the two women in question had been expelled. Neither defendant was an ordinary citizen: one, Michael Stojko, had fought Nazi Germany as a soldier in the Czech foreign army; the other, Otto Frank, had been the chairman of a postwar national committee. Although the former chairman had illegally traveled to occupied Germany after his loved one, he was tried not for violating the border, but for an offense against national honor, for which he received a sentence of two weeks and a 1,000-crown fine. Stojko was punished with a two-week jail sentence.[94] In another case, a "national administrator"—a Czech appointed to manage confiscated German property—was convicted for a night he spent with two German women a year after the war had ended. His crime apparently consisted of the fact that alcohol had been imbibed and, above all, that he had kissed them.[95] The three Czech men described here possibly parlayed their authority to entice or coerce German women, looking for a means to avoid deportation, into intimate relations. The difference between the sexes—that Czech women were punished for wartime offenses and Czech men for postwar ones—was in large part a consequence of power relations. During the war German men were the alpha males able to exploit sexual relations to their personal advantage; after the war Czech men took their place.

Conclusion

Jennifer Turpin writes, "Conventional views of the relationship between gender and war suggest that men make war, women make peace."[96] Traditionally, scholars viewed war as a male endeavor, barely mentioning women at all in their analyses. Over the past several decades, study of World War II has moved beyond an exclusive focus on men to a wider recognition of the role of women. Now, women on the home front are no longer invisible in historical accounts; they are no longer merely passive victims, but participants in societal mobilization. French, Italian, and Yugoslav women, in particular, are recognized as important contributors to resistance movements in their countries.[97] Where women have regained their agency, however, they have usually been portrayed as positive actors. They are victims, they are resisters, but they play little active role in repressive regimes. Despite the growth of interest in collaboration, study of the phenomenon has remained focused on men. Margaret and Patrice Higgonet warn, however, "But by focusing on their role as victims, rather than as agents, scholars have tended to exculpate and extricate women from history."[98] Like national histories, which took decades before they reluctantly began to appreciate collaboration's central role in wartime life, studies of war should also consider the multiplicity of women's responses to foreign occupation. After all, women were not just victims, they were perpetrators, too.

As this chapter has discussed, however, when women collaborated with the Nazis they were likely to do so in structurally gendered ways. The Nazi regime limited the opportunities for women to participate openly in repression, especially in occupied countries. Whereas men were active in fascist organizations and helped to administer foreign rule, women who collaborated more likely did so as individuals. As a result, perhaps the two most common avenues for female collaboration under Nazi rule were denunciation and fraternization. In the provinces of Bohemia, Moravia, and Silesia, however, neither practice was a particularly female vice. Czech men also fraternized with German women, both during and especially after the war. And men, both Czech and German, denounced acquaintances, co-workers, and relatives to the Nazi authorities. In fact, as the People's Courts' records indicate, there is good reason to think that men committed this supposedly feminine crime more often than women.

Notes

The author would like to express his gratitude to the editors, anonymous reviewers, and Peter Carroll for their comments and suggestions.

1. By January 1947 a total of 470 German suspects had been extradited to Czechoslovakia. Tomáš Staněk, *Odsun Němců z Československa 1945–1947* (Prague: Naše vojsko, 1991), 256.
2. Lida Baarová, *Útěky* (Toronto: Sixty-Eight Publishers, 1983), 254.
3. Ibid., 241–43, 254–55; and Stanislav Motl, *Prokletí Lídy Baarové: Příběh české herečky ve světle nově objevených archivních dokumentů a autentických vzpomínek* (Prague: Rybka Publishers, 2002), 152–53.
4. Slovakia had its own retribution law and tribunals and, therefore, will not be examined in this essay.
5. While the statistics on defendants' sex can be considered reliable, the nationality of a defendant was often a subjective and inconsistent determination. This was particularly true in cases where the accused had changed his or her official nationality during the war. The "German" total included inhabitants of prewar Germany and Austria, but most defendants had been Czechoslovak citizens before the war. In August 1945, they, together with nearly all of country's three million strong German community, were denaturalized in preparation for expulsion from Czechoslovakia. Monthly summary reports, Státní ústřední archiv (hereafter SÚA) Prague, f. MS (org), k. 1930–33, f. MS (Z.tr.), k. 2076–77. (Subsequent references to this collection will include collection, box, and document, followed by further relevant information, e.g., SÚA/MS (org)/1930–33; SÚA/MS (Z.tr)/2076–77.)
6. Calculations based on: Otakar Liška et al., *Vykonané tresty smrti Československo 1918–1989* (Prague: Úřad dokumentace a vyšetřování zločinů komunismu, 2000).
7. Baarová, *Útěky*, 264–65.
8. Adina Mandlová, *Dneska už se tomu směju* (Toronto: Sixty-Eight Publishers, 1976), 183–84; "Adina Mandlová odsouzena," *Mladá fronta* (6 February 1947), 3.
9. SÚA/MV-NR (B2220)/2017/sv. 2MV č. B-2220-12/8–47–I/2, "Informace pro pana ministra vnitra: výsledek činnosti národních výborů podle dekretu č. 138/45 sb." (18 August 1947).
10. Detlev Brandes, *Die Tschechen unter deutschem Protektorat: Besatzungpolitik, Kollaboration und Widerstand im Protektorat Böhmen und Mähren*, vols. 1 and 2 (Munich: R. Oldenbourg, 1969 and 1975); Vojtech Mastny, *The Czechs under Nazi Rule: The Failure of National Resistance* (New York: Columbia University Press, 1971); and Tomáš Pasák, *Český fašismus (1922–1945) a kolaborace (1929–1945)* (Prague: Práh, 1999).

11. The same applies to traditional studies of collaboration throughout Europe. Robert Paxton's *Vichy France,* the seminal work on the topic, treats women only as the objects of government policy designed to promote the family and reproduction. Paxton, *Vichy France: Old Guard and New Order, 1940–1944* (New York: Columbia University Press, 1972).

12. Paula Schwartz, "Redefining Resistance: Women's Activism in Wartime France," in Margaret Randoph Higgonet et al., eds., *Behind the Lines: Gender and the Two World Wars* (New Haven: Yale University Press, 1987), 142.

13. Jiří Hrbas, "Denunciant," *Rudé právo* (3 October 1945), SÚA/MZV-VA II(j81)/215.

14. "Doživotní žalář dr. Trpiškové," *Lidová demokracie;* "Žena číslo V 274 odsouzena na doživotí," *Práce,* "Lidový soud nad českou profesorkou-udavačkou," *Rudé právo* (28 September 1945), SÚA/MZV-VA II(j81)/215.

15. Mečislav Borák, *Spravedlnost podle dekretu: Retribuční soudnictví v ČSR a Mimoádný lidový soud v Ostravě (1945–1948)* (Ostrava: Tilia, 1998), 224, 274.

16. Václav Jiřík, *Nedaleko od Norimberku. Z dějin Mimořádného lidového soudu v Chebu v letech 1946 až 1948* (Cheb: Svět křídel, 2000), 376.

17. Phillipe Burrin, *France under the Germans: Collaboration and Compromise,* trans. Janet Lloyd (New York: The New Press, 1996), 209.

18. Robert Gellately, "Denunciations in Twentieth-Century Germany: Aspects of Self-Policing in the Third Reich and the German Democratic Republic," in Sheila Fitzpatrick and Robert Gellately, eds., *Accusatory Practices: Denunciation in Modern European History, 1789–1989* (Chicago: University of Chicago Press, 1997), 215.

19. §11 Decree no. 16/1945, Karel Jech and Karel Kaplan, eds., *Dekrety prezidenta republiky 1940–1945: Dokumenty* (Brno: Ústav pro soudobé dějiny AV ČR, 1995), 1:241.

20. As noted earlier, the assignation of nationality was sometimes arbitrary, especially in cases where the accused had been legally considered Czech before the war but had officially adopted German nationality during the occupation. Nonetheless, the records are remarkably complete: the archives of the Cheb court, for example, are today missing only 50 of the 2,037 case files. Archiv Ministerstva Vnitra (hereafter AMV) Prague, no. 12365 "Přehled činnosti MLS v době od 1. do 30.6.1946," MS no. 49.500/46–IV/5 (All further references to this archive will be archive, internal number, and manuscript number, e.g., AMV, no. 12365/49.500/46–IV/5); Jiřík, *Nedaleko od Norimberku,* 20.

21. On 8 June 1945 the Brno court convicted three male defendants in what was the first legally sanctioned Czech retribution trial. Czech retribution officially came to an end on 4 May 1947. (After the February 1948 coup d'état the communist regime restarted retribution, but 1948 trials are not considered here because of the markedly different political circumstances of those cases.)

22. Both the conviction rate and average sentence steadily declined over the course of postwar retribution. Monthly summary reports, SÚA/MS (org)/1930–33; SÚA/MS (Z.tr.)/2076–77.

23. "Přehled činnosti MLS v době od 1. do 30.6.1946," AMV no. 12365/49.500/46–IV/5. The calculations in the subsequent text are based on these records.

24. Borák, *Spravedlnost podle dekretu,* 224.

25. Perhaps the most evocative illustration of this hatred was a contemporary pamphlet, "The Devil Speaks German." Ivan Herben, "Ďabel mluví německý," in *My a Němci: Dějinný úkol strany národně socialistické při vystěhování Němců z Československa* (Prague, 1945).

26. Jiřík. *Nedaleko od Norimberku.*

27. Benjamin Frommer, *National Cleansing: Retribution against Nazi Collaborators in Postwar Czechoslovakia* (New York: Cambridge University Press, 2005), 135–38.

28. Verdict against Zdenka Holubová and Anna Velíšková (7 February 1947), Státní oblastní archiv (hereafter SOA) Prague/MLS-PR/Ls-II-1026/45, 82.

29. "Přehled činnosti MLS v době od 1. do 30.6.1946," AMV, no. 12365/49.500/46–IV/5.

30. Vojta Beneš, the Czechoslovak President's brother, once estimated that 240,000 Czechs were falsely accused by their fellow citizens after the war. Pavel Tigrid, *Kapesní průvodce inteligentníženy po vlastním osudu* (Toronto: Sixty-Eight Publishers, 1988), 374.

31. Baarová, *Útěky,* 255.

32. Mastny, *The Czechs under Nazi Rule,* 62.

33. Hitler once apparently proclaimed, "For me a women in politics is something repulsive." Jiřík, *Nedaleko od Norimberku,* 373.

34. Melissa D. Feinberg, *The Rights Problem: Gender and Democracy in the Czech Lands, 1918–1945* (Ph.D. dissertation, University of Chicago, 2000), 320–21.

35. Ibid., 342–43.

36. "Činnost Národního soudu v Praze," *Svobodné noviny* (8 May 1947), SÚA/MZV-VA II,(j41)/k. 213.

37. Burrin, *France under the Germans,* 209.

38. Jan T. Gross, *Revolution from Abroad: The Soviet Conquest of Poland's Western Ukraine and Western Belorussia* (Princeton: Princeton University Press, 1988), 120.

39. Claudia Koonz, *Mothers in the Fatherland: Women, the Family, and Nazi Politics* (New York: St. Martin's Press, 1987), 163.

40. A People's Court gave her nine years. "Udavačka z heydrichiády před soudem," *Národní osvobození* (22 November 1946), SÚA/MZV-VA II (j81)/216.

41. In 1946 a People's Court sentenced them each to ten years in prison. *Lidová demokracie* (26 February 1946), 2; *Právo lidu* (26 February 1946), SÚA/MZV-VA II(j81)/216.

42. On 7 October 1946 Kocinová was executed in Brno. "Trest smrti udavače," *Národní osvobození* (8 October 1946), SÚA/MZV-VA II(j81)/216.

43. "Julie Mušková před lidovým soudem," *Kutnohorský kraj* II:7 (15 Feb. 1946), 2. See also the cases of M. Trojanová and the newsstand owner Šteníčková, who both earned ten-year sentences after the war for their denunciatory letters to the newspaper. "Další zrádci národa potrestání," *Kutnohorský kraj* II:2 (11 January 1946), 1; "Šteníčková 10 let těžkého žaláře," *Kutnohorský kraj* II:36 (6 September 1946), 2.

44. Schwartz, "Redefining Resistance," 150.

45. The Taufners had changed their nationality from Czech to German during the occupation. Verdict against Jiří (Georg) and Vilemína Taufner, SOA-PR/MLS-KH, Ls 264/46.

46. After the war the Ostrava People's Court sentenced Kupčíková to twenty-five years in prison. She was released in 1953. Borák, *Spravedlnost podle dekretu,* 228.

47. Štěpánka Bortoliová and Augustina Musiálková, for example, denounced their husbands to pave the way for extramarital relationships. Ibid., 228–29.

48. Verdict, SOA-Praha/MLS-PR, Ls 1026/45, 89.

49. She served seven years of the sentence before being deported to Germany in 1953. Václav Jiřík, "Retribuční realita a Chebsko," in Frank Boldt, ed., *Velké dějiny, malý národ* (Havlíčkův Brod: Český spisovatel, 1995), 217.

50. "Rozsudky lidového soudu v Praze," *Lidová demokracie* (5 October 1945), "Esesácký surovec a udavačka odsouzeni lidovým soudem," *Rudé právo* (5 October 1945), SÚA/MZV-VA II(j81)/215.

51. Gross, *Revolution from Abroad*, 117.

52. He also ordered Reich flags for the small village of Vrdů near Kutná Hora and then forced the villagers to pay for them. The court sentenced Kamberec to fifteen years in prison and the loss of all of his property. L. Kamberec verdict (22 Feb. 1946), SOA-Prague/MLS-KH, Ls 19/46.

53. He was acquitted after the war because of his "weak intelligence." Borák, *Spravedlnost podle dekretu*, 227.

54. Ibid., 228.

55. Ibid., 229.

56. K. Svoboda verdict (11 Sept. 1945), SOA-Prague/MLS-KH, Ls 1/45.

57. Alice Kaplan, *The Collaborator: The Trial and Execution of Robert Brasillach* (Chicago: University of Chicago Press, 2000), 163–64.

58. V. Spike Pederson, "Gendered Nationalism: Reproducing 'Us' versus 'Them,'" in Lois Ann Lorentzen and Jennifer Turpin, eds., *The Women and War Reader* (New York: New York University Press, 1998), 44.

59. Fabrice Virgili, *Shorn Woman: Gender and Punishment in Liberation France*, trans. John Flower (Oxford: Berg, 2002), 238.

60. The concept of a "Protectorate" was based on the 1881 document establishing French colonial rule over Tunisia. Mastny, *The Czechs under Nazi Rule*, 41; Jeremy King, *Budweisers into Czechs and Germans: A Local History of Bohemian Politics, 1848–1948* (Princeton: Princeton University Press, 2003), 177.

61. Virgili, *Shorn Women*, 239.

62. Kaplan, *The Collaborator*, 163–64.

63. Virgili, *Shorn Women*, 240.

64. Estimates of deaths during the "Wild Transfer" range from a few thousand to several hundred thousand. The Czecho-German Historical Commission concluded that 19,000 to 30,000 Germans were killed. Společná německo-česká komise historiků, *Konfliktní společenství, katastrofa, uvolnění: Náčrt výkladu německo-českých dějin od 19. století* (Prague: Ústav mezinárodních vztahů, 1996), 29–30.

65. Norman Naimark, *Fires of Hatred: Ethnic Cleansing in Twentieth-Century Europe* (Cambridge: Harvard University Press, 2001), 118–19; Tomáš Staněk, *Tábory v Českých zemích 1945–1948* (Opava: Tilia, 1996), 85.

66. Prokop Drtina, *Na soudu národa: Tři projevy Ministra spravedlnosti dr. Prokopa Drtiny o činnosti Mimořádných lidových soudů a Národního soudu* (Prague: Ministerstvo spravedlnosti, 1947), 53–55.

67. She escaped vigilante retribution by offering her services to the new alpha males—Soviet soldiers. Jaroslav Drábek, *Z času dobrých a zlých* (Prague: Naše Vojsko, 1992), 98.

68. "Stýkala jsem se s Němci a štítím se práce," *Lidová správa* 1, no. 3 (30 October 45), 10.

69. MS no. 49910/45, "Excesses," SÚA/MS (Drtina)/2111.

70. SÚA/MS (Drtina)/2111, "Excesses"; Archiv Kanceláře Prezidenta Republiky (hereafter AKPR), f. D-11169/47 "Anonymy," věc: D; AKPR #R-7678/45 (28 July 1945).

71. Anonymous letter to the President, AKPR no. R-7678/45 (28 July 1945), AKPR/D-11169/47 (Anonymy), D.

72. Úřad předsednictva vlády, II/2 no. 4775-II-1051/46, SÚA/ÚPV-běž./1032, sign. 1364/2.

73. Benjamin Frommer, "Expulsion or Integration: Unmixing Interethnic Marriage in Postwar Czechoslovakia," *East European Politics and Societies* 14, no. 2 (2000), 390–92.

74. MV č. B-2220-12/8-47-I/2, "Informace pro pana ministra vnitra: výsledek činnosti národních výborů podle dekretu č. 138/45 sb." (18 August 1947), SÚA/MV-NR (B2220)/2017, sv. 2.

75. Jindřich Stach, *Provinění proti národní cti* (Brno: ZÁŘ, 1946), 11.

76. Jaroslav Fusek, *Provinění proti národní cti* (Prague: V. Linhart, 1946), 30.

77. For a sense of the punitive effect of the fines, consider that the average worker earned 834 crowns per month in 1948. According to Jan Michal, Czech wages increased only slightly between 1947 and 1948, while inflation remained relatively low. Milan Kučera, *Populace České republiky 1918–1991* (Prague: Česká demografická společnost, 1994), 57; Jan M. Michal, "Postwar Economic Development," in Victor S. Mamatey and Radomír Luža, eds., *A History of the Czechoslovak Republic, 1918–1948* (Princeton: Princeton University Press, 1973), 436, 446–47.

78. Trestní nález no. R14/419/46 (1 August 1946), Státní okresní archiv (hereafter SOkA) Kutná Hora/ONV-KH/88, sign. III/21b.

79. Trestní nález no. R14/83-46 (11 January 1946), SOkA Kutná Hora/ONV-KH/88, sign. III/21b.

80. TOK 12/46 (10 April 1946), SÚA/ZNV-Pr, sign. TOK, k. 373.

81. "Protokoly o schůzích TNK" (1945–46), SOkA Kutná Hora/ONV-KH, kniha no. 31, 16.

82. Trestní nález, TNK Kutná Hora no. R14/421/46 (31 May 1946), SOkA Kutná Hora/ ONV-KH/88, sign. III 21b.

83. "Mlčivé trpitelky," *Dnešek* I:10 (30 May 1946), 147–48.

84. Anonymous letter to the President, KPR no. R-7678/45 (28 July 1945), AKPR/ D-11169/47 (Anonymy), D.

85. Mandlová, *Dneska už se tomu směju,* 163.

86. Letter from Josef Miřatský to Interior Ministry Prague (21 March 1947), SOA-KH/ ONV-KH,/90, s/4-106.

87. Although the authorities did not ban interethnic marriages, they did force Czechs to undergo humiliating race examinations. Mastny, *The Czechs under Nazi Rule,* 134–36.

88. Jaroslav Kopecký, a Czech forced laborer, was arrested in 1943 for having intimate relations with a German woman. Kopecký was held for two months in the custody of the Carlsbad Gestapo and then another seven months in Dachau. His German girlfriend was imprisoned for six months in the Ravensbrück concentration camp. After the war the German woman who had denounced both of them to the Nazi authorities was herself sentenced by the Cheb People's Court to twelve years in prison. Jiřík, "Retribuční," 216.

89. Report from JUDr Jan Pavel Pringsheim (pt. II.j.), Columbia University, Bakhmeteff Archive/Jaromí Smutný Collection/"Reports from Czechoslovakia (Zpráva z domova) 1942–1943"/box 12.

90. Joseph B. Schechtman, *Postwar Population Transfers in Europe, 1945–1955* (Philadelphia: University of Pennsylvania Press, 1962), 67.

91. "Seznam osob zajištěných . . . ve věznicí okresního soudu v Čáslavi ve věci týkající se kolaborantů a zradců," SOkA Kutná Hora/ONV Čáslav75.

92. "Hlasy čtenářů," *Rudé právo* (16 February, 27 February, 9 March 1946), 3.

93. "Czech women—married to Germans," Archiv Akademie věd České Republikly, f. Zd. Nejedlý, veřejná činnost, k. 22.

94. TNK no. 18718/47 (3 May 1947) and no. 19789/47 (3 May 1947), SOkA Lovosice/ ONV Litoměřice/141.

95. Josef Plzák, "Malý retribuční dekret (Dekret pres. rep. č. 138/1945 Sb.) ve světle judikatury Nejvyššího správního soudu," *Právní prakse* XI (1947/48): 129.

96. Jennifer Turpin, "Many Faces: Women Confronting War," in *The Women and War Reader*, 3.

97. Margaret Collins Weitz, *Sisters in the Resistance: How Women Fought to Free France, 1940–1945* (New York: J. Wiley, 1995); Barbara Jancar-Webster, "Women in the Yugoslav National Liberation Movement," in Sabrina Ramet, ed., *Gender Politics in the Western Balkans: Women and Society in Yugoslavia and the Yugoslav Successor States* (University Park: Pennsylvania State University Press, 1999), 67–87; Jane Slaughter, *Women and the Italian Resistance, 1943–1945* (Denver: Arden Press, 1997).

98. Margaret R. Higgonet and Patrice L.-R. Higgonet, "The Double Helix," in Higgonet et al., eds., *Behind the Lines*, 46.

7 Family, Gender, and Ideology in World War II Latvia

Mara Lazda

Latvia won its independence after World War I, with the defeat of Germany and the fall of tsarist Russia. World War II, however, brought this independence to an end. On 23 August 1939, Soviet foreign minister Vyacheslav Molotov and Nazi foreign minister Joachim von Ribbentrop signed a nonagression agreement. Significantly for Latvia, the secret provisions added to the Molotov-Ribbentrop Pact secured spheres of influence for Joseph Stalin and Adolf Hitler. Latvia and neighboring Estonia and Lithuania were assigned to the Soviet Union, and Stalin moved quickly to annex them.[1] Following negotiations between Latvian and Soviet leaders whose proclaimed intent was to secure cooperation between the two countries, Soviet troops occupied Latvia on 17 June 1940. On 1 July 1941, the Nazis ended the Soviet occupation; the Nazis remained until 1945, when the Red Army reoccupied the country.[2] Thus, within five years, Latvians experienced the rule of two ideologically opposing total states: Stalin's class-determined regime and Hitler's racially determined state.

The manipulation of gender relations was integral to the construction of power hierarchies for both occupying powers, despite their conflicting ideologies. The roles assigned to men and women were important components of military, economic, and political policies of both occupations. At the same time, Latvians sought to protect the traditional gender relations they associated with Latvian independence. The national authoritarian government (1934–1940) had promoted the image of an ethnic Latvian nation—a nation in which women as mothers held a special responsibility for protection of the nation-state. By striving to maintain such gender "norms" associated with independence, Latvians could carve out a sphere of limited autonomy even under rule by a total state and distance themselves from the occupation regime.

This essay focuses on the Latvian family to illustrate the interplay among gender, the total wartime state, and the Latvian nation under occupation in World War II. The family provided a space in which Latvians could claim limited autonomy, but the family was also a channel through which the occupation regime sought to legitimize its rule, recruit support, and counter resistance. In 1940, by condemning independent Latvia's policies toward women and children, the Soviet regime made a clear break with the interwar Latvian nation. Declaring the "liberation" of Latvian women from the home, the regime promised that in Soviet Latvia women would be able to realize their true potential: "There is no job that a woman could not do."[3] The Nazi regime, in contrast, portrayed itself as the true protector of the Latvian family, resurrecting traditional gender and family roles—images that Latvians associated with interwar independence—to promote their own agenda: the National Socialist, anti-Semitic, race-based ideology.

Scholars have addressed the Soviet and Nazi regimes' intrusion into the private sphere of the family[4] and the gendered iconography[5] of their propaganda. This essay extends the discussion outside their centers of power in Soviet Russia and Nazi Germany to consider how the Soviet and Nazi regimes designed gender policies in the occupied territories during wartime, as a means of building both material and moral support for the war. The very fluidity of gender roles and the ambiguity between public and private[6] made gendered images particularly effective tools of propaganda for these ideologically opposed regimes in the attempt to control the Latvian population. At the same time, Latvians looked to the spaces between public and private to protect their national identity, when political, economic, and cultural institutions had been destroyed by the occupation powers.

Independent Latvia 1918–1940

Soviet and Nazi concepts of the Latvian nation and the effectiveness of their use of gender roles as propaganda for their regimes must be evaluated in the context of interwar Latvian independence. The population of the Republic of Latvia was diverse: in addition to the Latvian majority, it included significant German, Russian, and Jewish communities.[7] The republic had been founded on a civic concept of nation; automatic citizenship was granted based on *jus solis* to all former citizens of the Russian empire who had lived within the borders of the Republic of Latvia.[8] Minorities elected representatives to the parliament,[9] and the state supported minority schools and cultural societies.[10] The worldwide economic crisis of the 1930s and government instability, however, bolstered conservative politicians' calls for protection of the rights of ethnic Latvians in the new nation-state.[11] As the ethnic concept of the Latvian nation gained supporters, conservative politicians and women's groups called upon women to see themselves as mothers of both their own families and of the nation. The connection between motherhood and the ethnic nation became especially prominent under the authoritarian government of Kārlis Ulmanis (1934–1940), the leader of the Agrarian Union.[12] Ulmanis's ties to the countryside shaped his ideology and his policies as he emphasized the rural roots of Latvian culture. Ulmanis stressed the role of the Latvian family, in which fathers and mothers played vital roles, as representative of the future of the Latvian nation.[13] Ulmanis's mobilization of the family to strengthen the nation-state incorporated ideas already being promoted by women's organizations and integral to feminist goals. Conservative middle-class women in particular welcomed Ulmanis's emphasis on the family. In her 1935 article, "Women as the Uniters of the Nation," activist Līlija Branta noted: "[T]he family shapes the nation and the state . . . Women must not forget that they bear the same responsibility for our nation's fate as do men."[14]

Latvian women were politically active throughout the interwar period with representatives in municipal and national government. The Ulmanis government's increased focus on women's roles as mothers of the family and the nation did not mean that women retreated from political engagement.[15] Rather, the connection between the family and the nation was instrumental in broadening the foundation for interwar politics and in shaping the interwar image of the Latvian nation. The experience of Latvians during independence influenced their actions in World War II, and the politics of the nation as family and the family as nation helped shape Latvian attitudes toward the Soviet and Nazi regimes. Although Ulmanis's government lasted only six years before the Soviet invasion, he consolidated an ethnically based national culture in which the family played a central role and which Latvians quickly came to associate with sovereignty and stability. The Soviet occupation immediately followed this period of ethnic nationalism.

Soviet Occupation 1940–1941

After the invasion, Soviet prosecutor general Andrei Vyshinskii oversaw the centralization of political, cultural, and economic structures according to directions from Moscow. Ulmanis initially remained as a figurehead to "approve" the changes Vyshinskii instituted. In July Vyshinskii formed a new cabinet that established a People's Government (*Tautas valdība*) with Augusts Kirhenšteins, a microbiology professor at the University of Latvia, as its head.[16] Ulmanis was placed under house arrest, then deported to Siberia, where he died in 1942. The new regime organized single-list elections for a People's Assembly (*Tautas Saeima*) to create the illusion of legitimacy and to appear to observe the constitutional process. The new People's Assembly "applied" for membership in the USSR, and on 5 August 1940, the All-Union Supreme Soviet "granted" the assembly's request. A Soviet Latvian constitution soon followed.[17] Consistent with Soviet practice, despite the establishment of the People's Assembly, actual decision-making power remained in the hands of Vyshinskii and Soviet ambassador Vladimir Derevianskii.[18]

The principle of centralization was extended to all spheres of society—economic, social, and cultural as well as political. Interwar institutions were liquidated and replaced with Soviet ones. By 3 August 1940, the Soviet state had nationalized 804 businesses and absorbed their assets. Landholdings of over thirty hectares, including forests, lakes, and rivers, came under state control.[19] The regime dissolved independent Latvia's cultural and social organizations, among them the Boy and Girl Scouts, women's organizations, and ethnic cultural associations, including Latvian, German, Russian, and Jewish community groups.[20] In their place, the Soviet regime organized theater groups and choirs centered around the factory; Soviet officials pressured teachers to encourage children to join the Young Pioneers, which replaced the Latvian 4-H.[21]

In the Soviet construction of Latvian society under occupation, the family played a central role in policies and in propaganda. The regime used the relationship between family, gender, and the state to sever ties to the interwar period and to create new allegiances, binding Latvians to the USSR. On 6 November 1940, the Russian Soviet Code on Marriage, Family, and Guardianship replaced the interwar regulations.[22] According to this code, the responsibility for overseeing child raising and welfare fell to the People's Commissar of Education.[23] The Soviet code linked education, marriage, and family, reflecting the significance of the family as a channel through which the Soviet regime could seek to disseminate its ideology and win Latvian support for the occupation regime.[24]

The Soviet Latvian press portrayed these political, economic, and social changes as innovations that would rescue Latvians from their backwardness and bring them closer to other members of the "Soviet family."[25] The Latvian-language daily newspaper *Cīņa* (The Struggle) replaced interwar daily publications. A semimonthly women's journal, *Darba Sieviete* (Worker Woman), was sent directly to women who had subscribed to cultural, middle-class interwar women's magazines.[26] *Cīņa* articles redefined the interwar Latvian nation-state, in which ethnic categories had become central, to one in which class took priority over ethnicity.[27] Family and gender images were prominent in articles that sought to shape a class-based Soviet Latvian identity as well as justify the Soviet takeover. To undermine Ulmanis's definition of the nation, the Soviet regime targeted interwar gender roles, particularly the narrow definition of women as mothers. The Soviet regime brought "freedom" for Latvian women and true equality between Latvian women and men, which, according to the press, Ulmanis had denied. "Worker woman, now you are free!" cried a July 1940 front-page article. The author condemned the interwar Latvian government as discouraging women from developing their talents. Now, the author told women readers, "you may put your skills, your brain, and your muscles to use in the work in which you feel your calling. You are a human being, an equal comrade with man on the work front."[28]

The general narrative of *Darba Sieviete* mirrored that found in *Cīņa* in contrasting the modernity and progress of Soviet Latvia with the backwardness of interwar independence: "Never had the situation of women been so like the Middle Ages as it was in Ulmanis's time. Women were held back from participating in society, in education, in science." *Darba Sieviete* was therefore necessary to replace interwar periodicals that represented the "medieval" mindset.[29] The new periodical printed assertions of Latvian women's happiness and the success of the progressive Soviet policies: "we are infinitely thankful to the socialist state order for freedom . . . for women's independence and self-sufficiency."[30] Through such testimonials, both publications stressed the participation of women in redefining their roles under the new regime.

As scholars such as David Hoffmann have stressed, Soviet propaganda did not deny women's roles in the family and acknowledged their "natural duties as mothers."[31] An article in *Darba Sieviete* noted that "the most unhappy woman is one who can not have children."[32] This maternal rhetoric, however, was a tool to criticize the interwar period and to distinguish the Soviet worker collective from the Latvian ethnic concept of nationhood. While authors acknowledged some of the positive innovations of independent Latvia, such as kindergartens and childcare allowances, they generally dismissed Ulmanis's social and pronatalist policies. One author stated blankly, "I think it is not necessary to spend any more time looking at the benefits that the fascist government claimed to give the mother and child."[33]

Darba Sieviete stressed the social nature of the family and the significance of work, rather than the cultivation of Latvian tradition. While in interwar Latvia, Ulmanis and women's leaders such as Berta Pīpiņa had appealed to women to foster Latvian culture in their families; now the Soviet regime asked women to dismantle these "backward" traditions in light of the new, modern worker culture. Women's interest in handicrafts—the intricate weaving and knitting characteristic of Latvian traditional cultural handiwork—should not become a "cult-like" obsession: "[I]s it rational in this modern age, when many machines are capable of fast production, to devote so much time to renewing traditions of the Middle Ages, as in recent years many women from all classes, but especially bourgeois women [had done]?"[34] The author admonished women that, above all, they should use their time wisely. Handicraft was not art, she argued, because the work was not original but based on patterns. In interwar Latvia, in contrast, middle-class women's organizations had held workshops in cities and rural areas to teach women traditional Latvian handicrafts. Women had even attended the opera in self-made folk costumes for the purpose of advertising Latvian culture. That propaganda against handicraft was not fully supported by all members of the Soviet regime in Latvia is evident, however, from articles that appeared in *Cīņa*. Žanis Spure criticized the *Darba Sieviete* denouncement of handicraft, insisting that "handicraft does not interfere with political education," and promised that in fact the new regime would support craft competitions.[35]

The concept of the family was useful and even necessary for the Sovietization process to provide an image of stability and reassure Latvians that the Union of Soviet Socialist Republics and the presence of the Soviet Army promised a peaceful and prosperous future. However, the regime promoted the image of the family of Soviet peoples. This concept of family became central to Sovietization as it softened the fact of the militarism of occupation and established an image for the hierarchy of Soviet rule: Stalin as the head of the family, ruling over a collective of brothers and sisters. Returning from the mission to Moscow that completed the annexation process, each member of the official Latvian delegation stressed the fraternal ties between the Soviet peoples. The Latvian Communist Party Central Committee's First Secretary Jānis Kalnbērziņš repeatedly referred to Latvia's acceptance into the new brotherly family of the Soviet Union, where it would join the other brother-nations (*brāļu tautas*). Stalin took his place at the head of the family as "friend, teacher, and genius."[36]

Latvian women delegates had met Russian women in Moscow and warmly reported of their experience in *Cīņa.* Latvian women's speeches focused on "women's issues" such as the protection of women's and children's rights and on sisterhood among all women of the Soviet Union. Delegate Ieva Paldiņa described her experience in Moscow, where the "woman worker delegates to the Supreme Soviet, who [in Soviet Russia] are many in number, treated me as a sister, as a best friend among them. They thus accepted not only me and my person, but all of the women of Latvia's collective of workers." The women in Moscow had asked Paldiņa about the conditions for women in Latvia. Paldiņa reported that her Russian colleagues spoke proudly about their accomplishments for their families: "—my son is now the head of the railroad station . . . my son is an engineer. Women comrades, women workers," concluded Paldiņa, "this will also be the future path of our children."[37] It is striking, however, that they cited their achievements through the language of the family, as the success of their male children.

The Soviet authorities also offered Latvian parents a new and powerful paternalist guardian—the Soviet Red Army—praising the soldiers' physical strength and understanding. An article in *Cīņa,* "Spring of the Revolution," described the ideal:

> Down the crowded street rolls a motorcycle with a sidecar, in which sits a Red Army officer—one of those who returned freedom to Latvia's workers . . . A mother with two children—a girl and a boy—approaches. The officer takes the children and places them gently on his lap, and the mother gladly entrusts her children to him. Smiling, they drive off. Where? Off into tomorrow, into the future, which they want to shape into a more valuable and beautiful time than today.[38]

Latvians, as members of the Soviet family, had a common mission with the Red Army, which took on the role of parents. Not only did this redefine the image of occupation soldiers as friends rather than enemies, it also offered new models of masculinity. The soldier was a brave hero, father, and model of sophistication: "The armed forces of the Soviet Union have entered our country as [our] protectors and bringers of peace, and at the same time they are also representatives of the highest, socialist culture." This was in contrast to the drunkards, the author wrote, of the army of independent Latvia, or even that of the Russian tsar.[39]

Apprehension about the Soviet policies was addressed by reassuring women that the Soviet state would not take away their nurturing rights; rather, the desire to raise children in a communal environment should come from the mothers themselves. Writers recognized the significance of the family sphere for Latvians: "We must make sure that our children are not torn away from their mother on their day of birth, so that we have a strong and tight family bond . . . so that in their preschool and school years they have the proper upbringing and become responsible citizens of their class." The ultimate goal was "social upbringing" that benefited both child and mother. Mothers could finally be free to participate in political and social work: "The social upbringing of children frees the worker-mother from worrying about them, giving her opportunities to participate in production and cultural-social work. In the Soviet system, this social upbringing is coordinated with the goals of the working class. For this reason the purpose of kindergartens is to raise children in the communist spirit."[40] A draft of children's educational goals reinforced the image of Soviet society as a united family. In discussion of "cooperation with children's parents," the Commissar of Education downplayed the active role of the parents, and emphasized the need to introduce parents to the "families of Marx, Ulyanov . . . [and] the child raising ideas of Krupskaya, Gorky, and Dzerzhinski."[41]

Whereas in the interwar period Ulmanis made appeals to women to recognize their responsibility to the Latvian nation and to raise a moral, patriotic family, Soviet policies and propaganda presented an idealized image of the bond among the collective, work, and the family to build support and to attack interwar conceptualizations of Latvian identity. The Soviet claims of fighting for workers' rights did attract supporters. Latvians such as Ieva Paldiņa supported the regime, as did others who had felt marginalized by the increasingly ethnic, rural-based definition of the Latvian nation.[42] However, the deportations at the end of the first year of Soviet occupation provided a brutal example of the Soviet use of family relations to attack the Latvian nation—including ethnically non-Latvian citizens.

Latvians who supported and were loyal to the Soviet family were promised protection. Those who had "betrayed" the Soviet family of workers were deported to Siberia with their family members. The largest mass deportation in the first year of occupation took place during the night of 13–14 June 1941, when, in the middle of the night, Soviet officials and local Latvian delegates woke families and told them to prepare to leave within a half an hour. None of the deportees was officially charged or tried.[43] Often the reason for arrest was owning property or alleged anti-Soviet activity. The Soviet regime also accused women themselves of such treasonous behavior, but family relationships were often sufficient reason for deportation. Wives of Latvian army officers and mothers of "counterrevolutionary" sons were included on deportee lists. In some cases, Soviet officials arrested women as "heads of the household" in place of their husbands, who were in hiding or had been arrested earlier.[44] In other instances, if wives were not present at the time of their husband's arrest, the officials searched for them and brought them home.[45] In this one night, 15,424 Latvian citizens, including Latvians (81.27 percent), Jews (11.7 percent), Russians (5.29 percent), and Germans (.39 percent) were arrested. Of those deported, 46.5 percent were women, and 15 percent were children under the age of ten.[46]

The separation of families, of women and children from husbands and fathers, was an integral part of the deportation process. Families had no advance warning of the planned separations.[47] When they were loaded onto the cattle cars it was announced that men would have to go in separate cars to be more comfortable, but they would all be together in the end.[48] Men often had carried the family's belongings with them so that the women would not be burdened.[49] While women were sent to work settlements in the Kransoyarsk and Novosibirsk regions, men went to more brutal labor or prison camps or were simply shot. The deportees interpreted the deportations as a direct attack on the family. Rozmarija Zemīte, who was deported in 1941, called the separation a calculated policy to "destroy the Latvian nation."[50]

Women's stories of exile illustrate how reconstructing family ties became an important force for survival and resistance. Although the Soviet deportation procedure had exploited family ties to attack the Latvian nation, in exile, concepts of family helped the deportees to survive. Women created new families by "adopting" strangers. One woman accepted an older Latvian woman as her mother because the elderly would not receive food rations if they could not work.[51] Others took care of women's children, as one wrote: "It was not meant for me to be a mother, but I became convinced I could be useful, helping mothers with sick and dying children. The mothers themselves had fallen into apathy or insanity from the tension and sleepless nights."[52] The concept of the family had been used by the occupying powers to disseminate ideology and to attempt to control the population, but, at the same time, Latvians mobilized and reshaped family relationships to survive.

Nazi Occupation 1941–1945

The invasion of the Nazi army ended the Soviet deportation. On 17 July 1941, Latvia, with the occupied eastern territories of Estonia, Lithuania, and Belorussia, became a part of Reich Commissariat Ostland under Alfred Rosenberg. Initially, some Latvians considered the Nazis liberators who had saved them from further Soviet deportation. Emilija Vasara remembered, "We had no particular affection for the Germans [but] we welcomed [them] because of the 14 June deportations."[53] Latvians soon understood from Germanization policies and the Holocaust,[54] however, that the Nazis had no plans for an independent or autonomous Latvia, and support for the "liberators" diminished.

The vivid memory of the Soviet deportations is a partial explanation for the initial welcome Latvians gave the Nazi soldiers. The Nazi regime also gained support in Latvia by resurrecting interwar Latvian cultural and social organizations. Many saw this as a step toward stability and autonomy for Latvians. While the Soviet regime had condemned interwar independent Latvia and distanced itself from any association with its organizations, the Nazi regime allowed symbols of Latvian nationhood such as occasional display of the interwar flag—but in fact planned to institute Nazification and Germanization. For the Nazi regime, as for the Soviet regime, the family represented a channel for disseminating the occupying regime's ideology, in this case one based on anti-Semitism and racism. However, in a society that was based on "racial categories," strengthening the Latvian family could also pose a threat to the German *Volk*. Thus while the Nazi regime used the malleability and flexibility of the concept of the family to recruit supporters for its policies, at the same time Nazi officials were aware that the Latvians could pose a threat to the German nation.

The long-term plans for Latvia and the Ostland territories clearly were annexation and Germanization. On 20 June 1941, Rosenberg announced at a meeting in Berlin that the Reich would ban "all expressions of loyalty [to Latvia] or autonomy."[55] In the short term, however, Nazi policy in Latvia included measures that suggested autonomy might be possible. In August, the occupying power established a Latvian self-administration (*pašpārvalde*) headed by Oskars Dankers, who had left Latvia with the repatriating Baltic Germans in 1939 and now returned.[56] Although the establishment of a self-administration suggested autonomy on the local level, its activities were subject to the approval of the occupation authorities, and its power was largely symbolic.[57] Correspondence between regime officials points to the growing distrust the Nazis had of the self-administration, even with such limited powers. German officials complained that the self-administration members were overly nationalistic and anti-German.[58] Administrative and legislative control remained in the hands of the Nazis, under the Reich Commissioner in Riga, Heinrich Lohse. German was the official language of the Reich Commissariat, and Latvian was permitted only at the local level.[59]

The construction of gender policies and the regulation of family and marriage played a central role in the Nazi regime's quest to achieve its racial, administrative, and military goals, and to legitimize these goals in the eyes of the Latvian population. Legislation regarding marriage and the family distinguished the Nazi occupation from the preceding Soviet occupation and, by drawing ties to interwar independence, suggested continuity of the Latvian nation-state. In September 1941, for example, the General Commissioner of Riga reinstated family civil law valid before 17 June 1940.[60]

Like the Soviet occupiers, the Nazis also employed the press to present their ideal images of the family in the effort to discredit the previous regime and to claim legitimacy. The Latvian-language newspaper *Tēvija* (Fatherland)[61] replaced the Soviet *Cīņa* as the main official daily, and the woman's journal *Mana Māja* (My Home), featuring colorful pictures of women in Latvian folk costumes, replaced *Darba Sieviete* with its stories on women Stakhanovites.[62] The periodicals depicted the return of the traditional gender and family images that evoked the interwar period. Young women in folk costumes—embodying traditional culture and the handicrafts the *Darba Sieviete* had initially condemned—were seen on the pages of *Mana Māja*, greeting the arrival of German soldiers.[63]

Images of the family and stories of violence committed against mothers and children were used by the press as a way to disseminate racial, anti-Semitic ideology. The deportations "carried out by Jews and Bolsheviks," an anonymous author wrote, represented "a most horrid battle against Latvian families. The battle was no longer only with men, but infants, and old, sick women were also arrested and all taken away by Jews and Bolsheviks. Women who had just given birth, children ill with scarlet fever and pneumonia were torn from their beds."[64] From the first days of Nazi occupation, *Tēvija* praised the Wehrmacht for saving Latvian families, women, and children from the horrors of "Jewish-Bolshevism." In an article describing "The First Days of Freedom," the author contrasted the image of the Latvian mother and small children with the threat of the "Jewish agitator" the Germans had chased away.[65]

Tēvija journalists observed that Soviet claims to protect mothers and families had been nothing but empty slogans: "When communists attacked our peaceful towns and rural communities, no one was the subject of loud phrases more than women." Now, under the Nazis, the Latvian woman began a new path—one in which her primary responsibility was the family.[66] The first issues of *Mana Māja* in particular described the happy lives of women and families in National Socialist Germany, stressing the differences between Soviet and Nazi policies. In Germany, women could dedicate themselves to the family, and "the first step [when the Nazis came to power had been] liberating women from laborious factory work."[67] However, as the occupation continued and German victory no longer seemed certain, the Nazi regime increased its demands of Latvian women as workers. Still, articles stressed that this policy was very different from that of the Soviets, and, moreover, was temporary. The experience of German women was again cited as a model: "[In Germany] women have stepped up to take the place of men who have been called to war. But, in contrast to the Soviet Union, in Germany women work only in jobs that are appropriate for their strength and mentality [*garīgā struktūra*] . . . In Germany everything is done in order to lessen the workload for women. Women are never forced to compete with men, as they are in the Soviet Union—National socialism . . . sees German women as the mothers of the next strong, capable, and healthy generation."[68]

Correspondence between Nazi officials also revealed the conflict between garnering local support to fight the war under conditions of growing material and labor shortages, on the one hand, and observing racial ideological ideals, on the other, as well as the conflict between allowing some illusion of future autonomy for Latvians while at the same time exercising control over and monitoring expression of Latvian national identity. Military officers argued for flexibility in permitting marriages between Germans and "racially unobjectionable" Latvians because they believed a ban would inevitably result in the embitterment of the Latvian population and damage the honorable reputation of the German soldier.[69] Nazi officials' reports praised the growing trust the "Latvian farmer population" held for German soldiers and the bravery of Latvians at the battlefront. The increased presence of Germans in Latvia had resulted in intimate relationships between German men and Latvian women. "[The] Latvian girl has given herself to the German soldier based on her faith in his word. Her parents, having faith in the word of a German soldier, have allowed this intimate relationship." The German soldier, officers argued, had honorable intentions to marry his Latvian lover, who was often also expecting his child. Nazi officials presented these relationships as a way to gain the trust of the local "farmer population" and the German soldiers as representing the honest intentions of the Nazi regime.[70]

The significance of marriage regulation in occupation policy and the conflict between racial ideology and military expediency were evident at a January 1943 meeting in Berlin held to consider a ban on marriages between German citizens and residents of the former Baltic states. This meeting brought together representatives of the Nazi Party, the Reich Interior Ministry, the Wehrmacht, the Reich Ministry of Justice, the Reich Commissariat of Ostland, and several representatives of the Reich Ministry for the Occupied Eastern Territories.[71] The concern with Latvian-German relationships had grown with the expansion of the Reich Labor Service (*Reichsarbeitsdienst*, RAD), which had enlisted Latvian men in January 1942, to include the recruitment of young Latvian women in November 1942. The RAD brought approximately 14,000 Latvians to Germany.[72] The relationships between Latvians and Germans were no longer contained within occupied Latvia, but, with the introduction of the labor service, also extended to Reich Germany. The debates at this meeting illustrate the recognition that gender and family issues were instrumental not only to insuring the support of Latvians, but also to maintaining the loyalty of German soldiers to the *Volk*. Although they consistently referred to the admirable, honest, responsible conduct of German soldiers, officials did not entirely trust the soldiers and feared they had lost touch with the ideological vision the homeland provided, stating that "the soldier who has not been home [in the *Heimat*] for a long time has unfortunately lost the correct vision."[73] Moreover, admirable German characteristics were also a weakness, for the soldier's "good nature and decency . . . will cause considerable difficulty in the instruction of soldiers who already feel committed . . . The marriage of the best German men in the current battle for the destiny of our *Volk* represents not a private issue, but rather a duty for the future of the entire German *Volk*."[74]

Nazi propaganda that resurrected the family roles associated with Latvian independence had facilitated friendly relationships between Germans and Latvians. However, Nazi officials now feared that the Latvian mother or the Latvian family posed a threat to the German *Volk*. Through their relationship with Germans, argued Dr. Runter of the Reich Ministry for Occupied Territories in Berlin, "foreign people of the East are, by having illegitimate children with Germans, supplied with German blood, and simultaneously the German *Volkstum* loses valuable strength." Runter argued that these children should be registered and observed in order to determine whether they would develop into candidates for ethnic Germandom.[75] Some officials proposed that strict instruction of German soldiers to teach them restraint with local women would solve the problem and at the same time would avoid suggesting to Baltic peoples that they were being "demoted."[76] With the participation of Latvian soldiers in the war effort, Nazi officials argued that marriage and family policies were directly linked to higher goals of Germanization, labor, and military needs. Outright banning, thus, was considered increasingly "no longer politically responsible."[77]

The dilemma Nazi officials faced in disseminating ideology while controlling assertions of sovereignty provided a space for Latvian nationalists to employ family and gender roles to work for Latvian autonomy. While Nazi officials intended to use marriage regulations to build loyalties and recruit supporters, Latvians co-opted the family as a sphere in which they could exercise their own power.[78]

The attempt to use family policies to carve out a space for autonomy is particularly evident in the activities undertaken by the organization *Tautas Palīdzība* (People's or Nation's Aid; in German *Volkshilfe*), approved by General Commissioner Otto Drechsler on 30 October 1941. *Tautas Palīdzība* (TP) used Nazi anti-Soviet and racial rhetoric to claim a sphere of activity apart from both the Soviet and Nazi occupations. In addition, it increasingly referred to the need to strengthen the nation, although which nation it meant—an independent Latvian nation or one within the Nazi vision of New Europe—remained ambiguous. TP received the property of fifteen social welfare organizations the Soviets had liquidated, including the Latvian Children's Aid Society, the Riga Latvian Charity Society, and the Women's Aid Corps of Latvia. The Nazi officials closed the Latvian Red Cross and the Latvian Society of Friends of Children. Drechsler had the final word in all decision making and appointed the general director of self-administration Dankers as the head of TP. Initially, TP's work focused on aiding "victims of Bolshevism," but as the war dragged on and the German governing structure cut support for families and children, TP also took on the responsibility of providing support for them. There was no official relationship between the Latvian self-administration and TP, except in the person of General Dankers, and in the establishment of this welfare organization the Nazis were careful to avoid reference to Latvian autonomy. Nazi officials made compromises because of their need for an organization to administer aid to Latvians and help families, but they also sought to control of Latvian expressions of national identity and the founding of nationally based organizations.[79]

Tautas Palīdzība, however, succeeded in representing a Latvian identity separate from that of the Nazi occupation regime. TP members wore distinctive insignia, approved by the general commissioner, offering a visual reminder of the Latvian nation.[80] In addition, TP made direct institutional connections to the work and activities of the interwar Latvian Red Cross and the Latvian nation. At Christmastime, TP announced it would renew the tradition of the Red Cross and hold Christmas parties at hospitals and clinics.[81]

Tautas Palīdzība directly appealed to Latvian loyalty to the nation. A 15 November 1941 circular called for volunteers to aid with collecting donations, which, with members' dues, were the main source of income for TP. Anyone, man or woman, over the age of eighteen, "with a flawless past and national mindedness" was welcome.[82] TP was cautious and did not explicitly state its support for the *Latvian* nation. In official correspondences with Nazi officials, TP leaders focused on their work in aiding families that were victims of Bolshevism. Their pleas to Latvians, however, revealed additional aims. In a newsletter by the "Care of Mothers and Children" section, the author stressed that "a large family is the strength of the nation and . . . respect for the multichild family must be promoted."[83] This language was reminiscent of Ulmanis's and conservative women's groups' calls for strengthening the family in interwar independent Latvia. Within the constraints of occupation, the family again served as a point of mobilization in World War II.

In December 1941 TP addressed Latvian women and men and directly connected Latvian nationhood with the protection of women and girls. Bolshevism was not the only source of peril. Dankers wrote of threatening "moral dangers, which concern our young women. Often thoughtless playing with fire can be fatal for our young women, drawing them closer to the abyss, from which there is no return." Without clearly naming the "fire," TP condemned Latvian women's relationships with Germans. The circular urged TP members to be aware of this danger, which could ultimately mean the "death of our nation." TP had an obligation, according to this memo, to focus on providing the right environment for girls and realizing the "sacred responsibility" the Latvian home and family had in protecting and raising young women. Schools and parents had to guarantee that lessons took place during daylight hours so that girls would not be especially vulnerable walking home in the dark. Most importantly, adult Latvian men and women had to lead by example with their moral strength and determination.[84]

Correspondence among Nazi officials reveals that they realized they had underestimated the degree of independence Latvians exercised in family policies. In February 1942, Dr. H. Marnitz urged closer observation of TP, fearing that it was operating in the tradition of the Red Cross that had existed in the interwar period.[85] Others expressed disappointment and concern regarding the lack of National Socialist ideology in TP and warned of the presence of interwar sentiments. Nazi official Bönner recognized that the National Socialist People's Social Welfare organization (*Nationalsozialistiche Volkswohlfahrt*) activities were rather foreign to *Tautas Palīdzība*. He criticized TP's use of insignia from the interwar period, observing that officials wore the emblem of the Latvian Red Cross. Bönner noted that according to the decree of 2 February 1942, these signs should have been removed from clothing as well as buildings and transport vehicles. At the same time, he saw an opportunity to win favor with the organization and with the Latvian people more generally by allowing them to keep the symbols. This would be interpreted, he argued, "as a gesture of good faith for which the Latvians will be grateful." Furthermore, he asserted, such an action was still in keeping with Germanization: "The essence of these guidelines does not give up Germanization of this country or a slowing down of the tempo, but rather recognizes another, better way to achieve this goal."[86] Nazi officials continued to negotiate with Latvians over control of the family sphere, at least on the surface; this provided a space in which Latvian leaders of TP could seek to strengthen the Latvian nation.

Tautas Palīdzība leaders became ever bolder in claiming a role as defenders of the nation, yet the appeal was issued within the frame of racial rhetoric. Bruno Pavasars (who succeeded Dankers as head of TP) stressed that the work of TP was based on the need to go "forth with broader tasks [than interwar organizations] and to strengthen our nation's living strength [*dzīvais spēks*]."[87] Pavasars made a distinction between "elements" that should be supported and those that should not: "It is not the responsibility of TP to support those elements who do not wish to engage as useful members of the united nation, who do not sense nor recognize any responsibilities toward this community." The nation or community was not specifically named. Still, Pavasars stressed the need to help "co-nationals" (*tautieši*) return to Latvia from the Soviet Union, where some had lived since World War I. Pavasars countered critics who accused him of bringing "communists" to Latvia. Such people, wrote Pavasars, "do not understand the meaning of the national community [*nacionālā kopība*] . . . Even if ten or even twenty percent of the returnees turn out to be useless [*nederīgi*] . . . [we will] continue our work because of the children."[88] Working within the Nazi occupation structure and an official organization, without explicitly emphasizing the ethnic Latvian nation, Pavasars carved out a sphere of autonomy and sent a clear message—*Tautas Palīdzība* aimed not only to protect the Latvian family and nation but also intended to expand and strengthen it.

Conclusion

Joan Wallach Scott has argued in her well-known essay "Gender: A Useful Category of Historical Analysis" that gender as a fluid, contested concept challenges the "fixity" of political categories and definitions of power, providing key insight into political institutions as processes.[89] Including gender in the study of Soviet and Nazi-occupied Eastern Europe affirms Robert Gildea's statement in his study of German-occupied France that the "straightjacket of interpretations based on the Resistance/collaboration version of events" has restricted broader analysis.[90] Both the Soviet and Nazi regimes reshaped and redefined gender and the family in the attempt to legitimize their regimes and to gain support for their ideologies. Certainly there were Latvian collaborators, as well as resisters, under both occupations. Focus on gender does not ignore the violence of Stalinism and Nazism and the crimes committed by all groups, including Latvians, nor does it overlook the limitations of living under occupation. However, the ambiguity and malleability of the concept of the family that was central to these ideologically opposed regimes enabled Latvians to construct some autonomy within the constraints of occupation. The acknowledgment of the categories between and outside resistance and collaboration facilitates the incorporation of Eastern Europe's experience into the narrative of World War II not just as societies under occupation but also as societies that actively engaged with and shaped their relationship with the occupying regimes.[91]

Notes

The author would like to thank Maria Bucur, Nancy Wingfield, Toivo Raun, and Chad Bryant for their comments on drafts of this essay. All translations unless otherwise noted are by the author.

1. Gerhard Hass, *23. August 1939. Der Hitler-Stalin-Pakt: Dokumentation* (Berlin: Dietz Verlag, 1990), 194-204, 236–51. Lithuania was not officially part of the Soviet sphere until an additional clause was signed 28 September 1939.

2. The Soviet Army reached Latvia in July 1944, and Riga fell on 13 October. The western province of Kurzeme came under Soviet occupation only at the end of war in Europe in May 1945. Romuald Misiunas and Rein Taagepera, *The Baltic States: Years of Dependence 1940–1990,* rev. ed. (Berkeley: University of California Press, 1993), 45, 71. Latvia remained under Soviet occupation until August 1991.

3. "Nav darba, ko nevarētu veikt sieviete," *Darba Sieviete* (1 March 1941): 17.

4. For example for the Soviet Union, see Gail W. Lapidus, *Women in Soviet Society: Equality, Development, and Social Change* (Berkeley: University of California Press, 1978); Lynne Attwood, *The New Soviet Man and Woman: Sex Role Socialization in the USSR* (Bloomington: Indiana University Press, 1990); Wendy Z. Goldman, *Women, the State, and Revolution: Soviet Family Policy and Social Life, 1917–1936* (Cambridge: Cambridge University Press, 1993); David L. Hoffmann, "Stalinist Family Values" in *Stalinist Values: The Cultural Norms of Soviet Modernity, 1917–1941* (Ithaca: Cornell University Press, 2003), 88-117. Scholarship on Nazi Germany includes: Jill Stephenson, *Women in Nazi Society* (New York: Barnes and Noble Books, 1975); Rita Thalmann, *Frausein im Dritten Reich* (Munich: C. Hanser, 1984); Gisela Bock, *Zwangsterilisation im Nationalsozialismus: Studien zur Rassenpolitik und Frauenpolitik* (Opladen: Westdeutscher Verlag, 1986); Claudia Koonz, *Mothers in the Fatherland: Women, the Family, and Nazi Politics* (New York: St. Martin's Press, 1987); Renate Bridenthal et al., eds., *When Biology Became Destiny: Women in Weimar and Nazi Germany* (New York: Monthly Review Press, 1984); Lisa Pine, *Nazi Family Policy, 1933–1945* (New York: Berg, 1997); Elizabeth Heineman, *What Difference Does a Husband Make? Women and Marital Status in Nazi and Postwar Germany* (Berkeley: University of California Press, 1999); Elizabeth Harvey, *Women and the Nazi East: Agents and Witnesses of Germanization* (New Haven: Yale University Press, 2003).

5. See Koonz, "'More Masculine Men, More Feminine Women': The Iconography of Nazi Racial Hatreds," in Amir Weiner, ed., *Landscaping the Human Garden: Twentieth Century Population Management in a Comparative Framework* (Stanford: Stanford University Press, 2003), 102–34; Victoria Bonnell, *Iconography of Power: Soviet Political Posters under Lenin and Stalin* (Berkeley: University of California Press, 1997); Choi Chatterjee, *Celebrating Women: Gender, Festival Culture and Bolshevik Ideology, 1910–1939* (Pittsburgh: University of Pittsburgh Press, 2002).

6. On the fluidity of gender, see the introduction to this volume. Kirsten Heinsohn argues that "[n]o political system politicised and made public the private sphere like Nazism did, for it offered many different possibilities for political involvement in both spheres." Heinsohn, "Germany," in Kevin Passmore, ed., *Women, Gender, and Fascism in Europe 1919–45* (Manchester: Manchester University Press, 2003), 34. Scholars have debated the construction of separate spheres of public life and domesticity for some time. See Linda Kerber, "Separate Spheres, Female Worlds, Woman's Place: The Rhetoric of Women's History," *Journal of American History* 75, no. 1 (June 1988): 9–39.

7. According to the 1920 census, of a total population of 1,596,131, inhabitants, 124,746 were ethnic Russian (7.82 percent); 79,644 were Jews (5 percent); 58,113 were German (3.6 percent); and 54,567 (3.4 percent) were Poles. Other minority communities included Belorussians, Lithuanians, Estonians, and Ukrainians. Census cited in J. Rutkis, *Latvia: Country and People* (Stockholm: Latvian National Foundation, 1967), 292, 302.

8. A 1927 amendment granted citizenship to all subjects of the former Russian em-

pire who had lived in Latvia since 1 January 1925 and had lived either within the territory of Latvia within six months of 14 August 1914 or had been permanent residents before 1881. This right was also extended to their descendents. Alfreds Bilmanis, *Latvia as an Independent State* (Washington, D.C.: Latvian Legation, 1947), 52–56.

9. There were ten minority parties; the Russians had the most (five) followed by Jews (three) and Germans and Poles (one each). V. Stanley Vardys, "Democracy in the Baltic States, 1918–1934: The Stage and the Actors," *Journal of Baltic Studies* 10, no. 4 (1979): 328.

10. Between 1919 and 1933, there were 124 Russian elementary schools; 100 Jewish schools; 72 German, including both private and state-supported schools. The state supported minority schools even under Kārlis Ulmanis's dictatorship; their numbers, however, decreased. Leo Dribins, ed., *Mazākumtautību vēsture Latvijā* (Riga: Zvaigzne, 1998).

11. The election law encouraged political participation—any group of 100 voting-age citizens (men and women twenty-one and older) could form a candidate list—but resulted in a high number of parties represented in the parliament, which impeded coalition formation. In the four parliaments, between twenty and twenty-seven parties obtained delegates. Andrejs Plakans, *The Latvians: A Short History* (Stanford: Hoover Institution Press, 1995), 127. Yet scholars suggest that the government was more stable than its critics claimed: Jānis Ikstens, "Partiju darbības paradoksi Latvijā starpkaru periodā: Par 15. maija apvērsumu domājot," *Latvijas Zinātņu Akadēmijas Vēstis* (1999): 117.

12. On Ulmanis's coup, see Andrejs Plakans, *The Latvians*, 153–54; Georg von Rauch, *The Baltic States: The Years of Independence: Estonia, Latvia, Lithuania 1917–1940*, Gerald Onn, trans., 2nd ed. (New York: St. Martin's Press, 1995), 146–47, 151–56, 159–61; Martin Blinkhorn, *Fascism and the Right in Europe 1919–1945* (Harlow: Longman, 2000), 81. Also: Edgars Dunsdorfs, *Kārļa Ulmaņa dzīve: Ceļinieks, diktātors, moceklis* (Stockholm: Daugava, 1978); Aldis Purs, "Creating the State from Above and Below: Local Government in Interwar Latvia" (Ph.D. dissertation, University of Toronto, 1998).

13. From 1938, "Family Day" replaced "Mother's Day." In celebration of this day, the Ministry of Social Affairs organized a ceremony where Ulmanis presented money to poor families. Berta Pīpiņa, "Ģimenes dienas svinības," *Latviete* (January 1938): 14–15.

14. Līlija Branta, "Sieviete kā tautas vienotāja," *Latviete* (May/June 1935): 69–71.

15. Six women were elected to the Constitutional Convention in 1920. Although women were represented primarily on the city and local government levels, three women made political gains on the national level: Aspāzija (Elza Pliekšāne) of the Social Democrat Party was elected to the first parliament in 1920; Valerija Seile of the Latgale faction, a regional party, was appointed Minister of Education in 1921; Berta Pīpiņa of the Democratic Center Party was elected in 1931 as a parliamentary deputy. Līlija Brant, *Latviešu sieviete* (Riga: A/S Valters un Rarpa, 1931), 193–99; Pārsla Eglīte, ed., *Latvijas sieviete valsts 75 gados: Pētijumi, statistika, atmiņas* (Riga: Zvaigzne, 1994), 190–91.

16. Latvian communists played a small role in the Soviet occupation regime in 1940. In the interwar period, the communist party was banned and forced underground. Most Latvian communists who had then emigrated to the Soviet Union were victims of Stalin's purges. Some of these Latvians did return to hold leading positions in the occupation regime, such as Latvian Communist Party head Jānis Kalnbērziņš. Plakans, *The Latvians*, 146–48. Vyshinskii and Soviet ambassador to Latvia Vladimir Derevianskii requested that trustworthy aides be sent from Moscow. See telegram from 22 June 1940, published in Elmārs Pelkaus et al., eds., *Okupācijas varu politika Latvijā 1939–1991: Dokumentu krājums* (Riga: Latvijas Valsts Arhīvs, 1999), 78.

17. On the growing tensions between the Soviet Union and Latvia and the first year of Soviet occupation, see Seppo Myllyniemi, *Die baltische Krise 1938–1941*, Dietrich Assmann, trans. (Stuttgart: Deutsche Verlags-Anstalt, 1979); Misiunas and Taagepera, *The Baltic States*, 19–22; Pelkaus et al., eds., *Okupācijas varu polītika Latvijā*, 61–63, 95.

18. See "Decision no. 1716-688-s" by Molotov and Stalin that authorized Derevianskii to oversee the implementation of orders issued by Moscow. Pelkaus et al., eds., *Okupācijas varu politika*, 104.

19. Arnolds Aizsilnieks, *Latvijas saimniecības vēsture 1914–1945* (Stockholm: Daugava, 1968), 851; E. Žagars, *Sociālistiskie pārveidojumi Latvijā 1940–1941* (Riga: Zinātne, 1975), 60.

20. Misiunas and Taagepera, *Baltic States*, 15–43; Plakans, *The Latvians*, 141–48; Rolfs Ekmanis, *Latvian Literature under the Soviets 1940–1975* (Belmont, Mass.: Nordland, 1978), 44–45; Pelkaus et al., eds., *Okupācijas varu politika*, 118–19.

21. Latvian State Archive (hereafter, LVA)/f. 700, apr. 1, l. 349, 4.

22. LVA/f. 700, apr. 1, l. 412, 127–28.

23. LVA/f. 270, apr. 1, l. 16, 188.

24. On the family as "state mobilizational tool" under Stalinism in Russia, see Hoffmann, *Stalinist Values*, 105.

25. Joshua Sanborn examines the role of "metaphoric kinship" in his analysis of the Russian army in "Family, Fraternity, and Nation-Building in Russia, 1905–1925," in Ronald Grigor Suny and Terry Martin, eds., *A State of Nations: Empire and Nation-Making in the Age of Lenin and Stalin* (New York: Oxford University Press, 2001), 93–110.

26. A local office of VAPP (*Vserossiiskaia assotsiatsia proletarskikh pisatelei*; All-Union Association of Proletarian Writers), established 7 August 1940, controlled all aspects of publishing. Copies of all publications had to be sent to VAPP. See Ekmanis, *Latvian Literature*, 45. *Cīņa* initially had a circulation of 10,000 to 25,000 copies but expanded to 200,000. The circulation of *Darba Sieviete* ranged between 20,000 and 30,000 copies. *Darba Sieviete* was not sent to former subscribers of Latvian journals with an explicitly nationalist content. The sources for the first issues of *Cīņa* were largely articles translated from Moscow's *Pravda*, Soviet Russian and Latvian officials' speeches, and instructions to the Latvian people from the local government. Authorship is difficult to determine; most articles had no signed author or only initials. Latvian editors and writers worked on the staff of *Cīņa* and *Darba Sieviete*, though under the supervision of VAPP. The assistant editor of *Darba Sieviete*, A. Balode, was also on the staff of *Cīņa*. See E. Flīgere, comp., *Latviešu periodika: Bibliogrāfisks rādītājs*, vol. 4 (Riga: Latvijas Akadēmiskā Bibioteka, 1995), 43–46.

27. Sheila Fitzpatrick discusses the malleability of class in Stalin's Russia in "Ascribing Class: The Construction of Social Identity in Soviet Russia," in Fitzpatrick, ed., *Stalinism: New Directions* (New York: Routledge, 2000), 20–46, originally published in *Journal of Modern History* 65, no. 4 (December 1993): 745–70.

28. K., "Darba Sieviete, nu tu esi brīva!" *Cīņa* (1 July 1940), 1.

29. *Darba Sieviete* (1 August 1940), 2. See also Douglas Northrup's discussion of Uzbek identity in "Nationalizing Backwardness: Gender, Empire, and Uzbek Identity," in Suny and Martin, eds., *A State of Nations*, 191–220.

30. I. L., "Par jauno ceļu," *Darba Sieviete* (15 October 1940), 16–17.

31. See Hoffmann, *Stalinist Values*, 88–117; also the work by Wendy Z. Goldman and Lynne Attwood, who have analyzed the relationship between ideology and women in Russia, noting the combination of maternal rhetoric with images of worker women:

Goldman, *Women, the State, and Revolution;* Attwood, *Creating the New Soviet Woman: Women's Magazines as Engineers of Female Identity, 1922–53* (New York: St. Martin's Press, 1993); Attwood, *The New Soviet Man;* also Chatterjee, *Celebrating Women.*

32. I. Alksne, "Padomāsim par mātes un bērna aizsardzību," *Darba Sieviete* (1 August 1940), 3–4.

33. Alksne, "Padomāsim," 4.

34. "Bērnu stūrītis," *Darba Sieviete* (1 August 1940), 20.

35. Ž. Spure, "Ko un kā raksta mūsu prese," *Cīņa* (4 August 1940), 2. Spure was a secretary of the Soviet Latvian Communist Party.

36. See speeches printed in *Cīņa* (14 August 1940). See also discussion in Yuri Slezkine, "The USSR as a Communal Apartment, or How a Socialist State Promoted Ethnic Particularism," *Slavic Review* 53, no. 2 (Summer 1994): 415–52; Sanborn, "Family, Fraternity, and Nation-Building," in Suny and Martin, eds., *A State of Nations,* 93–110.

37. "Biedrenes Paldiņas runa," *Cīņa* (14 August 1940), 3.

38. "Revolūcijas pavasaris," *Cīņa* (26 June 1940), 2.

39. "Sarkanā armija—tautu audzinātāja," *Cīņa* (26 June 1940), 1.

40. "Bērnu dārzu nozīme un organizēšana," *Darba Sieviete* (1 August 1940), 3.

41. LVA/f. 700, apr. 1, l. 398, 8, December 1940.

42. Latvians of urban, working-class background remember that they had initially hoped their lives would improve under Soviet rule. Mara Lazda interview with Jānis Vilciņš, 14 August 2000, Riga, Latvia. I have used pseudonyms for the authors of all interviews cited in this essay.

43. Jānis Riekstiņš, "1941. gada 14. jūnija deportācija Latvijā," in Latvijas vēsturnieku komisija et al., eds. *1941. gada 14. jūnija deportācija—noziegums pret cilvēci. Starptautiskas konferences materiali* (Riga: Latvijas Vēstures Institūts, 2002), 23.

44. Iveta Šķiņķe, "1941. gada 14. jūnija deportācija arestētās un izsūtītās sievietes. Ieskats problēmā," in Latvijas vēsturnieku komisija, et al., eds., *1941. gada 14. jūnija deportācija,* 332–33.

45. Some women escaped this fate. Ruta recalled that her mother had gone to visit Ruta's grandmother. Although Ruta's mother was found and deported, her grandmother was allowed to stay because the "criminal"—Ruta's father—was her son-in-law and a relative by marriage only. National Oral History Archive, Riga, Latvia (hereafter NMV), no. 504.

46. See Heinrihs Strods, "Septītā pļauja (1940–1949)," in Anda Līce, ed. *Via dolorosa: Staļinisma upuru liecības,* 4 vols. (Riga: Preses Nams and Riga: Liesma, 1990–1995), 2:11. See Sindija Dimanta and Indulis Zālīte, "Četrdesmito gadu deportāciju struktūranalize," in Tadeušs Puisāns, ed., *Okupācijas varu nodarītie postījumi Latvijā 1940–1990: Rakstu krājums* (Stockholm: Memento, 2000), 148; Zālīte and Sindija Eglīte, "1941. g. 14. jūnija deportācijas struktūranalize," in Latvijas vēsturnieku komisija et al., eds., *1941. gada 14. jūnija deportācija,* 40–50. Although the exact numbers are not known, scholars have calculated recently that approximately one-fifth of the deported population survived life in exile. See Riekstiņš, "1941. gada 14. jūnija deportācija Latvijā," in Latvijas vēsturnieku komisija et al., eds. *1941. gada 14. jūnija deportācija,* 28.

47. Deputy Minister of Interior I. Serov instructed that officers should bring all family members together to the embarkation point and only then separate men from their families. Serov suggested that the arresting officers could ask men to pack their belongings in a separate suitcase and give the reason that men would undergo a health inspection separately from the women and children. Families were allowed to pack up to

100 kilograms. See the order as published in Pelkaus et al., eds., *Okupācijas varu politika Latvijā,* 146–51.

48. Lidija Vilnis, "Manas dzīves melnā lapa," in Līce, ed., *Via dolorosa,* 3:98.

49. Vizma Stūre, "Aiz mežiem, mežiem . . . mājas," in Līce, ed., *Via dolorosa,* 3:64.

50. NMV/1704.

51. NMV/374.

52. Irēne Dumpe, "Mūsu lielais 'rūpju bērns,'" in Līce, ed., *Via dolorosa,* 1:335.

53. Lazda interview with Emilija Vasara, 2000, Riga, Latvia.

54. The Germans and their Latvian collaborators, most notoriously the Arājs commando, murdered almost all of Latvia's 70,000 Jews. Latvia's prewar Jewish population was approximately 93,000. Approximately 15,000 Jews fled with Soviet forces to the Soviet interior. Leo Dribins estimates that 14,000 Jews returned to Latvia, including 2,000 who survived Soviet deportations. Leo Dribins, *Ebreji Latvijā* (Riga: Latvijas Zinātņu Akadēmijas Filozofijas un Socioloģijas Institūta Etnisko Pētijuma Centrs, 1996), 25, 31.

For more detailed information on the Holocaust in Latvia, see Andrew Ezergailis, *The Holocaust in Latvia 1941–1944: The Missing Center* (Riga: The Historical Institute of Latvia, with the United States Holocaust Memorial Museum, Washington, D.C., 1996). Other sources on Latvian collaboration include Robert G. Waite, "'Reliable Local Residents': Collaboration in Latvia, 1941-1945," in Latvijas vēsturnieku komisijas et al., eds. *Latvija otrajā pasaules karā: Starptautiskās konferences materiāli* (Riga: Latvijas Vēstures Institūta Apgāds, 2000), 115–44; Katrin Reichelt, "Between Collaboration and Resistance? The Role of the Organization *Pērkonkrusts* in the Holocaust in Latvia," in Latvijas vēsturnieku komisija et al., eds., *Holokausta izpētes jautājumi Latvijā* (Riga: Latvijas Vēstures Institūta Apgāds, 2003), 279–98. Uldis Neiburgs has several publications on resistance, including "Nacionālās pretošanas kustības organizācijas Latvijā padomju un vācu okupācijas laikā (1940–1945)," *Latvija otrajā pasaules karā.* See also Dzintars Ērglis, *Latvijas Centrālās Padomes nezināmās lappuses* (Riga: Latvijas Vēstures Institūta Apgāds, 2003). On the problems of Holocaust research in Latvia: Latvijas vēsturnieku komisija et al., eds., *Holokausta izpētes problēmas Latvijā.*

55. Pelkaus et al., eds., *Okupācijas varu politika,* 173.

56. According to the supplementary agreement of the Molotov-Ribbentrop Pact, Soviet leadership would not interfere with the repatriation of Baltic Germans. In October 1939, Latvian and Reich representatives signed an agreement facilitating repatriation, and between 1939 and January 1941 approximately 55,000 Baltic Germans left Latvia for Germany. For the supplementary agreement see Alfred Seidl, comp., *Die Beziehungen zwischen Deutschland und der Sowjetunion 1939–1941: Dokumente des Auswärtigen Amtes* (Tübingen: H. Laupp'sche Buchhandlung, 1949), 126. Also: Seppo Myllyniemi, *Die Neuordnung der Baltischen Länder, 1941–1944: Zum nationalsozialistischen Inhalt der deutschen Besatzungspolitik* (Helsinki: Suomen Historiallinen Seura, 1973), 45.

57. See Proclamation of 28 July 1941 as cited in Raphael Lemkin, *Axis Rule in Occupied Europe* (Washington, D.C.: Carnegie Endowment for International Peace, 1944), 300–304; Plakans, *The Latvians,* 148–52.

58. Latvian State History Archive (hereafter, LVVA)/f. P-69, apr. 1a, l. 6, 118. 1 March 1944.

59. Order issued by H. Lohse, 18 August 1941, as cited in Lemkin, *Axis Rule in Occupied Europe,* 301–02. Also: A. Rosenbergs's confidential order issued to the Reich Commissioner in Ostland and the General Commissioner in Riga regarding language use 2 January 1942. Cited in Pelkaus, et al., eds., *Okupācijas varu politika,* 174–75.

60. LVVA/f. P-812, apr. 1, l. 5, 1–2. From the General Commissioner.

61. The editors and writers of *Tēvija* were Latvian but worked under the supervision of the Nazi regime, which distributed Confidential "Press Instructions" to the top editors of all approved periodicals. Several of the authors and editors had ties to the interwar Latvian extreme right group, Thundercross (*Pērkonkrusts*). The extreme right, however, had also exhibited anti-German tendencies. There was open conflict between the Latvian editors and their supervisors. On 5 February 1942, editor Ernests Kreišmanis questioned the second-class status of Latvians, demanding to know why Latvians received fewer rations than Germans. LVVA/f. P-70, apr. 5, l. 3, 227.

62. The first issue of *Tēvija* appeared on 1 July 1941. Its circulation reached 280,000 and included the provinces of Latvia. *Mana Māja* was published first in January 1942. Its purpose, according to introductory letters from the editors, was to help women both in urban and rural areas run their households in wartime. On the surface, the publication of *Mana Māja* appeared as the continuation of the interwar periodical published by the Board of Agriculture (*Lauksaimniecības kamera*). The staff was primarily Latvian, but the publisher was *Deutsche Zeitung im Ostland*, later *Deutsche Verlags un Druckerei Gesellschaft*. *Mana Māja* had a circulation of approximately 60,000 issues per year. E. Flīgere, comp., *Latviešu periodika*, vol. 4, 14, 92–93, 125. See also LVVA/f. P-74, apr. 1, l. 2, 27; Arturs Žvinklis, "Latviešu prese nacistiskās Vācijas okupācijas laikā," in Latvijas vēsturnieku komisija et al., eds., *Latvija otrajā pasaules karā*, 354.

63. See the cover of *Mana Māja* on the first anniversary of the German occupation. "Pateicības un prieka gaviles 1. jūlijā 1941. g.," *Mana Māja* (10 July 1942).

64. "No žīdu vadītām boļševiku laupītāju un slepkavu bendēm brīvi!" *Tēvija* (1 July 1941), 2.

65. J. K., "Pirmās brīvās dienas," *Tēvija* (12 July 1941), 3.

66. K. Vanga, "Latvju sieviete jaunās gaitās," *Mana Māja* (20 January 1942), 28.

67. "Sieviete un ģimene nacionālsociālistiskajā Vācijā," *Mana Māja* (20 January 1942), 26.

68. "Kā dzīvo vācu strādniece?" *Mana Māja* (10 November 1942), 467.

69. The position of Latvians and the other majority ethnic groups in the Reich Commissariat Ostland on the Nazi "racial scale" was not outlined clearly. This ambiguity was a key factor in the fluidity of Nazi policies regarding the Latvian family that at times Latvians interpreted as steps toward autonomy. The northernmost group in the commissariat, the Estonians, was considered "racially akin to the Germans," but Latvians and Lithuanians, along with Czechs were "partially Germanic." The majority population of the fourth administrative district in Ostland, the Belorussians, was "racially alien": Ihor Kamenetsky, *Secret Nazi Plans for Eastern Europe: A Study of Lebensraum Policy* (New York: Bookman, 1961), 83, 89–90. The evaluation of Latvians and their potential for Germanization changed throughout the war: Katrin Reichelt, "Latvia and Latvians in the Nazi Race and Settlement Policy: Theoretical Conception and Practical Implementation," in Latvijas vēsturnieku komisija et al., eds., *Latvija otrajā pasaules karā*, 267; Myllyniemi, *Die Neuordnung der baltischen Länder*, 146–47.

The Czechs, too, used their ambiguous status under the Nazi regime, exploiting Nazi gendered rhetoric to advance the cause of the Czech nation. See Melissa Feinberg's contribution to this volume, "Dumplings and Domesticity.".

70. LVVA/f. P-69, apr. 1a, l. 6, 284. Report of Mitau Commissioner to General Commissioner in Riga.

71. LVVA/f. P-69, apr. 1a, l. 6, 303 Participant list of meeting, 28 January 1943. Heineman also notes the significance of reproductive and marriage policies throughout the

Nazi governing structure in the Reich proper in *What Difference Does a Husband Make?*, 17–43.

72. Arveds Švābe, ed., *Latvju Enciklopēdija* (Stockholm: Apgāds Trīs Zvaigznes, 1950), 432–33.

73. LVVA/f. P-69, apr. 1a, lieta 6, 295. Poremski's report of meeting of 28 January 1943.

74. LVVA/f. P-69, apr. 1a, l. 6, 309. Dietl's letter.

75. LVVA/f. P-69, apr. 4. l. 105, 2. Berlin, 9 October 1942. Runter.

76. LVVA/f. P-69, apr. 1a, l. 6, 289.

77. LVVA/f. P-69, apr. 1a, l. 6, 285; LVVA/f. P-69, apr. 4, l. 105, 2. 9 October 1942.

78. In her study of the Protectorate of Bohemia and Moravia, Feinberg points to the Czech "aping of [German] ideals, while at the same time defending Czech national autonomy." Feinberg, "Dumplings and Domesticity." The Latvians also sought to protect the Latvian nation from within institutions that the Nazi regime had approved, such as *Tautas Palīdzība*.

79. A draft of the statutes in German first listed the name of *Tautas Palīdzība* as the Latvian (*lettisches*) Self-Help Organization. This reference to nationality, however, was crossed out and replaced with "local, native" (*einheimisches*). LVVA/f. P-69, apr. 6, l. 1, 31.

80. LVVA/f. P-69, apr. 6, l. 1, 13.

81. LVVA/f. P-1015, apr. 2, l. 1, 86 TP Newsletter no. 42.

82. LVVA/f. P-1015, apr. 6, l. 1, 3.

83. LVVA/f. P-1015, apr. 2, l. 1, 9.

84. LVVA/f. P-1015, apr. 2, l. 1, 10. TP Newsletter no. 8. 12 December 1941. Signed by Dankers and Skrapce.

85. LVVA/f. P-69, apr. 6, l. 5, 8–11. Confidential memo from Dr. Marnitz regarding TP to the General Commissioner. 27 February 1942.

86. LVVA/f. P-69, apr. 6, l. 5, 12–17.

87. LVVA/f. P-1015, apr. 2, l. 4, 24–31.

88. LVVA/f. P-1015, apr. 2, l. 4, 25.

89. Joan Wallach Scott, "Gender: A Useful Category of Historical Analysis," in *Gender and the Politics of History*, rev. ed. (New York: Columbia University Press, 1999), 42–43, 48–49.

90. Robert Gildea, *Marianne in Chains: In Search of the German Occupation 1940–1945*, paperback edition (London: Macmillan, 2002), 403; also Feinberg, "Dumplings and Domesticity."

91. See Jan T. Gross, "Themes for a Social History of War Experience and Collaboration," in István Deák et al., eds., *The Politics of Retribution in Europe: World War II and its Aftermath* (Princeton: Princeton University Press, 2000), 15.

Part Three. *Remembering War: Gendered Bodies, Gendered Stories*

8 Kosovo Maiden(s): Serbian Women Commemorate the Wars of National Liberation, 1912–1918

Melissa Bokovoy

Shortly after the end of World War I and the unification of the Serbs, Croats, and Slovenes into one kingdom, the Serbian National Women's Union invited the representatives of fifty women's organizations from throughout the newly created Kingdom of Serbs, Croats, and Slovenes (hereafter Yugoslavia) to attend a meeting in Belgrade, the nation's capital. Convening in September 1919, the organizers and participants decided to bring their organizations together into a single entity—the National Women's Union of Serbs, Croats, and Slovenes—to develop women's humanitarian, ethical, cultural, feminist, social, and national activities, and to represent Yugoslav women in international women's organizations.[1]

Tempers flared and tensions among the participants emerged during the meeting. According to the Croatian journalist, Zagorka (Marija Jurić), the Serbian delegates sought to dominate the meeting and assert a position of first among equals based on their suffering, sacrifices, and heroism during the Balkan Wars (1912 and 1913) and World War I (1914–1918). Zagorka observed:

> To understand the psychology of this congress, one needs to understand the mood and the skill of the women, especially the Serbian women who are in the majority. Mainly, they show two sides: a strong natural intelligent strength and an unshakable, traditional patriotism. . . .
>
> In their national and political mood the majority of these women breathe powerful Serbian nationalism. The war suffering of the Serbian women still tempers their feelings. These women are the Mothers of the Nine Jugovići. They understand *Jugoslavenstvo* as a territorial concept, and not as a national idea and a banner of *jedinstvo* [unity]. One can discern in their eyes and in their words the iron strength of Serbian patriotism that one must remember is a tribal patriotism that accepts sacrifice, which as of now, they can't overcome.[2]

The historical and mythical terrain from which Serbian women drew their claims was one not only strewn with military and civilian bodies, citizen suffering and persecution, and alleged atrocities and brutalities, but also peppered with victories and triumphs. In the early months of the war, the Serbian army achieved several of these victories by defending its border and capital city, Belgrade, from the attacks of Austro-Hungarian troops. By 1915, however, Serbia succumbed to a typhus epidemic and the combined forces of the Austro-Hungarian and Bulgarian armies. Fleeing the enemy, tens of thousands of civilians, including the elderly, women, and children carrying only the basic necessities, went south. Eventually some remnants of the population and the army made their way to Greece, where they joined British and French forces. Other civilians, primarily women and children, fell under the occupation of Bulgaria and Austria-Hungary. Reports noted the enormous suffering of this population under occupation through famine, deportation, imprisonment, executions, labor conscription, and the burning of villages. By mid-1917, South Slavs from the Habsburg Monarchy had joined the Serbian, British, and French forces in Greece. Together, these forces drove the Austrians, Germans, and Bulgarians from occupied Serbia in 1918. By war's end, Serbia had lost nearly a quarter of its prewar population of three million. Both men and women, young and old, experienced total war as combatants, refugees, prisoners of war and occupation, victims, and mourners of the dead.

Despite the visibility of Serbian women during the Balkan Wars and World War I, women's experiences were either relegated to secondary roles or largely ignored in the commemorative practices and traditions that emerged in Yugoslavia during the interwar period. In the aftermath of the war, military cemeteries and monuments were constructed, and commemorative ceremonies began to take place that honored the fallen soldier. Such memory sites represented war as a military conflict between soldiers and the soldiers as the ideal national citizens, sacrificing their lives so that the Serbian nation might live. The vast majority of the fallen soldiers were husbands, fathers, brothers, or sons, and the act of remembering and commemorating their lives and deaths was left to their wives, mothers, and sisters. In this chapter I examine how Serbian women's individual acts of mourning and remembering the fallen were collected, nationalized, and universalized by Serbian intellectuals and representatives of the nascent Yugoslav state in order to privilege Serbian sacrifice and suffering over the other nationalities in the new country. Serbian women, and by extension Serbian men, could claim the status of first among equals, not as individuals, but as mothers and bereaved daughters and sisters who had sacrificed their men (Serbian) for the creation of Yugoslavia.

Kosovo Maidens and Mothers

Zagorka's references to the wartime suffering of the Serbian women and their sacrifices for territorial gain allude to earlier sacrifices and sufferings of the Mother of the Nine Jugovići. Her sons, according to Serbian legend, perished at the hands of the Ottoman Turks at the Battle of Kosovo in 1389. Zagorka sensed among the Serbian women a patriotic allegiance and commitment to a national cause, which developed from the blending of recent experiences and events with collective memories of the Battle of Kosovo.

The songs of Kosovo tell of the glory of the medieval Serbian Kingdom, the necessity of struggle against tyranny, and self-sacrifice for the Orthodox faith and for Serbia. The key actor in the story is Prince Lazar, who was approached by a messenger from God on the eve of the battle and given a choice. God would intercede on the side of the Serbian nobles in order to preserve the Serbian state, thus securing for the Serbs an earthly kingdom; or the Serbs could face the Turks without God's intercession, perish, and ascend into God's heavenly kingdom. In the song, "The Downfall of the Serbian Empire," Lazar considered the choice:

> "Kind God, what shall I do, how shall I do it?
> What is the empire of choice?
> Is it the empire of heaven?
> Is it the empire of the earth?
> And if I shall choose the empire of the earth,
> the empire of the earth is brief,
> heaven is everlasting."
> And the emperor [Prince Lazar] chose the empire of heaven
> above the empire of the earth.[3]

Prince Lazar willingly sacrificed his earthly kingdom for a heavenly kingdom, a choice that "symbolized the enduring values of justice and righteousness."[4] According to legend, Lazar's choice resulted in the suffering of the Serbian people during its long years of subjugation to the Turks. The martyrdom of Lazar and his people, who gave their lives freely for the faith and for the land, would eventually be avenged. In the legend, the Serbs knew that God would protect his people, reward them for their faith, and return them one day from their captivity.

The tradition of Kosovo, in the form of the cult of the 1389 battle, had inspired the Serbian people, its leaders and intellectuals for centuries. By the early nineteenth century, the Kosovo idea had become deeply embedded in the emerging national history and narratives of the Serbian people as they began their hundred-year struggle for national liberation and emancipation from the Turks. From the early modern period to the present, the Serbs' defeat at Kosovo Polje and its mythologization and memorialization in epic song provided the Serbs a framework to understand their past, present, and future.[5] As the literary historian Svetozar Koljević noted, the oral epic songs about the Battle of Kosovo have provided the Serbs with both a way of "coming to terms with history and a means of getting out of it."[6] In addition, the Kosovo myths prescribed behaviors and values for the Serbian people, both men and women.

An early twentieth-century Serbian woman writer, Olga Kernić-Peleš, described accepted attitudes toward men's and women's roles in Serbian society for the first issue of the magazine, *Srpkinja* (Serbian Woman). Serbian men were "peace-loving, but decisive, ambitious, and self-willed, the Serb cared above all for his honor, loving justice and truth. He was unused and unwilling to be enslaved . . . Honest, sincere, reliable, faithful to his friends, for whom he would spill his own blood. Ever vengeful to his enemy, he was also magnanimous and patient. For honor and liberty, his own life was never too high a price to pay."[7] The heroes of the Kosovo myth, Prince Lazar, Miloš Oblić, and Prince Marko embody these traits.

During the nineteenth-century liberation struggles against the Turks, Serbian men were expected to be courageous, self-sacrificing, and loyal to the Serbian national cause. Kernić-Peleš framed women's roles against the same backdrop, writing: "In earlier times, Serbian women were peaceful, they wrote of their love of their homeland. . . . By the hearth, beside the cradle, a woman was the happy spirit of her home." And when the bloody times of battle and slaughter came, the woman stepped out of her family circle. She accompanied the armies to battle, tended their wounds, fed the wounded heroes with white bread, and gave them white wine to drink. The people immortalized her in the song about the Maiden of Kosovo:

> Mothers would see their sons off to battle with song, encouraging them, emboldening them, bequeathing us the eternal symbol of the Mother of the Jugovići, and beside her then as today there were countless other.
> And how wisely and thoughtfully did Serbian women wear the royal crown and help the armies under their rule—we have examples in Queen Milica, the Lady Rosanda, and Princess Jerina.
> And how ready were Serbian women to sacrifice themselves for the sake of the homeland may be seen in the example of lovely Mara, the daughter of Prince Lazar, who married Bajazit, the son of her people's enemy . . . [8]

The text, written at the time of the First Balkan War (1912),[9] interpreted and fixed for Serbs specific characteristics, traits, and roles which Serbian women should possess during times of war—sacrifice, selflessness, compassion, and comfort; the roles of helpmate, selfless and courageous mother, and martyr. The mythical figures of the Kosovo Maiden and the Mother of the Jugovići, the medieval persons of Queen Milica, the Lady Rosanda, and Princess Jerina, and the songs of Kosovo, as they became part of the Serbs' collective memory and commemoration of their struggles to be free of Ottoman rule, defined the place of women in this history. These images, memories, and tropes helped shape the ways in which women interpreted their role in the first of Serbia's twentieth-century wars, the "Wars of National Liberation, 1912–1918."[10]

Memorializing the Present in the Past

Before the twentieth century, Serbian men and women participated together in the creation, preservation, and transmission of the collective memories that recalled the events, heroes, martyrs, and notables of the Battle of Kosovo. Throughout the Balkan Peninsula, including Serbia, women were the principal transmitters of the song tradition. Since women's work often occupied their hands with weaving, knitting, carrying water and firewood, and cooking tasks, song in its vocally presented medium rather than instrumental music has been their main musical outlet.[11] Women's songs spoke of their love of homeland, family, home, children, and loss. Men dominated the singing when the subject turned to narrating war and heroism, and these songs spoke of men's heroism, sacrifice, loyalty, and courage. However, in their songs, men did not express the grief and sorrow of death that is often featured in women's singing. Expression of grief, loss, and sorrow was left to women in their laments.[12] As noted by the interwar Serbian ethnographer Novica Šaulić, who during and after the war recorded the death laments of Serbian women, women sang directly from their hearts and souls. Šaulić wrote, "women's emotions are deeply felt, created from sorrow, and born of tears." He observed that Serbian women were carrying on the tradition bequeathed to them from earlier generations and learned through the recitation of two poems from the Kosovo epic cycle: "The Kosovo Maiden" and "The Mother of the Jugovići."[13]

In the early nineteenth century, the abbot of the Serbian Orthodox monastery in Šišatovac at Srem, Lukijan Mušicki, recorded the poem, "Kosovo Maiden" from a blind woman living in the neighboring village of Grgurevci. In 1817 he forwarded the poem to Vuk Karadžić, the Serbian philologist who created the first grammar and dictionary for the Serbian language. The poem opens with the description of a bright Sunday morning following the battle. A young women looks for her betrothed among the wounded and the dead, carrying in her hands white bread and two gold jugs—one filled with cold water, the other with red wine. She turns the heroes over in their blood, looking for her fiancé and his two blood brothers. The story ends when one of the wounded heroes tells the girl that both her fiancé and his blood brothers are dead:

> And fortune fell on the hero, on Pavle Orlović, the young man who carried the Prince's battle-standard: and she discovered him alive, and his right hand had been cut off, and his left leg cut off at the knee, and his supple ribs were fragments, his liver showing pale; she took him from the floods of his blood, she washed him in the coldness of water, and she gave the sacrament of red wine, and she gives him the white bread to eat. And the hero's heart began to dance, and Pavle Orlović is speaking: "Kosovo girl, my darling sister, what troubles you so terribly, that you turn over heroes in their blood? Young girl walking the battlefield, who are looking for? Is it your brother? Is it your cousin? Or is it your father?"

The Kosovo Maiden's outpouring of grief upon learning that her fiancé is dead is personal but also conveys the full national pathos of the Kosovo battle. The poem ends:

> Kosovo maiden, my darling sister, look, my dear, at the battle lances, where they are so tall and so dense: that is where the blood of the heroes bled, stirrup-iron deep to a high horse, stirrup-iron deep and girth deep, and deep as the silk belts on fighting men. And that is where those three died. Go home now to your whitewashed house, with an unbloody hem, unbloody sleeve. And when the young girl heard his words she dropped tears down on her white face, she went away to her whitewashed house, and her white throat lamented: "Unhappy! Evil luck has come on me, Unhappy, if I were to grasp a green pine, even the green pine would wither!"[14]

The scene described above and the moving verses of the song were used not only by Kernić-Peleš during the First Balkan War as a model for Serbian women in the past and present, but also by a number of Serbian artists in the nineteenth and twentieth centuries, who chose to memorialize women's nurturing role and selflessness on canvas. The most familiar and popular work depicting the Kosovo Maiden is Uroš Predić's romantic-realistic work, painted in 1919. For art historians the painting is not particularly interesting, because it is both stylistically and thematically anachronistic.[15] For historians, however, the popularity of the work after 1919, when reproductions of this painting were found in many Serbian middle-class homes, is significant. The painting incorporated two motifs: war as noble and uplifting on the one hand, and tragic and unendurably sad on the other. The image of the handsome young man lying in the beautiful maiden's arms against the backdrop of the battlefield at Kosovo might have spoken to a family's grief and connected personal loss to the nobility of the sacrifice as represented by the Battle of Kosovo. In addition, the painting reminded Serbian households of their duty—men to fight and women to mourn and remember.

A mother's grief was presented in a series of powerful images in the song "The Death of the Mother of the Jugovići." Unable to wait for the news about the battle, the Mother of the Jugovići asked God to reveal to her the outcome. God granted her swan's wings, which enabled her to fly to Kosovo, and a falcon's eyes, which allowed her to see the battlefield. Upon seeing her husband and her nine sons dead, she did not cry out, but remained stalwart. The Mother of the Jugovići returned home with their horses, dogs, and falcons and was greeted by the other soldiers' grieving widows and orphans. Holding back her tears, she detailed the battle. However, when two ravens dropped the severed arm of her youngest son, she no longer repressed her grief. Holding the severed hand and whispering to it, she began a lament:

> My hand, O green apple,
> Where did you grow, where were you ripped off?
> You grew upon this mother's lap
> You were torn away on the Kosovo plain.[16]

At the end of the song, the mother's heart broke with pain and death came as a relief.

Conducting research on women's laments in the aftermath of the world war, Novica Šaulić drew a direct line between the Kosovo Maiden and the Mother of the Jugovići to Serbian women mourning the dead from Serbia's wars of liberation. In his research, he concluded,

> Serbian women, mothers, and sisters guard [the soldiers] from forgetting and remember warriors in their heartfelt songs, elevating them to immortal glory and everlasting life. Through the misty acknowledgment of life after death, heroes are brought back to life by grace, love, and imagination. . . . These women, as mothers and sisters and as lamenters, contribute moral strength and create a powerful bond of a people to the land.[17]

Writing in 1917 for a British audience, the Serbian princess Alexis Karageorgevitch described a scene of several Serbian women in full lament who were mourning their war dead. She noted, "The weird monotonous strains of their sad music, as it was wafted across the stream to me, hardly seemed to lend themselves to dancing, nor to suggest any form of gaiety; rather, they are the appropriate accompaniment to the national epic poems which immortalize the sufferings of this free spirited people when under the domination of the Turks."[18] Karageorgevitch not only described the recitation of parts of the epic cycle during women's work, she also observed an act of mourning for the victims of the typhus outbreak of 1915.

In early 1915, a devastating flu epidemic swept through both the Serbian military and civilian populations, weakening Serbia's position vis-à-vis its enemies to the north and east—Austro-Hungary and Bulgaria. It is estimated that this epidemic immediately claimed 100,000 civilian lives, killing 35,000 soldiers and infecting another 400,000.[19] Karageorgevitch witnessed a series of funeral processions during the epidemic. She observed:

> The pretty little cemetery with its daily increasing number of graves, some marked only by a plain wooden cross, some by crosses of stone, and others again by tattered banners, had become almost the center of the village life. One heard constantly the wail of "kuku mene" (Woe is me), a characteristic expression of grief. There is a pretty legend which connects the kuku with the death of Lazar. After the battle of Kosovo in 1389, when Lazar was captured and beheaded by the Turks, the souls of his daughters were permitted by the pitying gods to enter the bodies of cuckoos, whose melancholy notes has ever since embodied the soul of grief.[20]

For Karageorgevitch, this scene evoked not only the unbearable personal tragedies of the mourning women; their cry also harkened to the national past of the Serbian people.

Women's responsibility for remembering and commemorating the dead was well described by Karageorgevitch:

> In Serbia, Saturday is the day of the week usually set apart for visiting the cemeteries. From dawn to dark the roads are filled with women and girls carrying food and wine, which they set out, interspersed with lighted candles, on the family graves. Sitting about in groups, these women and girls work themselves up into hysterical wailing, which continues all day and fills the air for great distances, with the traditional lamentation.[21]

Lamentation by women has often been interpreted as an expression of personal loss in terms of emotional, economic, and social deprivation. The reader senses the individual pathos of the women in Karageorgevitch's description of the act of mourning. However, her commentary, as a representative of the state, appropriates these women's grief for the state and conjures up the image of past sacrifices of Serbian women in time of war and liberation. In her study on lamentation in Greece, Gail Holst argued that there is often a tension between public and private burial and commemoration of soldiers. The tension can only be resolved when the state convinces the families, particularly the mothers of soldiers, that the glory of dying for the fatherland outweighs private grief, and compensates them for their loss. Is the fixing of woman as Kosovo Maiden and the Mother of the Jugovići an attempt to co-opt women's individual sorrows and substitute national sacrifice? Karageorgevitch, a representative of the state, described the private burial of war victims and the expressions of individual grief and loss by women and related their grief to that of the daughters of Prince Lazar. In the introduction to his collection of laments, Šaulić did not deny the importance of laments to individual mourning, but he ascribed a larger meaning to women's grief. He argued that women's laments were "national songs and national laments" despite the fact that they "often went unnoticed."[22] Šaulić believed women and their laments to be a significant factor in transmitting the collective memories of Serbia's wars past and present.

Motherhood, Womanhood, and the Nation

Serbian women contributed to the collective mourning for the war dead and commemoration of Serbia's heroes and martyrs not only through their laments; as in other national movements, Serbian women were also designated as the bearers of national memories and stories because of their role as mothers. An oft-told story about the Serbian conquest of Kosovo during the First Balkan War reveals the place women were given as preservers of national and collective memories. In the 1932 Vidovdan (the feast day of St. Vitus, celebrated on 28 June)[23] issue of the official journal of the Ministry of the Army and Navy, *Vojnički Glasnik*, an officer recalled his emotions as his unit headed for Kosovo and battle with the Turks in 1912:

> The single sound of that word—Kosovo—caused an indescribable excitement. This one word pointed to the black past—five centuries. In it exists the whole our sad past—the tragedy of Prince Lazar and the entire Serbian nation. Each of us created for himself a picture of Kosovo while we were still in the cradle. Our mothers lulled us to sleep with the songs of Kosovo, and in our schools our teachers never ceased in their stories of Lazar and Miloš . . . When we arrived on Kosovo and the battalions were placed in order, our commander spoke: "Brothers, my children, my sons!" His voice breaks. "This place on which we stand is the graveyard of our glory. We bow to the shadows of fallen ancestors and pray God for the salvation of their souls." His voice gives out, and tears flow in streams down his cheeks and grey beard and fall on the ground. He actually shakes from some kind of inner pain and excitement. The spirits of Lazar, Miloš, and all the Kosovo martyrs gaze on us. We feel strong and proud, for we are the generation which will realize the centuries-old dream of the whole nation: that we with the sword will regain the freedom that was lost with the sword.[24]

According to this recollection, this officer believed that he and his comrades-in-arms learned their duty at their mothers' breasts. Their mothers' songs inspired them to act and fight during the Balkan wars, and these soldiers fully expected that their actions and lives would be remembered in the same fashion.

Women's centrality in the creation, promotion, and preservation of the idea that the Wars of National Liberation were a continuation of the centuries-old struggle against the Turks was well expressed by Natalija Bjelajac (nee Antonija Javornik), who was attached to a military hospital during the First Balkan War. In an interview during the 1970s she recalled the scene of her medical unit arriving at Kosovo Polje after the Serbian Third Army took Priština on 22 October 1912:

> The soldiers lay on the ground and kissed it. Then all of them hugged each other, kissed, and talked about how they had waited for over five hundred years for this moment, how Kosovo had been avenged . . . I understood that from June 1389 to October 1912 generation to generation lived to realize this dream—during times of happiness and grief Kosovo was talked about, and now the soldiers had arrived at this hour to drive the Turks out and free Kosovo . . . They had fulfilled the oath of many generations.[25]

While Bjelajac's recollections were those of one woman, her presence at the scene demonstrates Serbian women's close proximity to and participation in the wars and how the Kosovo legend structured individual and collective memories. Both men and women drew the connection between 1389 and 1912–1918, but Serbian women played an important part in the construction of Serbia's collective memory of the Balkan Wars and World War I by blending the memories of the wars of national liberation with those of the battle of Kosovo.

Serbian women's organizations before, during, and after the wars of national liberation consciously tied their efforts to humanitarian, cultural, and above all national tasks dealing directly with the effects of war. Initially some of these groups saw their mission as providing humanitarian aid to wounded soldiers, the families of fallen soldiers, war orphans, and refugees. Such work was associated with Serbia's national survival, and after the war these organizations took it upon themselves to commemorate the war dead and comfort those left in the war's wake. Some of the organizations considered mourning and commemorating Serbia's fallen soldiers as one of their main tasks. The Žensko Društvo Južne Srbije (Women's Society of Southern Serbia) stated, "The heavy wounds remaining on the souls of our people after 500 years of the Ottoman yoke and the traces on our spirits and our language from various foreign influences before liberation require long and serious healing. Our association . . . heals the old wounds and errors and prepares women for their future as wives and mothers, giving them a Serbian education and a useful craft."[26]

In the interwar period, a number of Serbian women's organizations regularly held requiem masses for and built monuments to various Serbian military heroes from the "Wars of National Liberation, 1912–1918." One such organization was the Dobrotvorna Zadruga Srpkinja in Sarajevo. At a memorial requiem for Vojvoda Stepi Stepanović, the president of this society described the great services and sacrifices of Little Serbia, the Piedmont of Serbdom and Yugoslavism, for the liberation of Bosnia-Hercegovina and the Serbian motherland.

> She [Serbia] sacrificed hundreds of thousands of her best sons, gave up her name, flag, existence, and eventually the blood of her king. But still they aren't satisfied

and want more, they want to kill her spirit, rip out her heart, wipe out every trace of her, but this will never be! Mother Serbia will give more sacrifices, take more blows for the good of the King and our fatherland Yugoslavia, but she will endure.[27]

Other organizations, like the Kola Srpskih Sestara (Circle of Serbian Sisters, hereafter KSS), were founded to provide educational opportunities for girls and to instruct the girls in proper attitudes and behaviors toward the nation. The KSS school for girls in Belgrade stated that its mission was to "develop a sense of sisterly love and learn to sacrifice for their families and their nation."[28] This call for sacrifice came on the heels of Serbia's wars and its liberation; Serbian girls were to prepare themselves for any task or sacrifice for the love the nation. One such task was the organization and execution of fund-raising drives for the design and building of both modest and elaborate memorial sites to the soldiers and victims of war. Local committees of the KSS, like the one in Jagodina, not only sought funds to erect a modest monument in front of the church where many soldier's bones were interned; they also organized the dedication ceremony, which entailed a visit from a representative of the royal family, a mass, a speech by the president of the Jagodina chapter of the KSS, poetry readings by local schoolchildren, lunch, and a lecture about the role of women in Serbian society. The conflation of past and present events in this ceremony sent a clear message to its participants: men were to fight and women were to mourn.

Conclusion

After 1918 all of Serbia appeared to be in a somber and commemorative mood, needing, like other Europeans, to understand the meaning and significance of their enormous losses. Individually and collectively, through narration, performance, or collection, Serbs remembered their suffering, sacrifice, and heroism. Absent from the vast majority of their ceremonies, their commemorative activities, and memories were the wartime experiences or sacrifices of the other peoples of the Kingdom or those who had suffered at Serbian hands. In the multinational Kingdom, the commemoration of the sacrifices and sufferings of the Serbian people elevated the Serbs to a claim of first among equals, a position that they collectively remembered, commemorated and believed to be rightfully theirs. Blending the personal, the political, and the cultural, commemoration of the wars of national liberation in Serbia forged a consensus version of the war among Serbs. Serbs articulated memories that connected to experiences they deemed as significant and important: courage, self-sacrifice, and suffering. As holders of these memories, they accorded themselves special status and a claim on the resources, institutions, and conscience of their new state.[29]

What is becoming increasingly evident is how the individual memories of Serbs were not obscured by the political symbolism that was inscribed on top of mourning. Individual and collective Serbian memory of the wars of national liberation were marked by certain recurring themes and symbols derived from folklore, the history and myth of the Battle of Kosovo, Orthodox Christian belief, and national iconography. Thus the work of commemoration in interwar Serbia was not only personal, bereavement and mourning, or political, remembering or forgetting in pursuit of national interest, but also cultural. It inscribed a set of symbolic codes, ordering discourses, and master narratives that recent events, like the wars of national liberation, had disrupted, challenged, or newly established.[30]

In the interwar period in Serbia, the urgency of injunctions to remember the experiences of the Balkan Wars and World War I produced a culture of commemoration which not only excluded the other national groups, but in fact, faced opposition in other types of commemorative activities seen in Croatia, such as memories of Croatian suffering, heroism, and sacrifice which were not associated with the Great War. Examples of this are found in the Zagreb city elite's embrace of monuments, memorials, and commemorative activities around "the Croatian Greats" and the suffering of the Croatian people since medieval times. This is not to say that some Zagrepčani did not commemorate World War I and Croatian participation and suffering. The commemorative activities of veteran groups in Zagreb who were volunteers with the Serbian and Allied forces on the Salonika Front were noted and documented. However, their commemorative activities and efforts were small compared to those in Serbia or to other types of commemorations taking place within the Croatian capital. Attempts to broaden commemoration outside volunteer circles were met with obstructionism as was the case of a group of city leaders who tried to name a street after King Petar Karadjordjević (postponed after the death of Radić in 1928) and the construction of a war monument in Croatia's main cemetery, Mirogoj, which was not erected until 1939.

Commemorations in both Serbia and Croatia after the war privileged certain kinds of experience and excluded others. Not only did commemorative activities tend toward privileging one national group over another, but commemoration of the wars of national liberation privileged male experience over female experience. Despite the visibility of women during the Balkan Wars and World War I, as combatants, non-combatants, refugees, and victims, women's experiences became either secondary considerations or largely ignored in the commemorative practices and traditions which emerged in Yugoslavia during the interwar period. In the case of Serbia in the aftermath of the wars, military cemeteries, monuments, and commemorative ceremonies began to be built that honored the fallen Serbian soldier. Such memory sites represented war as a military conflict between soldiers, and the soldiers as the ideal national citizens, sacrificing their lives so that the state and the nation might live. The vast majority of the fallen soldiers were husbands, fathers, and brothers and the act of remembering and commemorating their lives and deaths was left to their wives, mothers, and sisters. Official commemoration assigned to Serbian women the responsibility for the practical aspects of mourning and they publicly mourned masculine sacrifice.

The meaning that interwar commemoration sought to impose on the war, as a basis for the kingdom's post-war nation and state building politics, involved the unity of the nation in recognizing masculine [and Serbian] sacrifice as its highest value. Women's participation in the recitation of the epic cycle, their primacy in death ritual and lamentation, their active participation in commemorating the military war dead, and their cultural representation as descendants of the Kosovo Maiden and Mother of the Jugovići contributed to this process. Through private grief and public mourning, Serbian women wove the myth of Kosovo into the political rhetoric and culture of the Serbs during the interwar period. The intent of such conflation was to privilege the longtime suffering and sacrifices of the Serbian people, both men and women, above the sacrifices and suffering of their fellow citizens in the new enterprise of Yugoslavia. Serbian women played a central role in creating and maintaining Serbian collective memories of the Balkan Wars and World War I. They asserted themselves or were inserted by others into the Serbian national mission not as warriors or as victims of the war. Instead they participated in the mission of nationalism through their assigned commemoration of the dead.

Notes

All translations are the author's unless otherwise noted.

1. Neda Božinović, *Žensko pitanje u Srbijii u XIX I XX veku* (Belgrade: Dvadesetčetvrta, 1996), 104–105; Thomas Emmert *Serbian Golgotha Kosovo, 1389* (Boulder, Col.: East European Monographs, 1997), 35–36; Jovanak Kecman, *Žene Jugoslavije u radničkom pokretu i ženskim organizacijama 1918–1941* (Belgrade: Narodna knjiga), 163–67. By 1921, the Union included 205 organizations representing 50,000 women from all over the country.
2. Zagorka, "Snimke iz Beograda," *Jutarnji List* (8 October 1910), 3.
3. Anne Pennington and Peter Levi, *Marko the Prince: Serbo-Croat Heroic Songs* (London: Duckworth, 1984), 17.
4. Celia Hawkesworth, *Voices in the Shadows: Women and Verbal Art in Serbia and Bosnia* (New York: Central European University Press, 2000), 21.
5. Emmert's *Serbian Golgotha Kosovo* is an excellent survey of how Kosovo and its legacy and unique ethos played an important role in the preservation of Serbian identity. He discusses how many of the themes of the Kosovo legend found their way into the dramas, poems, and paintings of nineteenth-century Serbian intellectuals and artists. He also discusses the public ceremonies planned for the 500-year anniversary of Kosovo Polje in 1889. See the chapter "A Legend's Legacy," 121–42. Also Wayne Vucinich and Thomas Emmert, eds., *Kosovo: The Legacy of a Medieval Battle* (Minneapolis: Minnesota Mediterranean and East European Monographs, 1990).
6. Svetozar Koljević, *The Epic in the Making* (Oxford: Clarendon Press, 1980), 320. Quoted in Celia Hawkesworth, *Voices in the Shadows,* 20.
7. Ibid., 28. According to the poems, Miloš was the greatest of Lazar's warriors, a rival of Vuk Branković, and the man who slew the Ottoman Sultan Murad. One of the poems makes Miloš a participant in the battle at Kosovo, while another legend says that

he infiltrated the Turkish camp and murdered Murad in his tent. Prince Marko (1371–1395) was a Turkish vassal from Prilep who was purported to have protected the population from Turkish violence and was praised as a great hero in the Kosovo epic songs.

8. Ibid., 29.

9. In October 1912, the first of the twentieth-century wars in the Balkans broke out. In the first Balkan War, the four Balkan states, Montenegro, Serbia, Bulgaria, and Greece, fought and defeated the Ottoman Turkish army and drove the Turks from the Balkan Peninsula. Shortly after the cessation of hostilities, a second war broke out between Bulgaria and its former allies over Macedonian territory recently vacated by the Turks. Having suffered substantial losses against the Turkish army as it advanced toward Istanbul in the first Balkan war, Bulgaria could not defend itself against the onslaught of its former allies.

10. The new state embraced this phrase immediately after 1918 to convey a variety of meanings. Depending on the context, liberation could signify liberation of the Serbs from the Ottoman Turks, the removal of Austria-Hungary from Balkan affairs, the driving out of the Germans and Bulgarians from ethnically Serb areas, the liberation of all of the South Slavs from their overlords, or any combination of the above. As World War I ended, Serbs, both men and women, began to ascribe meaning to their wartime experiences by remembering and commemorating their suffering, sacrifices, and losses in relation to the memory of the Battle of Kosovo.

11. Timothy Rice, "A Macedonian *Sobor:* Anatomy of a Celebration," *Journal of American Folklore* 93 (April–June 1980): 121.

12. Patricia K. Shehan, "Balkan Women as the Preservers of Traditional Music and Culture," in Ellen Koskoff, ed., *Women and Music in Cross Cultural Perspective* (Urbana: University of Illinois Press, 1989), 45–53.

13. Novica Šaulić, *Srpske narodne tužbalice* (Beograd: Grafički institut "Narodne misao," 1929), 19.

14. Pennington and Levi, *Marko the Prince*, 24.

15. Ljubica D. Popovich, "The Battle of Kosovo and Battle Themes in Serbian Art," in *Kosovo: Legacy of a Medieval Battle*, 252.

16. Pennington and Levi, *Marko the Prince*, 26.

17. Šaulić, 21.

18. Princess Alexis Karageorgevitch, *For the Better Hour* (London: Constable and Company Limited, 1917), 9.

19. Dragan Živojinović, "Serbia and Montenegro: The Home Front, 1914–1918," in Bela Kiraly and Nandor Dreisziger, eds., *East Central European Society in World War I* (New York: Social Science Monographs, 1985), 243.

20. Karageorgevitch, 42–43.

21. Ibid., 53.

22. Šaulić, 17.

23. Vidovdan is the feast day of Saint Vitus celebrated on 28 June. It has become a sacred day in Serbian history. It is purported that on this day in 1389 the Ottoman Turks defeated a united Serbian army on the Field of the Blackbirds in Kosovo (Kosovo Polje). In addition, the assassination of Archduke Francis Ferdinand took place on 28 June 1914 and the centrist constitution of Yugoslavia was adopted on 28 June 1921.

24. Emmert, *Serbian Golgotha: Kosovo, 1389*, 121.

25. Natalija Bjelajac and Antonije Durić, *Šene—Solunci govore* (Belgrade: Književne novine, 1987), 24.

26. Letter to the king from Žensko društvo Južne Srbije, 15 March 1926, Arhiv Jugoslavije (AJ), 74–106. Quoted in Carol Lilly, "Serbia," in Kevin Passmore, ed., *Women, Gender and the Extreme Right in Europe, 1918–1945* (London: Macmillian Press, 2003), 127.

27. Letter from Čedomir K. Jovanović, Kragujevac, 2 June 1939, AJ, 74-253-379. Quoted in Lilly, "Serbia," in Passmore, ed., *Women,* 128.

28. Letter from Council of KSS of Banja Luka to Queen Marija, 15 January 1927, AJ, 74: 418–618; "Izveštaj Glavnog odbora KSS," in *Izveštaji Kola Srpskih Sestara za 1927 godinu,* Beograd, 1928, AJ, II 7875. Quoted in Lilly, "Serbia," in Passmore, ed., *Women,* 129.

29. There are many ways that I could conclude, but because I am in the midst of my research on this subject, I would simply like to share some of the various directions that this project will be taking. A large part of this story is about the ways individuals and groups use commemoration to identify as a people who share a past and future defined in national terms. Readings that inform my conclusions are: Rudy Koshar, *From Monuments to Traces* (Berkeley: University of California Press, 2000) and Susan R. Grayzel, *Women's Identities at War: Gender, Motherhood, and Politics in Britain and France during the First World War* (Chapel Hill: University of North Carolina Press, 2001).

30. Daniel Sherman, "Monuments, Mourning and Masculinity in France After World War I," *Gender and History* 8, no. 1 (April 1996): 82.

9 Women's Stories as Sites of Memory: Gender and Remembering Romania's World Wars

Maria Bucur

The two major European wars of the past century (1914–1918 and 1939–1945) were intensely personal events. The direct experience of these ravaging conflicts encompassed entire populations, civilians and soldiers, and the full territory of the countries engaged in the war, through combat and/or occupation. This is certainly the case in Romania. Yet the official memory of the two world wars incorporates the personal recollections of these experiences in ways that almost always privilege political and diplomatic institutional events over individual quotidian perceptions. How have the individual and collective forms of remembering these wars related to each other over time? What has been preserved and what has been forgotten, especially in the official avenues of collective memory, and with what consequences? This essay focuses on one particular aspect of this broad question: How are narratives about wartime experiences specifically encoded to include expectations about heroism, sacrifice, patriotism, and gender roles? And how have women's narratives of such experiences been incorporated differently from men's narratives into the collective memory of war?

My analysis foregrounds experience as historically bounded. Thus, self-representations of wartime experiences enable me to reflect on how ideological discourses about the nation and wartime sacrifice were gendered and also to examine how, in constructing their experience of the war, individuals made gender a component of their selves. The texts I employ in this study open themselves to multiple readings of self-representation of experience as both reflective of gender expectations and also constitutive of the author's gendered identity.[1]

This analysis incorporates autobiographical writings of three types: (a) memoirs written after the wars, focusing on wartime experience; (b) diaries written during the war and published afterwards; and (c) postwar oral testimonies of people who lived during World War II. The choice of memoirs is obvious, as they represent an exercise in self-representation and are a clear form of recollection, situating the personal experience presumably in the center of the narrative. Even this assumption is not always borne out by some memoirs, as in instances when the focus of the narrative is on description of the outside world and events, rather than the author's personal involvement in them, or his/her reflections about these occurrences. Yet the premise of these memoirs is clearly to bear witness, to situate the "I" in the center of the events and to privilege that vantage point as a knowledgeable one, by virtue of having experienced those events. For both writers and their audience, memoirs reflect the assumption that personal experience renders the memory of the event more authentic than a narrative about the same event told by a distanced observer, someone who was not there. More intriguing for the historian is *how* that representation of personal experience constructs the gendered self in historically contingent ways.

Though diaries are less clearly such a form of self-representation for the purpose of remembering, I have included them for several reasons. Journals, even those written for personal use and without the expectation of later publication, represent an effort to set down for immortality a personal experience, a reaction, or a reflection connected not only to the outer world (and thus historical reality), but also to the transformation of the self over time. A journal is thus an attempt to construct the possibility of remembering, recollecting one's experiences in the future, and to render them retrospectively meaningful as "authentic" experience. The observations made are always at the same time oriented towards the present (writing down what one feels or thinks), towards the future (how one thinks s/he will react to these observations when rereading them in the future), and towards the past (how do these notes compare to what one wrote yesterday or at some other point in the past). Thus, although diaries do not reconstruct events of the past, the experiences noted therein are also a form of autobiographical writing that helps construct the individual memory of the period. Another reason to include diaries is the clear intent of some of the authors to publish these writings as a form of correcting the misunderstandings about events that took place during the war. They offer their own notes from that period as an alternative log, truthful either to other recollections or to polemics about what had "really" taken place. Most texts analyzed here fall into this category.

Finally, I have included oral personal narratives about the war. They are part of a study that focused on a specific event during the war: a massacre of civilian population in 1940.[2] An important difference between oral testimonies and the two kinds of autobiographical texts mentioned above is the very orality of these narratives, which makes them no less subjective, but renders them "self-censored" in a different way from written accounts, in the sense that the process of communicating them does not include the additional step of writing them down and thus constructing the memory into a finite text. At the same time, oral testimonies, especially those recorded long after the events, are part of a continuum of self-representation and *re*membering, and thus as much a product of this process as a product of the immediate recollection of events related to the war. Written memoirs are also part of this process, but less obviously so.[3]

These three forms of autobiographical narrative help highlight particular ways of remembering, connections between the personal and the larger historical context, relations between gender identity, specific experiences, and their representation. The following discussion will enable me to begin analyzing the gendering of both personal memory of the war and also of the relation between individual memory and collective or official forms of recollection or commemoration.

World War I

Though Romania entered the war only in August 1916, it suffered great casualties both because of the extent of the front on which it was engaged and also because of the disintegration of the Russian army. In addition, Romania was not prepared militarily or economically for a long-term total war. Half of the country was occupied within three months, the casualties of the army were tremendous (over 300,000 dead, more than 50 percent of the total fighting force), and much of the population had to retreat to Moldavia between November 1916 and April 1918. The crowding of the refugees and armies in Moldavia led to a typhoid epidemic that killed over 100,000 people. Since the violence of the war was very broad in terms of combat zone and also very close to all civilians because of the size of the country and its inverse "L" shape, World War I directly touched every inhabitant of Romania. Residents of the occupied territories had to deal with the new wartime administration or went into exile in Moldavia, while people from Moldavia were overwhelmed by the civilian and military crowds that overran them. Poverty, illness, and fear of further human and territorial losses dominated the experience of most Romanians, men and women, soldiers and civilians.[4]

How have Romanians remembered World War I? Though autobiographical writing had become a common literary genre by 1914, the number of memoirs, recollections, and diaries published in the two decades after 1918 surpassed any previous such phenomenon. The most important aspect of this new trend was that individuals without literary pretensions were now publishing their autobiographical writings, emphasizing the historical content and veracity of the account, rather than the literary quality of the material. It is not surprising, then, that Romanian literary critics have paid little attention to these writings, considering them unimportant from a literary perspective.[5] One historian has written that "during the interwar period autobiographical writing was pushed into a shadowy corner more than any other literary genre."[6] He acknowledges, however, that "[autobiographical writings] continued to be read. Maybe not as literature, but possibly even more than literature."[7] This author suggests indirectly that there was a growth in autobiographical writing and especially in the market for it, but he is unwilling to concede that such books contributed to the development of Romanian literature.

Yet people read these war memoirs and diaries voraciously. Through their discussion we can begin to analyze the construction of not only the individual but also the collective memory of World War I. People of different political persuasions, ages, classes, and genders published autobiographical writings about the war. Reading their stories opens up windows into a variety of experiential angles. It does not, however, provide a global picture of wartime experience, because all of the authors tend to be relatively well, if not highly, educated and to come from urban areas.[8] Therefore, what follows is an evocative rather than comprehensive analysis of the personal experience of the war.

Many women published autobiographical writings after World War I, although very few women non-writers had engaged in such endeavors before 1918.[9] The explanation for this change can probably be found in greater access on the part of women to both education and other forms of participation in the public sphere, giving them the self-confidence and skills necessary to think of themselves as publishable authors. Though women did not receive the vote until 1929 (and then only in municipal elections and with significant educational and marital restrictions), by the beginning of the war many women's organizations were active in Romania. Some were political and suffragist in focus, while others were primarily welfare-oriented or philanthropic.

In addition, women's war experiences became more intensely political and public as the conflict continued. Women were forced to become the providers for their families, as well as the mediators between the home and the civil and military authorities (Romanian or occupiers). These external developments prompted women to constitute themselves differently as subjects of the state and as gendered selves. And women chose to insert their personal narratives as relevant to broader discussions about patriotism, heroic actions, treason, and other heated polemic debates that ensued after the war. Some female authors clearly stated such motivations as the reason for publishing their memoirs, while others only intimated them in their narratives. In the preface to her wartime journal *The Woman-Soldier* (1928), Jeanna Col. Fodoreanu, a nurse who worked as a volunteer close to the front throughout the war, asserted:

> If I dare bring to light my modest war Journal after so much time, it is because I kept waiting for others more capable than me, more competent at writing to speak and remember those who fulfilled their duty under the folds of the holy Flag of the Red Cross, raised here by the greatest and dignified Queen of our days. I waited, I searched, but I did not find more than two-three lines here and there.[10]

She continued by dedicating the book to Queen Marie as a leader in the war effort and to the memory of all heroes dead in the war.

This preamble suggests a self-effacing attitude with regard to the author's agency in terms of providing historically significant recollections of the war. Yet the author clearly situated herself as an authoritative arbiter of what constituted proper representation of fulfilling one's duty towards the Red Cross and the nation. The inconsistencies between what Fodoreanu considered an accurate representation of these actions, as shaped by her interpretations of wartime experience, and the texts that were published in the first decade after the war prompted her to constitute her narrative as important for the collective memory of the war.

What is remarkable about Fodoreanu's journal is that she clearly considered the actions of the auxiliary medical personnel in charge of the wounded soldiers memorable (i.e., worthy of inclusion in the collective memory of the war) as well as heroic. While many of those whose actions appear as heroic were men, the volume also included many stories of women who acted with greater dignity and courage than men. In her narrative courage ranged from moving with the ambulance train in the front lines in the midst of enemy artillery fire to standing up to the military officers to preserve the well-being of the wounded and personnel in charge of the ambulances. In the author's view, many of the female volunteers appeared more dedicated and brave facing these challenges than doctors who were commissioned officers. Fodoreanu and other women who published wartime memoirs, such as Sabina Cantacuzino, attempted to bear witness to women's dignified and selfless participation in the war effort and to the effects of the war on their lives, to counterbalance the almost exclusive emphasis in writings that appeared soon after the war on the military and political action of men.

Indeed, most of the autobiographical writings published right after 1918 were those of military and political leaders or other prominent male public figures, including writers or journalists. A search through the collection of the library of the Romanian Academy revealed almost seventy such titles in the first decade after the war. Some of the most familiar of this group were *The Capital under Enemy Occupation, 1916–1918,* by the well-known journalist Constantin Bacalbaşa, and *Impressions and Personal Opinions from Wartime Romania,* by the lawyer and politician Vasile Th. Cancicov. Both contained a wealth of detail and were penned in a rich and captivating prose.[11]

Why did these men want to publish their wartime diaries? In the dedication to his volume, Cancicov professed to have wanted to keep the diary as a private document for his children. Yet he did publish it before his death, with a letter of introduction from Take Ionescu, a prominent politician, as a guarantee of the journal's veracity.[12] This self-presentation suggests that Cancicov wanted to establish his lengthy memoirs as an unequivocally authoritative account for posterity. Bacalbaşa did not provide any explanatory introduction, but his narrative is one that simultaneously placed the author's personal opinions about the meaning of the wartime events at the center of the narrative and also provided countless anecdotes, most based on what Balcabaşa had *heard* from others, but not seen during the war. These stories aimed to "document" his indictment of the cowardly behavior of many civilians (especially women) under occupation and his call for justice in recognizing the self-sacrifice of many who had gone unknown after the war: "I don't know . . . of a single case of public and resounding recognition for those who stayed put to defend honor and patriotism; I know, however, that there were true press campaigns for those who did the opposite."[13]

These and other similar autobiographical writings by well-known and respected public figures established a series of authoritative perspectives on the war. Cancicov and Bacalbaşa, for instance, focused mostly on the political and administrative actions of the occupying authorities and on the fate of the Romanian army, rather than other aspects of everyday life. However, there was little verifiable information about the actions of either the Central Powers or the Romanian government-in-exile.

The authority of Bacalbaşa's account rested as much on his reputation as a journalist as on his experiences. A significant portion of his book comprises anecdotes the author heard during the war. The narrative itself makes this position of indirect witness clear. Yet even such honest acknowledgement did not prevent both contemporary audiences and, later, historians from using Bacalbaşa's book as *documentary* evidence about life in Bucharest under the German occupation.[14]

The daily problems of securing food, fuel, and medicine for those at home were present but not prominent for Cancicov until he was himself imprisoned. Forced into prison and deprived of decent food, heating, and medical help, he began to address these issues more directly. After he was liberated, Cancicov resumed his focus on political and military issues. There is little mention of his family in the book—1,343 pages long! Bacalbaşa also focused primarily on the events he observed or heard about on the street and in government institutions, offering little insight into the daily life of people living under occupation and indicting those who fraternized with the occupiers: "The whole foreign population is on the streets . . . throwing flowers and giving cigarettes. Nine parts out of ten are women."[15]

Many of the male autobiographical writings published in the first decade after the war, such as *Daily Notes from the Front* or *Combat Journal*, were little more than logs from military officers, documenting their troops' activities in combat, often in technical language and seldom with any details outside strict military data.[16] Still, some of these books were published by prestigious publishing houses and went through several editions. The public was interested in these types of documents as pieces of the puzzle which was still largely unknown to most people—civilians or military—right after the war, because of the censorship of news in both the occupied and the free zones.

This wealth of predominantly male autobiographical writings had a direct, profound impact on the first and, to this date, most influential history of the war, first published by Constantin Kiriţescu in 1921. In his preface to the first edition, Kiriţescu acknowledged the paucity of archival material and his use of personal testimonies: "Aside from my personal notes, [I used] all I could find, published or not, here and elsewhere . . . as a faithful image of our war, under its various manifestations."[17] The result was a narrative that emphasized almost exclusively political and military actions, with little reference to daily life under the occupied territories or overcrowded Moldavia. Meant as a popular work, especially with the aim of educating the younger generations, Kiriţescu's history of the war is at once a compilation of personal recollections of the war and at the same time an attempt to transform them into a collective authoritative narrative.[18] The author did not credit publications or documents individually, leaving the reader unable to identify the particular sources of the author's claims.

In spite of that, the book went through numerous editions, praised by historians and nonspecialists alike to this day.[19]

Missing from Kirițescu's narrative were women. Marginal, if at all present in most of the male autobiographical writings published in the war's aftermath, women did not appear to have played a very important public role during the war. While Kirițescu was careful not to vilify them in the same way Bacalbașa had,[20] Kirițescu also glossed over the important contributions women made especially in the medical field, taking care of Romanian POWs in the occupied zone and even helping some escape, and providing most of the staffing, often as unpaid volunteers, in hospitals in the free zone.

Because individual memoirs and collective commemorations of the war ignored women's experience of and contribution to the war effort, more women began to publish their memoirs or wartime journals. In addition to Fodoreanu, many other women published similar texts about their wartime experiences.[21] In 1935 Queen Marie published such a memoir, *Ordeal. The Story of My Life.*[22] These women provided a very different picture of the war than their male counterparts. Though they did not represent a cross-section of all Romanian women, presenting rather a few highly educated individual voices mainly from the upper echelons of society,[23] these authors brought into focus the hardships of daily life during war and the sometimes incredible exertions of the civilian population to survive and even help the war effort.

The diaries are particularly interesting, as they represent immediate reactions to the onslaught of violence from the perspective of people who were caught very much unprepared by the beginning of the war. They are also written from a perspective that places the author's personal experiences and thoughts in the center of the narrative. This group of autobiographies seems to contradict the claim that women tend to have relational narratives more than men.[24] The female authors dwelled upon their emotions and the effects of the war on their individual selves. At one point, Nelli Cornea contemplated her own feelings towards the enemy: "A terrible hatred seems to grow in me against them [the Germanophiles] . . . But it doesn't turn into thirst for revenge." Further on, she wrote about her growing depression brought on by the strange feelings of hatred towards the enemy.[25]

Women writing about the war also focused on relationships, especially their immediate family. Fodoreanu wrote little about the young daughter and mother she left in occupied Bucharest, probably because this constituted the most emotional and potentially demoralizing subject for her self-composure while she was serving in the medical volunteer corps in Moldavia. Yet she wrote often about her father and brother, both on the front, acknowledging a breakdown of several days when she found out about her brother's death.[26]

Sabina Cantacuzino also focused a great deal of attention on her family. However, the discussion of her relatives amounted to a combination of personal stories with political commentary, as the people whose activities she described were the leader of the National Liberal Party in exile, Ion I. C. Brătianu, the head of the hospital administration in Bucharest, Constantin Cantacuzino, and other individuals from the highest echelons of the National Liberal Party.[27] She provided numerous details about family life and the troubles of daily life under occupation, which served not only to illustrate Cantacuzino's own experience but also to reinforce the bonds of suffering between the Brătianu-Cantacuzino family and the average Romanian.[28] Published two decades after the war, her memoirs contributed to a campaign of rescuing the reputation of the Brătianu name and the Liberals, under severe attack at that time.[29] Thus, her stakes were far higher than simply bearing witness to the experience of the war from a female perspective. Cantacuzino's sharp pen also attacked a number of well-known persons, especially women of the upper class, for their cowardly—even treasonous in some instances—attitudes under the German occupation.[30]

If the focus of these memoirs was often on family relationships and emotions, the language also tended to be more impassioned than that found in the autobiographical writings of most men, who attempted to preserve an air of distance and objectivity vis-à-vis their recollections. That is not to say that the writings by Cancicov or Bacalbaşa, for instance, lacked emotional charge. But they dwelled very little upon their own reactions and feelings and focused more on what they remembered having seen, representing themselves as objective rational observers rather than embattled actors or even vulnerable victims, as women's self-representations often suggested. Thus, emotions were somewhat removed in their discourse. The closest Bacalbaşa came to acknowledging his feelings was when describing the early days of the occupation. About 23 November, the day when the Central Powers entered Bucharest, he simply stated: "It is a cursed day!"[31]

A great sense of fear is apparent in the pages of women's writings, especially at the beginning of the war. After the initial enthusiasm of entering the war, the radical changes from the very first days—mobilization, militarization of the economy and government institutions—made all women aware of their vulnerability. Their livelihood was further threatened by the deterioration of the domestic situation after only a few weeks of fighting, when the Romanian armies began to incur great losses and thousands of refugees appeared in Bucharest. By the end of August, Cornea had become desperate and fearful: "War is something awful . . . All of a sudden all hospitals are full."[32] Yet fear gave way to frustration about the civilians' reaction to the occupation or deprivations during the war, and finally to a state of depression when the war efforts did not bring any victories, only sacrifices: "We are crucified . . . Crucified, mocked by the pagans and devil's hands . . . "[33] Some women expressed hatred of the enemy and desire for revenge when they became increasingly despondent. Cantacuzino reflected from the distance of twenty years on the brutality of her own emotions: "Sometimes I was scared of my own [cruelty] and accused myself of barbarism."[34] Cornea referred to the enemy as a monster and "the German hoof."[35] All of the authors displayed some degree of hatred towards the Central Powers.

Almost all of the women also made strongly anti-Semitic remarks that betrayed a deep-rooted mistrust, if not hatred, of the Jews as unpatriotic or outright treasonous.[36] Cantacuzino often commented on Jewish fraternization with the Germans, referring to them as "kikes" (*jidani*).[37] While some of these anti-Semitic statements were based on actual encounters, in others her anti-Semitism took on mythic proportions. In one case, Cantacuzino wrote: "My mother arrived in Mihăeşti . . . dead tired. They had been ten in a compartment [on the train], and, of course, eight were Jews, because they were the only ones to travel freely." [38] Her statement simply reflected the assumptions her mother and Cantacuzino herself made about the collaboration between the Jewish population and the German occupiers.

Likewise, these authors showed no sense of empathy or loyalty towards women in general. Rather, they were eager to separate themselves from what they considered the dishonorable attitude of many other women, who for instance worked for the occupying powers or fraternized with them. This ambivalent position was reflected in some contradictory remarks. On the one hand, Sabina Cantacuzino acknowledged the behavior of some women as courageous, such as Alexandrina Cantacuzino's attitude when taken prisoner by the Germans.[39] But she was critical of the same woman's showy patriotism as something "she could afford," because of her husband's official position under the occupation.[40] Cornea differentiated between nurses who gave their all and those who refused to help or held back in some instances. Yet in the same breath she stated with frustration: "This [the administration of the hospital] will not prosper until it falls into women's hands."[41]

For some authors frustration and powerlessness became overpowering: "Our country, whose fate was in the balance [at the beginning of the war], is now lost." [42] Cornea, in particular, dwelled a great deal on her misfortunes as a woman. During the war she lost her husband and saw her material situation deteriorate to the point that she became penniless and suicidal. A staunch feminist, she responded by railing against the injustices done to all women in her predicament:

> Women have no rights, widows even fewer. After widows are squashed like a lemon, they are thrown out on the street by the law . . . Democracy, democracy, when will your time come, to rule here like in France and America, so that a person could win based on merit, work, and talent, not inheritance.[43]

Finally, as more family and friends perished in the war, mourning took over a large part of women's emotional life. The final victory of the Romanian troops in the war was reflected differently in their writings. Some rejoiced with a sense of revenge and righteousness:

> The messengers of victory were arriving. Our brothers, beautiful, as the Latins are supple, after the heavy trunks, the sinister Teutons . . . The noble army of our allies, the liberators of the world![44]

Others did not recover from the losses in the war. After working as a volunteer nurse in Moldavia for over two years, Fodoreanu wrote about the triumphal return of the king and queen to Bucharest:

> I am not going to the parade. I am no longer anything more than a poor woman who lost her father, mother, brothers, relatives, friends . . . I will remain between these walls where I was born to cry out my pain.[45]

Still, returning to the nursing war service at the beginning of 1919, she accompanied the Romanian troops that occupied Hungary.

The richness of these personal recollections about the war and the variety of experiences represented in these narratives complement men's autobiographical writings and greatly enhance our understanding of the scope of wartime experience, foregrounding the gender dimension of how these experiences were constituted as historically significant. Women's narratives also bring into question the equation of courage and heroism exclusively with combat. The dangers and hardships women faced throughout the war confronted them with the necessity of becoming resourceful, brave, and steadfast in their efforts to simply survive. In order to provide food for hospitals and other philanthropic institutions, women "had organized a whole system: meat in caskets, with women crying behind the carts . . . and lambs wrapped as children."[46] Those who worked as nurses had displayed even more courage and spirit of self-sacrifice, some working under fire very close to the front (Fodoreanu), others simply working close to the source of typhoid infection (Cornea), and a few even helping some Romanian prisoners escape (Alexandrina Cantacuzino).

Women were not the only ones to sing their praises. A few of the men who were hospitalized during the war also acknowledged in their autobiographies the important role played by nurses and other women volunteers.[47] One wrote: "[H]eroes are those . . . who died on the battlefield defending the country; but in no way inferior to them are those who willingly sacrificed themselves for the same goal . . . How many doctors and nurses, who left freely for the same love [of country], . . . died in the claws of the other enemy, typhoid fever?"[48]

Women's experiences of courage and sacrifice were at best marginally represented in the collective forms of remembering the war. In addition to Kiriţescu's lack of attention to women's wartime actions, this silence was also reflected in many forms of collective commemoration. Thousands of war memorials mushroomed throughout Romania in the first decade after 1918. Most were small, local efforts in every village to remember those who died in wartime combat—a form of mourning. In addition to these memorials, several larger projects attempted to raise money from the government and general population. Only one of these represented the female contribution to the war—the project for a monument to the only Romanian woman known to have died in combat, Ecaterina Teodoroiu. Other projects included a monument for all teachers who engaged in combat, a monument for the infantry, and a mausoleum for the Mărăşeşti battle, the Romanian Verdun.[49]

Only in 1932 was a monument to the medical heroes raised, representing not only men but also women as prominent contributors in the war effort. In fact, the most visible figure in the bas-relief of the monument is Queen Marie, who led the wartime nursing effort. Still, at the inauguration of the monument, the

Figure 9.1. Romanian Nurses in a Hospital on the Eastern Front, World War I. Courtesy of the National Military Museum, Bucharest.

allocutions focused exclusively on the sacrifices of male soldiers and doctors in uniform. No mention was made of the many women who also served as volunteers.[50]

To my knowledge, there was only one request from a veterans' organization to commemorate the sacrifices of women in the Red Cross through a plaque in the Military Museum.[51] It is not clear what the final response to this request was, but there is no such memorial today.[52] Such efforts suggest that, although not in the mainstream of collective recollections, women's personal memories of their wartime experience were somewhat valued and appropriated in the public discourse about the meaning and memory of the war, at least between the world wars. Women were themselves at the forefront of such efforts, though not exclusively.

Unlike women's writings in Germany, Hungary, or Great Britain, Romanian women's testimonies about their contributions to the war effort, their narratives of suffering and sacrifice, did not become an important vehicle for negotiating political power. Romanian activists' efforts to connect the value of women's contributions in the war with postwar demands for power were met with little sympathy among most politicians and even other women activists.[53] Most were happier simply to enable women to play a public role in the remembering of the war through mourning, building memorials, and organizing commemorations for the war dead. In such commemorations, however, the emphasis was almost exclusively on the soldiers and their heroism on the battlefield. This marginal presence of women as agents but not subjects of the collective memory of the war has remained largely unchanged.

World War II

The wartime experiences of men and women were gendered in a similar fashion as in World War I, with some minor but important differences. Generally speaking women were again not mobilized for the war effort, but by 1941 a much larger percentage of the female population was employed in the cash economy. Therefore, women were more involved in the wartime economy than they had been between 1916 and 1918. Discussions of their wartime roles still revolved, however, around images of women as mothers and moral guardians of the nation. Women thus continued to work as they had done before the war, without a radical disruption in employment patterns. In terms of more direct contributions to the war effort, the state created a welfare organization—the Patronage Council—which acted as an umbrella institution for various, mostly private, initiatives. This was somewhat of a departure from the previous world war, when private organizations were left to their own financial and administrative devices to care for the wounded, orphans, widows, and generally impoverished.

Another departure was to allow women to participate in the war effort on the front in a more regularized, if still marginal, fashion. In addition to male nurses, the army now included a regular ambulance and nursing service staffed by women. These women were not part of the regular army but were under the direct command of the army's sanitary service, as volunteers. It is not clear what these women thought of their activities and how they saw themselves in relation to the male medical staff, as no memoirs comparable to Fodoreanu's writings from World War I have surfaced. But although the changes described above suggest important departures for women in enabling them to play a more active role in the war, in reality these opportunities were limited. The state spent little money on either the Patronage Council or the women's nursing and ambulance service. Marshall Ion Antonescu, Romania's leader during World War II, and the public voices of his regime continued to speak about women's role as patriotic mothers, but they rarely made reference to any other contributions by women to the war effort.[54]

During World War II, commemorative activities began at the same time as combat did, so an official line of collective remembering was established from the start. Personal memoirs were not published until after 1945, and then in a much politicized and highly censored atmosphere. The Soviet Army had occupied Romania and the Communist Party was attempting to establish some legitimacy vis-à-vis older parties. Everyone, from the military-civilian leadership to the entire population, was trying to come to terms with Romania's about-face on 23 August 1944, when the country joined the Allies against the Axis, on whose side it had fought most of the war. To top it all off, Northern Transylvania was retro-ceded to Romania. The vastly different experiences of not only civilians versus soldiers, but especially people of different ethnicity—Romanians, Hungarians, Jews, Germans, Russians, Ukrainians, and Roma—during the war also made it impossible to begin establishing anything but a highly ideologized, Soviet-controlled memory of World War II.

Indeed, although people wrote about their wartime experiences between 1940 and 1944, very few such texts have surfaced. Most were probably destroyed by their authors or others to whom they were entrusted right after the war, out of fear of repercussions. Others were hidden and remained so until after 1989. Very few have been recovered and published. The authors of autobiographical texts that appeared in Romania between 1945 and 1989 were Jews writing about their experience in Axis-allied Romania or in deportation in Transnistria; Romanian soldiers who fought on the western front after August 1944, published at the request and with the express approval of the communist regime; and communist "partisans" who wanted to solidify their claims to power under the communist regime.[55] None of these categories included women.

Such an absence is even more glaring when considering the clearly stated goals of the communist regime to bring about gender equality. In other countries, such as Yugoslavia and the Soviet Union, the communist regime drew a great deal of attention to women's contributions to World War II, both as soldiers and as civilian participants in the war effort.[56] In Romania there was no such attempt to at least pay some symbolic homage to women. In part, this absence is certainly connected to the lack of prominence of women both in communist organizations and in the Romanian army. But such details did not prevent the Romanian Communist Party from fabricating a history of its partisan movement. Why no women, then? The more likely reason is that, in spite of having a woman, Ana Pauker, among its five most powerful members, the Romanian Communist Party simply chose not to focus on recruiting women in its initial years in power.

Another important factor is that from the beginning, the Ministry of Defense was given the responsibility of commemorating the war (i.e., generating the propaganda material that would help construct the "correct" official memory of World War II). Although women did work in the Ministry of Defense, they were not in decision-making positions about such propaganda matters. Professional soldiers and party activists in the army were not interested in showing the contribution of the civilian population (unless they were partisans) or auxiliary personnel on the battlefield, such as nurses. Thus, women's memories of the war remained buried during the communist regime. Finally, since there was no tradition in the official public memory of focusing on women's participation in the previous world war, the propaganda writers did not have to counter such a discourse in their newly fashioned narratives about heroism, patriotism, and proletarian struggle.

In fact, in the first two decades after 1947 there was no emphasis on individual experience in the official commemorations of the war. Large parades and mass meetings were meant to dwarf the contribution of any one individual and focus instead on the role of the Communist Party, the Soviet Union, and the working class. The one significant exception was Stalin's image as hero and protector.

With Nicolae Ceauşescu's rise to power and Romania's subsequent overtly nationalist course among other Soviet bloc countries, such commemorations shifted from an emphasis on the Soviet Union to one on Romania's own contribution to the war. One prominent change was the renewed interest in the stories war veterans had to tell. The official program of the twentieth anniversary of the liberation of the country from the "fascist forces" on 25 October 1964—Romania's Armed Forces Day—included for the first time presentations by veterans.[57]

Moreover, starting in the mid-1960s, the Propaganda Service of the Ministry of Defense, following party directives, began a campaign of reinvigorating the collective memory of World War I, including women's contributions to it. In several volumes of wartime recollections that celebrated the patriotic efforts of the proletariat (most of them in the lower echelons of the officer corps, or simple recruits), there were a few stories about women's heroism in assisting soldiers on the front, some by acting as scouts, others by hiding soldiers and spying.[58] But again, the writings by women who were nurses or contributed to the war efforts in other capacities than in combat were not highlighted. The apparent invisibility of women in Kiriţescu's history and other authoritative texts about the war, combined with an exclusive identification of heroism with combat, served again to render women at best marginal among the celebrated actors of World War I.[59]

Autobiography and Collective Memory of the Wars after 1989

After 1989 a flood of memoirs appeared, most of them focusing on the experience of the gulag but some also on World War II. The veterans of the eastern front in particular made great efforts to bring visibility to this wartime experience, especially since it had been a taboo subject in the official collective memory of the war. Reacting against the collectivist shaping of official memory before 1989, veterans' organizations published many personal narratives of soldiers on the eastern front, providing an alternative that focused on military action, the experience of soldiers in combat, and anti-Soviet nationalism. Women's experiences were again omitted.

There is one remarkable exception to this general trend: the journal kept by Alice Voinescu, a philosopher and professor at the Dramatic Arts Conservatory in Bucharest. While the journal spans a much longer period of her life (1929–1961), it also provides a vivid narrative of the experience of the war through the eyes of this one highly educated and articulate woman. After the death of her husband the journal is structured as a series of letters to him, and the period of the war is located in this part of her life (roughly one third of the book). Voinescu constructed her experiences as gendered, writing often about her vulnerability in society (not being able to teach at a more prestigious school because she was a woman) or in marriage (tolerating her adulterous husband as a matter of wifely duty). Her reflections also represented an embattled attempt to sometimes overcome and sometimes accept her vulnerability as woman.

Her comments about the experience of war were often expressed in the form of a lively, casual dialogue, sometimes showing fear for those around her (seldom for herself) and often looking for a partner with whom she could share her frustration with the injustices and misery, both material and moral, she saw around her:

> I seem to live in a dream—sometimes very ugly . . . I cannot struggle with the horror of barbarism, I start thinking that *I cannot react against barbarism except through kindness,* let them put me in [jail]! . . . Ică [Mihai Antonescu, the prime minister and Marshall Antonescu's right hand] must be sadistic and unimaginative, otherwise he wouldn't order the robberies and massacres against the Jews. If he realized what a horrible perversion of our soul he is provoking, he wouldn't be proud. Dear baby, am I so naïve not to understand certain needs? Well, *no.* Perversity and murderous bestiality cannot be necessities![60]

Voinescu offered an insightful window into the reactions of a civilian and woman to the conflicted realities of the war. While her writing reflected a semblance of the normalcy of everyday life, the journal contained many subtle reminders that civilians faced not only the reality of combat losses, but also the violence occurring at home against Jews:

> Nothing new on the front, but horrendous rumors about the horrible deeds against the Jews. Proof of frightening cruelty, which makes me shiver about humanity's future . . . This is not a return to barbarism, but rather a pathological deviation.[61]

Yet while decrying the violence against the Jewish population, Voinescu also showed her frustration about the reaction of the Jewish communities to these events:

> It is terrible what is happening to this unfortunate people, but the war is against them. What are they doing? How are they reacting? Do they dare take a position? No. They suffer and defend themselves in the shadows, they creep by. They have to risk directly, otherwise they won't come out alive . . . I feel great pity for them, but I want to be able to also admire them.[62]

Voinescu's journal is unusual in the detailed and engaged personal reactions about the fate of Jews during the war. Almost all other autobiographical writings from this period by ethnic Romanians keep silent about the experience of the Romanian Jews. It would be impossible to make a claim about gender differences in this regard, especially given the paucity of sources written by women. But Voinescu's journal does raise the question of how visible anti-Semitic policies were to civilians versus soldiers, and to what extent one could speak of a passive acknowledgement or even support by civilians of such policies.

Voinescu wrote less directly about the gendered aspects of her wartime experience than about particular family problems and the fate of the Jews (some of her relatives were in mixed Romanian-Jewish families, thus the fate of the Jews was partly a family matter). But the journal contains clear suggestions about her concern for women's suffering: "I know what it means to lose your husband, and I think about the millions of widows, fiancés, mothers, children, parents, brothers, friends, about all the links among people that give birth to humanness."[63]

Voinescu also repeatedly expressed a desire to do more for the war effort. Frustration and a certain boredom alternated in her tone, suggesting that at least this one woman considered herself unnecessarily marginal to the war effort. From her growing discouragement about the opportunities open to her, one can infer that women interested in becoming more active in the war effort did not have many options. Working in a hospital was one avenue. On 12 July 1941, less than three weeks after Romania's entry in the war, she wrote about wanting to volunteer in a hospital: "Tomorrow I will go to the hospital to make myself a bit useful, and also to reenter reality."[64]

Within a month she began to display both affection and even a maternal emotional need for the wounded soldiers, but also frustration because of the inadequate staffing and supplies. Her sentiments towards the soldiers became increasingly conflicted as she also showed a growing anger, even disbelief, upon hearing some of the hateful statements of the patients: "The conversation with the soldiers—some are *poisoned.* The criticism of the past regimes makes them profoundly unjust and especially indoctrinated monkeys of a cheap and dangerous propaganda."[65] This last statement seems an indirect but fierce attack against the anti-Semitic and profoundly xenophobic propaganda of the Antonescu regime.

Voinescu wrote in detail about women in her family, sometimes commenting also on women in Romanian society in general. At the beginning of 1943, as the Romanian armies were fighting alongside the Germans in Stalingrad, she wrote: "here [in Romania] women are narrow in their minds and hearts. Either mediocre dames, who aren't worth anything, or saints, or beautiful devils."[66] Other comments about women were similarly harsh. Voinescu seemed to consider women both intellectually and emotionally the weaker sex, although it was not clear whether she saw herself an exception to this categorization or a victim of it.

Still, she sometimes praised women individually. On one occasion she wrote about a meeting at the Orthodox school for girls, where she witnessed the work of the philanthropic organization that sponsored it (the National Society of Romanian Orthodox Women). She praised especially the actions of two women whose names have already come up in connection with the experience and memory of World War I: Alexandrina and Sabina Cantacuzino.[67] Her uneven appreciation for women's efforts during the war suggests Voinescu considered herself as both vulnerable and also underappreciated as a woman.

Voinescu's journal offers an in-depth yet by no means "typical" account of women's experiences in World War II. A wider array of women's personal memories of the war has begun to emerge in oral histories, however. The representation of wartime experiences in these narratives is, of course, not just a function of the subjects' personal recollections, but also of the manner in which they are produced. Constructed as a dialogue with the interviewer, these life stories are not a premeditated and self-censored description of a woman's experiences but are rather offered in a more spontaneous manner. The text that emerges is also very much a product of the interviewer's intentions, the questions asked, the very presence of the interviewer, in addition to the actual intentions and specific recollections of the subject. Even though these particularities may render oral histories more problematic as autobiographical texts, oral interviews are still an important site for enlarging and diversifying the public memory of wartime experiences, especially among the less educated and women.

Several years ago I interviewed several women subjects in a project focusing on the massacre of civilians on 9 September 1940 in a Northern Transylvanian village.[68] Of sixteen interviews conducted for this project, seven subjects were women. An interesting gendered aspect of the retelling of the story of this massacre grabbed my attention in two interviews. Both were taken with husband and wife present. In the first one, the man was the subject, though the wife had been present at the events and the husband had been away from the village, serving in the Romanian army. Not unlike other men, such as Bacalbaşa in World War I, the husband represented himself as an authoritative figure in recollecting the events of the massacre. While he was describing his memories of the event (clearly not his own, but a narrative he had heard from other people, including his spouse), the wife pretended to be busy working in the background, yet carefully listening in on the conversation. Occasionally she intervened in the story to correct her husband. She did not want to make herself the representative of her family in linking her personal reminiscences with my effort to connect them with the collective memory of the massacre. Yet she had a strong sense of her authority as a witness and wanted to make sure we got the story straight. In the second interview I spoke with both wife and husband. In this case, the wife kept asking for her husband to confirm her story, seemingly unsure of her own memories and authority as a witness. Though both men and women were witnesses to the massacre of Treznea of 9 September 1940, it is mostly men who discuss it publicly. These two interviews suggest that women may be less sure of their public authority to bear witness or be less self-assured about the historical significance of their personal memories. Other scholars working on gender and memory in oral history projects have arrived at similar conclusions.[69]

By the same token, my study and others by ethnographers and anthropologists suggest that in Romania women tend to play an important role in transmitting the oral narratives that help shape the collective memory of smaller communities.[70] Women are central in organizing the rituals of burial and remembering for the dead in their family. In fact, they constitute the living memory of these dead. Traditionally, they also keep the lists of the names of the deceased and make sure these names are read out in church at the appropriate religious holidays. Therefore, the role of women in constructing sites of memory is complex and has to be researched further in order to understand the relationship between their personal recollections and the collective memory in their local communities.

The reconstruction of the collective memory of World War II to include the perspective of personal recollections has only recently begun in Romania. In the past decade, the focus of most publications has been on bringing to the surface the experience of soldiers on the eastern front, on the one hand, and the trauma of the Jewish population, on the other hand. These two different (opposite in many ways) tracks have not been incorporated equally in collective representations of wartime experience. The Jewish experience remains much more marginal to the grand narrative of the war, though recent publications and official endeavors show some promising beginnings in demarginalizing this aspect of the war. The experience of other civilians is even more invisible, and although more gems like Voinescu's journal may come to the fore in the coming years, it is more likely that a more complete and gender-inclusive picture of the personal experience and memory of the war will take shape through oral histories. The difficulty, however, is in convincing women of this older generation that their personal stories have historical significance.

The starting point for such a shift has to be the reexamination of what constitutes "historical experience" during war along more gender-inclusive lines. To begin with, we need to pay closer attention to the overwhelming masculinist assumptions about what war heroism, trauma, self-sacrifice, and suffering mean. In the context of total war, women's experiences (especially as civilians) will help us begin to reevaluate the central role of subjective representations for constituting both ideological constructs such as "heroism" and "patriotism" and the identity of historical subjects. This means nothing less than moving away from an analysis of war that privileges almost exclusively combat and diplomacy, and starting to engage questions about the social and cultural aspects of war. Gender is a central component of all these approaches.

Notes

1. Joan Scott, "The Evidence of Experience." *Critical Inquiry* 17, no. 4 (Summer 1991): 773–97.

2. For a broader context in which the interviews were made, see Maria Bucur, "Treznea: Trauma, Nationalism and the Memory of World War II in Romania," *Rethinking History* 6, no. 1 (2002): 35–55.

3. This essay does not include discussion of either novels or other texts of fictional literature with autobiographical content, in part because such writings try to cross genres and represent more complex texts whose analysis a brief presentation such as this cannot afford to develop. The observations made here can be extended to such texts, which I intend to do in a larger book project.

4. Though my emphasis is on the subjective quality of valuation and self-representation of wartime experience, I believe that the horrendous material conditions of wartime Romania are an essential context for beginning to analyze the individual narratives about the war.

5. George Călinescu, *Istoria literaturii române de la origini pînă în prezent* (Bucha-

rest: Ed. Minerva, 1983), Dumitru Micu *Istoria literaturii române de la creația populară la postmodernism* (Bucharest: Ed. SAECULUM I.O., 2000); George Ivașcu, *Istoria literaturii române* (Bucharest: Ed. Stiințifică, 1969); Gheorghe Adamescu, *Istoria literaturii române* (Bucharest: Ed. Eminescu, 1998); Eugen Lovinescu, *Istoria literaturii române contemporane* (Bucharest: Ed. Minerva, 1973); Alexandru Piru, *Istoria literaturii române* (Bucharest: Ed. "Grai și suflet—Cultura Națională," 1994); Serban Cioculescu et al., *Istoria literaturii române moderne* (Bucharest: Ed. Eminescu, 1985); Dumitru Micu, *Scurtă istorie a literaturii române* (Bucharest: Ed. Iriana, 1994).

6. Micu, *Scurtă istorie*, 227.

7. Ibid.

8. Though I do not have evidence that all the women authors discussed below had university degrees, it is safe to say that they had far more education than the average woman in Romania. In the early years of the twentieth century, university education remained a more limited option for women than for men. Many women, especially among the social elites, such as Sabina Cantacuzino and Jeanna Fodoreanu, received their education with private tutors or abroad. Their level of education is difficult to assess according to regular university standards. However, their writing style and erudite references to political, historical, and literary matters suggest they had at least a level of cultural literacy comparable to that of university-educated male writers.

9. See Călinescu, *Istoria literaturii române;* Lovinescu, *Istoria literaturii române;* Micu, *Scurtă istorie.*

10. Jeanna Col. Fodoreanu, *Femeia-Soldat* (Oradea: Tipografia Somenfeld, 1928), 9.

11. Constantin Bacalbașa, *Capitala sub ocupația dușmanului, 1916–1918* (Brăila: n.p., 1921), Vasile Th. Cancicov, *Impresiuni și păreri personale din timpul războiului României. Jurnal zilnic, 13 august, 1916–31 decembrie, 1918* (Bucharest: Atelierele Societatei "Universul," 1921).

12. Cancicov, *Impresiuni și păreri*, iii–vi.

13. Bacalbașa, *Capitala*, 64–65.

14. One prominent case is a recent study by the well-respected historian Constantin Rădulescu-Zoner and Beatrice Marinescu, *Bucureștii în anii primului război mondial, 1914–1918* (Bucharest: Ed. Albatros, 1993).

15. Bacalbașa, *Capitala*, 41.

16. For example, Romeo Vidrașcu, *Jurnal de campanie. 15 august 1916–19 iunie 1918* (Bucharest: Convorbiri Literare, 1920); Marshall Alexandru Averescu, *Notițe zilnice de războiu* (Bucharest: Ed. Cultura Națională, 1937); Mihail Văgăonescu, *Viața în războiu. Insemnări zilnice de pe front, 1916–1919* (Bucharest: Casa Scoalelor, 1925); and Gen. N. Tătăranu, *Acum un sfert de veac. Amintiri din război* (Bucharest: Ed. Cartea Românească, 1940).

17. Constantin Kirițescu, *Istoria războiului pentru întergirea României, 1916–1919*, vol. 1 (Bucharest: Ed. Stiințifică și enciclopedică, 1989), 23. Though he did not provide a bibliography and footnotes in any edition of the book, Kirițescu suggested the importance of wartime journals in a foreword to a book published in 1925, *Life during War: Daily Notes from the Front, 1916–1918* [*Viața în războiu. Insemnări zilnice de pe front, 1916–1918*] by Mihail Văgăonescu (Bucharest: Casa Scoalelor, 1925): "Reading Mr Văgăonescu's pages, we see war as it is, we feel it, we live it . . . The documentary significance is just as great." (3–4) Kirițescu's characterization of the diary as "documentary" reflects his belief that autobiographical texts were truthful reflections of the events and authors' experiences, by virtue of the author's ability to write about what he saw and heard as the events were unfolding.

18. Kirițescu, *Istoria războiului,* 24.

19. Ibid., 1–2; see Rădulescu-Zoner and Marinescu for their uncritical use of Kirițescu.

20. At one point, Bacalbașa claimed to have said before 1916 that, in case of war, he would not be afraid of the peasants, as others were, but of "Jews and women," whom he did not consider trustworthy patriots. See Bacalbașa, *Capitala,* 132–33.

21. For example Sabina Cantacuzino, *Războiul 1914–1919* (Bucharest: Ed. Universul, 1937); Nelli Cornea, *Insemnări din vremea războiului* (Bucharest: Ed. Librăriei H. Steinberg și fiu [1921]); Ecaterina Raicoveanu (Fulmen), *Jurnalul unei surori de caritate, 1916–1918* (Bucharest: Ed. Librărici universalc Lcn Alcalay, 1920); and Sevcra Sihleanu, *Note și desminiţiri asupra amintirilor D-nei Sabina Cantacuzino* (Bucharest: n.p., 1938).

22. Marie, queen of Roumania, *Ordeal: The Story of My Life* (New York: C. Scribner's Sons, 1935).

23. Nelli Cornea was the only exception. Although she was the educated wife of a lawyer, she lacked access to the highest circles of Romanian society.

24. Richard Ely and Allyssa McCabe, "Gender Differences in Memories for Speech," in Selma Leydesdorff et al., eds., *Gender and Memory* (Oxford: Oxford University Press, 1996), 17–30.

25. Cornea, *Insemnări,* 48–50; quote from 48.

26. Fodoreanu, *Femeia-Soldat,* 51–54.

27. Cantacuzino, *Războiul 1914–1919,* 178.

28. Ibid., 198–99.

29. By 1937, due to internal tensions and also Carol II's (1930–1940) insidious efforts to undermine its stability, the National Liberal Party had splintered into two main sections. The weakness of the Liberals was powerfully demonstrated in the February 1937 elections, which paved the way for royal dictatorship. See Paul Quinlan, *The Playboy King: Carol II of Romania* (Westport, Conn.: Greenwood Press, 1995) and Maria Bucur, "Carol II," in Berndt Fischer, ed., *Balkan Dictators in the Twentieth Century* (London: Hurst and Co., 2005).

30. Cantacuzino, *Războiul 1914–1919,* 69, 97, 142–43, among them Alexandrina Fălcoianu and Severa Sihleanu, who in response published their own memoirs to cleanse their reputation.

31. Bacalbașa, *Capitala,* 33.

32. Cornea, *Insemnări,* 11.

33. Cornea, *Insemnări,* 63; "devil's hands" is a loose translation of "liftelor spurcate," which amounts to a curse in Romanian.

34. Cantacuzino, *Războiul 1914–1919,* 179.

35. Cornea, *Insemnări,* 58 and 61–63.

36. This is an attitude common to many of the autobiographical writings of men. Bacalbașa alone makes a point of distinguishing "the Jews" as a general category, separate from instances of fraternization with the Central Powers by individual Jews. See Bacalbașa, *Capitala,* 128–36.

37. Cantacuzino, *Războiul 1914–1919,* 88.

38. Ibid., 184.

39. Ibid., 34, 152.

40. Ibid., 174.

41. Cornea, *Insemnări,* 65.

42. Ibid., 115.

43. Ibid., 94 and 95.

44. Ibid., 137.

45. Fodoreanu, *Femeia-Soldat*, 74.

46. Cantacuzino, *Războiul 1914–1919*, 30.

47. Tătăranu, *Acum un sfert de veac*, 71–72; N. Russu-Ardeleanu, *Prizonier in ţara ta* (Botoşani: n.p., 1918), 20; and Corneliu Moldoveanu, *Majestatea morţei* (Bucharest: Ed. H. Stinberg, Librar, 1919), 49–50.

48. Dr. Anton D. Velcu, *Memoriei Detinsei Profesoare Elena Cancicov (Soră de caritate în timpul războiului)* (Bucharest: n.p., 1936), 16–17.

49. For a discussion of the monument to Ecaterina Teodoroiu, see Bucur, "Between the Mother of the Wounded and the Virgin from Jiu: Romanian Women and the Gender of Heroism during the Great War," *Journal of Women's History* 12, no. 2 (Summer 2000): 30–56; for discussion of the Mărăşeşti mausoleum, see Bucur, "Paying Homage: The Gendered Construction of Heroism in Interwar Romania," paper presented at the AAASS Convention, November 1999, St. Louis.

50. See *Universul* 49: 159 (11 June 1932), 4–5.

51. Muzeul Militar Naţional, fond. Muzeul Militar, dos. 5, ff. 3 and 12.

52. The building of the Military Museum was destroyed during World War II. After the war, the museum moved twice. I found no evidence of the plaque having been placed in the prewar building or the first post-1945 location of the museum. There are no plans to erect such a plaque in the current location.

53. See Bucur, "Between the Mother."

54. Mihai Antonescu, "Infăptuirile regimului Antonescu," *Porunca Vremii* 11, no. 2323 (6 September 1942), 1–4. See also Gh. Butnariu, "Meditaţii pentru femeile de astăzi," *Porunca Vremii* 10, no. 1946 (1941), 1 and 3.

55. Two other categories of individuals published wartime memoirs/autobiographical writings: Jews who had left Romania during or after World War II and members and sympathizers of the Iron Guard. I do not include them because these writings were published outside of Romania and were generally unavailable to the public in Romania, making them much less significant for the construction of the collective memory of the war inside Romania. Both categories of diasporic writings included men's and women's recollections.

56. See Barbara Jancar, *Women and Revolution in Yugoslavia, 1941–1945* (Denver: Arden Press, 1990) and K. Jean Cottam, "Soviet Women in Combat in World War II: The Ground Forces and the Navy," *International Journal of Women's Studies* 3, no. 4 (1980): 345–57.

57. Arhiva Ministerului Apărării Naţionale, dos. 11049/microfilm roll 51391, 126–27.

58. See Gh. Preda, comp., *Si-au făcut datoria (Amintiri din primul război mondial)* (Bucharest: Ed. Militară, 1968), esp. 20–29.

59. Although women's autobiographical writings published during the interwar period were readily available (they had not been catalogued in the secret index of the Romanian Academy and other libraries), few if any historians writing about women in twentieth-century Romania used them.

60. Alice Voinescu, *Jurnal* (Bucharest: Ed. Albatros, 1997), 262 [italics in the original].

61. Ibid., 258.

62. Ibid., 260.

63. Ibid., 289.

64. Ibid., 248.

65. Ibid., 264 [italics in the original].

66. Ibid., 437.

67. Ibid., 451.

68. See Bucur, "Treznea."

69. For example, Marina Malysheva and Daniel Bertaux, "The Social Experiences of a Countrywoman in Soviet Russia," in Leydesdorff et al., eds., *Gender and Memory.*

70. Gail Kligman, *The Wedding of the Dead: Ritual, Poetics, and Popular Culture in Transylvania* (Berkeley: University of California Press, 1988); and Katerine Verdery, *The Political Lives of Dead Bodies: Reburial and Postsocialist Change* (New York: Columbia University Press, 1999).

10 The Nation's Pain and Women's Shame: Polish Women and Wartime Violence

Katherine R. Jolluck

When disaster struck the Polish nation in September 1939, its members had a historical narrative and national mythology to provide meaning to the new calamity. The Nazi and Soviet occupations seemed to parallel the partitions of the late eighteenth century, after which the Polish nation endured 123 years of foreign domination. Linking their loss of statehood to their Christian beliefs, Poles came to see themselves as a martyred nation, required to make sacrifices to the "altar of the Fatherland" to ensure Poland's resurrection. During the period of partition, women had made important contributions to the Polish national struggle. A few "women-heroes," such as Emilia Plater and Henryka Pustowojt, took up arms in insurrections against tsarist rule. More often wives followed husbands—freedom fighters—into Siberian exile, while other women donned black clothing to mourn the martyrs for Polish independence. The national poet Adam Mickiewicz began a long tradition of poets and writers extolling patriotic Polish mothers who raised sons to fight for the fatherland, selflessly sacrificing their offspring for the cause. Generations of Poles credited females with keeping the spirit and culture of the nation alive despite foreign rulers' attempts to extinguish national expression. Women participated in the triumphal efforts to win Poland's independence in the final stages of World War I, sometimes fighting alongside men to secure its borders.[1] The reestablishment of a sovereign Polish state in 1918 seemingly fulfilled the promise of the romantic nationalists' characterization of Poland as the "Christ of Nations."[2] That it came crashing down in 1939 in no way diminished Poles' attachment to their national myths.

The endurance of Polish identity and culture despite the lack of statehood for more than a century bequeathed a set of deep beliefs and practices to the new victims of foreign aggression. Facing even more brutal attempts to destroy their culture and society, Poles looked to the achievements of their forebears for models of action and for faith in ultimate victory. With some exceptions, like the women who transported ammunition on the Italian front or fought in the Warsaw Uprising, Polish females tended to engage in gender-specific patriotic activities. Although men and women mostly played distinctive roles in maintaining and defending the nation, they placed their efforts in a common framework. Individuals of both sexes drew upon a shared national history, suffused with religious meaning, to shape a sustaining identity and a collective hope for the future. Within this context individual suffering acquired national and religious significance, compounding the story of the Polish national tragedy.

This chapter examines one aspect of Polish women's wartime experiences—forced exile to the USSR after the Red Army invasion in 1939. It investigates women's use of the idea and ideals of the nation in coping with the physical adversity and violence they endured as a result of their conditions and treatment in exile. National identity provided a clear and poignant framework for women to understand and express some of the agony they experienced at the hands of their nation's enemy. Connecting with the struggles of compatriots, past and present, and with Catholic and Polish notions of sacrifice, women could take solace in suffering in the name of the fatherland. They used the nation as a neutral space in which they could find meaning to articulate their hardships, which seemed a fundamental aspect of being Polish. Shared tragedy rendered the women Poles on par both with their ancestors and with men. Nationality thus provided a meaningful and comforting way to objectify some of the physical traumas the women endured in Soviet exile. Other violations affected women so specifically, however, that they could not talk about them in terms of the nation; the more gendered the indignities and assaults, the less relevant the category of the nation for discussing them. Women found it easy to discuss violations they shared with men, which they could construe in national terms. Transgressions of social norms regarding the female body, though, seemed impermissible in the traditional story of the martyred nation, and therefore were largely silenced.

Historical Background

In August 1939 the Soviet and German foreign ministers concluded the Molotov-Ribbentrop Pact, whose secret protocols proposed dividing up the Polish state. The German army invaded Poland on 1 September, and the Red Army moved in on 17 September to claim its portion. Soviet officials quickly incorporated the territories of eastern Poland into the USSR, and then set out to establish their control. The process entailed widespread arrests, removing national and local leaders in the military, political, economic, religious, and cultural spheres; economic and political reorganization; and attempts to extinguish expressions of Polish culture and patriotism, whether in schools, churches, or homes. Early in 1940 Soviet authorities began a more catastrophic attack on civilian life—mass deportations to the interior of the USSR. This procedure resulted in the forced resettlement of hundreds of thousands of Polish citizens, the exact number of which remains undetermined. High estimates place the number of deportees at nearly one million, while some scholars offer figures closer to 350,000.[3] Mass arrests continued, resulting in an additional 100,000 to 250,000 persons being transported eastward to Soviet prisons and labor camps.

Eight to ten percent of those incarcerated were women. Border transgressions and participation in activities of the Polish underground account for more than half of their arrests. The vast majority of females, though, was deported without being charged with any crime, simply administratively exiled to the interior of the USSR, "resettled" in Soviet parlance. I call this latter group "deportees," to distinguish it from those incarcerated—"prisoners"—and use the term "exiles" to refer to both groups as a whole. While most prisoners were adult males, over half of the deportees were women and children, many of whom were removed after the arrest of male relatives.

The exiled women came from all walks of life, for the occupier sought to rid eastern Poland of all elements it suspected would be disloyal to the new regime. This encompassed individuals whose national identity, class origins, political orientation, religiosity, or level of social activism did not conform to the dictates of the communist party, which declared itself the leading force in society. Not only government officials and cultural elites faced exile. Landowning peasants, even those with small plots, seemed to have too much of a stake in the former system. Individuals whose relatives went abroad out of dire economic necessity were suspect, while families of men interned during the military campaign became "socially dangerous elements." Refusing to vote in the plebiscite that led to incorporation into the USSR or declining a Soviet passport virtually assured one a place on a transport eastward. So, too, could denunciations. In sum, average citizens were taken as well as elites.

The deportees ended up on collective farms or "special settlements" in some of the more inhospitable regions of the USSR—Siberia, Central Asia, and the Arctic North. In this their lives resembled those of compatriots sent to the Gulag, the system of labor camps. By all accounts, the exiles lived in abominable conditions. Securing the basic physical necessities became nightmarish struggles. Whether female or male, incarcerated or resettled, the exiles performed hard labor in conditions that at the very best betrayed the Soviet regime's lack of regard for the Poles' well-being; at worst, it betrayed a calculated desire to make them suffer. Local authorities typically responded to Poles' pleas for help by snapping, "Get used to it or drop dead!"[4]

Many of these women perished in wartime exile, but some were rescued.[5] After the German invasion in June 1941, Soviet leaders negotiated a pact with the Polish government-in-exile providing for the formation of a Polish army in the USSR to fight the Nazis. The agreement also promised the release of the exiled Poles. In 1942 this Polish army transported 115,000 of the exiles across the Caspian Sea to Iran and asked them to write about their recent ordeals. The army circulated several questionnaires, to which some respondents provided brief answers, while others used them as springboards, filling composition books with expanded replies. Still others offered detailed narratives, numbering hundreds of pages long. Most authors were ethnic Poles, as the Soviet government declared exiles of Belorussian, Jewish, or Ukrainian origin to be Soviet citizens and hampered their evacuation. They represent a cross-section of Polish society, in terms of class, education, occupation, and place of residence. While some documents are comprehensive and eloquent, others are barely literate, written almost as stream of consciousness. They all reflect shared patterns of meaning and interpretation.[6]

"Generic" Offenses

Much of the adversity the Poles faced in the USSR stemmed from deplorable living conditions: overcrowding, hunger and thirst, frostbite or suffocation, exhaustion and disease. The women write freely about such problems, which plagued the body in the most basic ways, affecting women and men alike. They vividly depict both the effects of these circumstances on their bodies and their efforts to cope with them. Characterizing such hardships as crimes perpetrated by Soviet officials, the women appear unrestrained in speaking out and expressing their pain. It is the suffering of the Poles.

The exiles considered the Soviet regime the source of their agony and believed that its agents missed no opportunity to intensify it. The statements and memoirs frequently report the denial of medical attention to the Poles, complaining that commandants and collective farm chairmen refused to grant even brief absences from work to visit a doctor or care for a sick relative. Deportees recall vainly begging local officials to transport them to the nearest hospital, often hundreds of kilometers away. Zuzanna Nowosielska devotes her entire testimony to an accident that befell her son at work; the authorities would neither provide him transportation nor allow her to leave her job to help him.[7] Nowosielska tells the story of her son's accident "only to show how they treated us." Like many deportees, she asserts that Soviet officials deliberately treated the Poles worse than others, be they Soviet citizens or national minorities likewise deported from Poland. Reportedly, the pleas of Poles for assistance met only with contempt. When Irena Sroka sought help for her dying mother she encountered the laughter of the authorities, who said that they had no need for Poles—there was more than enough land for their graves. Similarly, Jadwiga-Helena Szymkowska asserts that when accidents occurred among the deportees in her settlement, those in charge merely hissed, "Let the Polack die."[8]

The bulk of the Soviet population endured the same poverty and stark conditions the Poles described, a fact that meant little to the exiles, who neither left their homes willingly nor chose where they ended up. What mattered was the fact that Soviet authorities had condemned the Poles to such forbidding locales. The harsh reactions to expressions of need intensified the Poles' suffering and seemed to reveal a vindictive attitude toward them. Most importantly, the exiles understood that it was their connection to the Polish nation that caused them to be forcibly taken from their homes and subjected to such misery. Soviet citizens continually underscored this perception. "Polish lords" and "Polish dogs" became stock phrases in official and popular usage. Many exiles felt that they received harder work assignments and lower food rations precisely because of their nationality. As one woman declares in recounting her miserable existence on a collective farm, "[T]he fact that I am a Pole was enough to sentence me and other deportees like me to living conditions comparable to slow starvation."[9]

The conduct of interrogators of the Soviet security police, the NKVD, provided Poles the clearest evidence of the effort to inflict pain on their nation; it did not matter that the Stalinist regime treated those it considered its enemies, regardless of national origins, in the same manner. The NKVD largely viewed the Poles as foes because of their Polishness and all the qualities Soviet ideology ascribed to it: an aristocratic or bourgeois nature, national chauvinism, religious devotion, and opposition to communism. Thus allegiance to the Polish nation alone signaled to the Soviet government and its agents a real or potential enemy; in the paranoia of the Stalinist years, the distinction was irrelevant. "The NKVD saw a counterrevolutionary in each Polish man and Polish woman," explains a teacher, arrested as a "dangerous element."[10] During interrogations the officers fired streams of insults at the women, including "Polish pig" and "Polish whore."[11] In the documents, women use the details of these interrogations, as those of the living conditions, to underline the current tragedy of the Polish nation.

Women recount repeated nighttime interrogations, often lasting ten to twelve hours at a time. According to Bronisława Dziedziecka, this maltreatment served to keep the prisoner in a state of constant tension and exhaustion.[12] Women also report the routine use of violence against them. NKVD agents hit women in the face, using their hands, rubber truncheons, or the butts of revolvers. They grabbed them by the hair and repeatedly slammed their heads against the walls. Interrogators frequently struck their victims' fingers and hands, twisted their arms, and kicked their legs.[13] Many women endured confinement in the *kartser,* a particularly severe basement cell—empty, cold, frequently flooded. Such confinement could last several days, typically without any provision of food or drink or opportunity to use the toilet.[14]

Following interrogation or detention in the *kartser,* the victims were dumped back in their cells, often unconscious, febrile, or bleeding profusely. Many women write of their horror at seeing damaged bodies, beaten in an "inhuman way," brought back to the cells in the mornings.[15] In one cell the inmates cried upon seeing a gray-haired woman return from her interrogation covered with blood. The beaten woman's response, recounted by Jadwiga Cwikowska, reveals an attitude commonly expressed by the Poles: "And that woman, seeing us crying, smiled, saying, 'It's nothing children, it's for the Fatherland,' her words sounded in my ears throughout the entire time of my investigation." "Our Poland endures suffering and torture," notes another exile, "and we do along with Her."[16]

Like many other Poles, these women downplay bodily pain. They boast of their ability to withstand physical pain and their refusal to cry in front of the perpetrators, expressing a view of suffering as ennobling and even necessary for a higher goal—an independent and sovereign Polish nation. In so doing, they appropriate the partition-era ideal of sacrificing oneself on the "altar of the Fatherland." Traditionally a male-gendered notion of sacrifice, it required men to give up their lives fighting for independence; women would bear and raise sons to continue the struggle. These exiled women see themselves as active agents in the national struggle. Claiming their own physical suffering to fall within the male tradition, the women effectively de-gender the notion of sacrifice and patriotic devotion. Configuring their suffering this way renders it both equal to men's and redemptive. The women consider themselves simply Poles, martyrs for the fatherland.

This holds true not only for those beaten by the NKVD. The nation provided women a framework for understanding and articulating the physical pain and violence they shared with male compatriots—when they were starved, left to the mercy of the elements, or refused medical care. Such privations and assaults can be called "generic" or ungendered—they affected women as physical beings, but not explicitly female ones; the salient factor of their social identity explaining their plight was nationality. Being hungry or cold, or enduring torture, did not elicit shame. Nor did it compromise a woman's sense of self as a Pole. Indeed, as the gray-haired woman quoted above suggests, for many exiles such pain only strengthened national identity and the resolve to maintain it. Speaking of their misery, women could clearly externalize the responsibility for their injuries: the culprits were Soviets (regarded essentially as Russians), whether government official, prison warden, NKVD agent, collective farm chairman, or neighbor. The wretched living conditions and brutal treatment, as well as their agonizing consequences, reflected not on the victims, but on the perpetrators. Themselves blameless victims, women openly discussed their mistreatment as Poles. In connecting them to the history and traditions of their martyred nation, such disclosures bolstered the individual's identity as a Pole and presented Soviet rule as criminal, executed by a people "disgusting and barbarous."[17]

Gendered Offenses

Not all of the hardships connected with the body could be externalized, despite the context of national oppression. Some circumstances of exile left the body in a state that violated social requirements and expectations, thus injuring the individual's identity. The meaning associated with a particular situation could cause intense suffering, which sometimes equaled or even exceeded the physical discomfort involved. In some cases the body was not even touched yet was the source of great distress, because the context compromised the individual's sense of self. Cultural notions about the proper deportment, condition, and treatment of the physical body, particularly the female one, create a social aspect to the body; the violation of which can prove as dangerous to the individual as direct physical injury.

The exiled women's sexuality became a weapon in the hands of men with authority, a tool with which to humiliate and control them. This category of offenses, which victimized the women specifically as females, encompasses a range of situations and conduct. In the ensuing discussion I separate them into three groups, on an ascending scale of violence to the individual: mixing, invasion, and sexual exploitation. Corresponding with the increase in the violence of the offense is an increasing level of internalization on the part of the woman and a greater tendency to take refuge in silence. Additionally, the nation increasingly loses its relevance for women's understanding and articulation of their suffering. These injuries to the female body and identity robbed the women of the ability to name them and to express their full impact.

Mixing

The problem of the female body most frequently arises in the women's testimonies in expressions of shock and disgust that women and men were not physically separated at times they presumed proper and necessary—which I refer to as mixing. Simply put, in the USSR women and men were brought together in places, in proximity, and at times that Polish women considered outrageous violations both of their human dignity and of nature itself. To the Poles, this habit of mixing betrayed a complete lack of understanding and respect for the "natural" differences between males and females on the part of the Soviets—an indication of a "primitive" character.

Mixing began with the journey to the USSR, in the cramped cattle cars, and often continued in prison cells and barracks. In each place men and women had to sleep and attend to bodily functions in each other's presence. One woman writes that in the first prison in which she was held, forty people were packed into a cell for ten, "women, men and children all together." Her misery lessened in the second prison, where "the conditions were so much better, the cells were only for women and children."[18] This separation seemed to restore a measure of normality to a chaotic and distressing situation. Some women record only the fact of this mixing in recollections of their cells. Many others include it in their list of agonizing conditions, such as intense heat or cold, lack of air, lice and bedbugs, severe overcrowding, and a foul stench. This list merits pondering. The body experiences literal discomfort or pain from the just-enumerated plagues; it is completely unaffected by the mixing.

Mixing also constituted a problem for deportees. The daughter of a forester notes, "The lack of space meant that women and girls had to sleep together with men." A farmer from the Wilno region describes her barracks: "men and women together in terrible crowdedness."[19] They do not recall any specific incidents stemming from these living arrangements; the simple description of the situation expresses its indignity. The frequency of the complaint points to the violation women felt and suggests a pronounced sense of modesty and even shame accompanying the female body, a body expected to be hidden from the public—particularly male—gaze.

Women felt particular humiliation in regard to bodily needs and functions, especially on the transports. "All physiological matters had to be done in the open in the car in spite of a mixed company it couldn't be helped," explains Stefania Ulanowska.[20] In some prisons, women were allowed to use the toilets only under the watchful eyes of male guards.[21] Deportees frequently found that there were simply no enclosed spaces for eliminating bodily waste, or they were not delimited by sex. The problem loomed large at the worksites. "Going to the toilet during work was disapproved of or even forbidden," writes a laboratory nurse forced to labor in the fields; "[W]e were not permitted to move even half a meter to some bushes, and had to take care of our needs in the eyes of the guard."[22]

In their testimonies, most women merely state these uncomfortable facts, without expressing their reactions. A few, though, try to convey their anguish. A teacher from Cracow writes: "At the stations or anywhere the train stopped we had to jump down from the high cars and, under the guard of the soldiers, crawl under the cars—everyone together, women, men and children. There was no shame. A person became an animal relieving the unavoidable bodily needs." What here elevates humans above animals? Mindfulness of the "necessary" separation of the sexes, and a sense of shame in relation to the body. Jadwiga Jeleniewrza described the same ordeal: "This occurred in the light of day, at the station, under your own car, in the eyes of the masses passing by and of the Soviet soldiers, everyone all together—women, men, the old and the young. Many people fell seriously ill from this."[23]

Part of the injury stemmed from the invasion of private space and violation of personal autonomy connected with the body. It was not only the lack of privacy per se that disturbed the women. No one writes of feeling shame that unfamiliar women, foreign or not, observed them urinating, but they repeatedly underline that they had to take care of these needs in front of members of the *opposite sex.* This exposed their bodies and physiological functions in a way that they found highly uncomfortable and offensive to their notions of modesty. In Polish Catholic culture, as in many others, the burden of hiding the body weighed more heavily on women than on men. Indeed, male deportees also note this predicament, but with considerably less frequency, stressing that the unaccustomed situation especially disturbed females. Referring to mixing on the transports, one Polish man notes: "[E]ach of us, and especially women and girls, was tormented."[24]

Women found bathing facilities even more agonizing. "Whoever goes through such a bath for the first time suffers a great deal," explains Eugenia Schmidt: "Inside the rooms, where you had to undress and bathe under a shower, was a male staff. The bath took place in their presence." "We had to strip and hand over our clothing to be steamed," recounts another woman: "We then had to approach the soldiers and get from them a ridiculously small piece of soap, and after having washed, return to receive a towel and prison underlinen, which . . . was handed to us, each piece separately."[25] A twenty-four-year-old offers a vivid account of her first trip to a Soviet bath:

> Long ago, when I was a child, a little girl, I fantasized, I tried to imagine everything that I heard. I heard about heaven and hell. A strange thing, when I entered the bath I saw hell, just as I had imagined it in my girlhood. Hot, steaming streams of water, turned on briefly by the men attending the bathhouse—tens, maybe even hundreds of naked women—the water steaming, men screaming, "Faster, Faster!"[26]

Several points merit attention. First, the women describe these baths at length, providing both physical and emotional detail; some even list the baths among their worst experiences in the USSR.[27] Second, the humiliation of having to bathe under the watchful eyes of men aroused some of the greatest anger expressed by Polish women toward the Soviets. "What could we do in the face of this one more humiliation?" asks a teacher incarcerated in a labor camp: "Contempt was our sole defense. Passing naked down the long corridor we looked at the men with their horrid smiles as if they were many pieces of wood, until little by little they stopped smiling." Anna Cieslikowska describes the self-control the ordeal required: "You had to overcome your embarrassment and humiliation, clench your teeth and control yourself in order to calmly bear the coarse jibes and not spit in those hideous faces, or not punch them between their eyes." She recalls having to wait, naked, while her clothes were disinfected:

> That waiting was the worst, as the whole band of Russkies attending the bath walked about the room, our escort guards also came in, under the pretext of watching so that none of us escaped. I don't know where I got so much strength to calmly bear all the humiliation. I was half-conscious from helpless rage. I felt that if one of those scoundrels approached me, I would douse him with boiling water or strangle him with my own hands.[28]

While women often write that they bore the trials of exile with silence and fortitude, the situation in the baths unusually provoked them. Many of them screamed and protested; some went on hunger strikes to force a change.[29]

Mixing in the baths represents one of the few circumstances impelling individual women to resist on their own behalf. Though physically unharmed, the exposure of their bodies to the eyes and jeers of Soviet men caused great emotional distress, for mixing in the baths was understood as the ultimate humiliation. Taken from their homes and loved ones, deprived of their material possessions, their bodies represented the final frontier; it was all that the women still possessed, the last space of privacy and individuality. Expressing outrage served to reject the status of objects, to reclaim the right to privacy and to their bodies, to their identity as individuals and as a collective of females.

The strength of their reaction partly stemmed from the attempted deprivation of autonomy and individuality. In this sense the offense is a "generic" one. But gender plays a critical role. Private life, Gérard Vincent suggests, can best be understood as "the range of the inarticulate"—the secret.[30] As for privacy in relation to the body, it is precisely those parts of the anatomy that constitute physical sexual difference, and serve as the basis for social distinctions of the same, that are considered "private," and which individuals seek to protect from the intrusive gaze of strangers, above all, *those of the opposite sex.* That which most clearly announces one's sex, which reveals the individual as a sexual being, is considered above all else the person's "own" and the most necessary to hide from others. The need to conceal these body parts and functions tends to be greatest for women, who are traditionally regarded as "different" from the male norm, their bodies viewed as the "other."[31] Before the war, Polish Catholic women continually received reminders of the necessity of covering their bodies. Catholic writers denounced short skirts, thin material, low-cut or sleeveless blouses, skin-colored stockings, and short hair—anything that revealed or highlighted the contours or skin of the female body.[32] Immodest dressing, they cautioned, would cause females to lose respect, and could harm the health of family and nation. It was the duty of *women* to defend public and private decency.[33]

The exposure of the exiled women's most private parts to members of the opposite sex called attention not only to their nakedness and defenselessness but to their femaleness, in a carnal sense, causing both shame and anger. The severity of the insult alone, however, does not account for their strong and vocal reaction. The relative anonymity of the women in this setting appears critical in enabling them to protest. Solidarity among the women made resistance possible, for the group offered support and encouragement to find an outlet for anger, and no doubt reduced the fear of painful consequences. Though it had little tangible result, protesting at least helped to relieve some of the profound feelings of helplessness that individual women report experiencing.

The bond of nationality also played an important role, for they were targeted as a group of *Polish* females. Their protests served to oppose a further national conquest—the appropriation of their bodies. While they recognized themselves as victims of males, the men's different, antagonistic nationality mattered, for it provided for an opening to speak. A woman who protested with a hunger strike notes that the director not only failed to remedy the situation, but told them that they were no longer in Poland and had better get used to the mixed baths. Some women assert that the practice of staffing the baths with men did not bother Russian women, thus signaling the latter's perceived unnaturalness. An office worker wrote, "The male presence in the bathhouse during the women's bathing throws a suitable light on and adequately characterizes those who employ such methods."[34] Presumably, the Russian women's lack of shame "adequately characterizes" them, as well. The trauma Polish women experienced due to mixing helped to show the suffering Russians inflicted on the Polish nation, as well as to demonstrate the perceived inequality of the two societies. Mixing thus represents a transitional category—a gendered offense reflecting on its perpetrators that therefore could still be told as part of the story of the nation in exile.

Invasion

As violations of the body became more individualized and invasive, and more focused on its femaleness, women progressively internalized the breaches. This began with body searches. Arrested women were routinely and repeatedly forced to strip and endure meticulous searches of their belongings and bodies. Few women offer details about these procedures. "The searches were conducted in a vulgar manner," writes one prisoner, "offending female dignity." In a commonly vague fashion, Antonina Wawrzyńkowska notes, "The night searches tormented us immensely, as we were ordered to strip to nakedness—etc."[35]

Some women are a little more explicit, revealing to what the "etc." refers. "At night we were summoned to interrogations," explains Eugenia Pióro, "torturous searches were made, humiliating and offending female dignity (gynecological searches)."[36] Many women endured these invasive examinations, but only those probed by female agents—a rarity—offer details. In these cases male guards remained in the room.[37] Cecylia Czajkowska recalls her experience:

> [T]he nurse announced that I had to undergo a search. I didn't realize what that would be like, I thought it meant looking through my purse, pockets and overcoat, something of that sort. And then a horrible moment, the search was a medical body one. I suggested to the nurse, even begged, that she dismiss those soldiers during it, telling the nurse that I couldn't undress in front of them. I encountered loud, coarse laughter and profanities . . . I will never forget the moment of that search.[38]

Sabina Ziółkowska, noting her possessions were taken by twenty "vultures," continues describing that episode with the following staccato narration:

> But that's not the end. They see yet to the possibility that I surely could have hidden gold, or some kind of papers. Despite the fact that I am nearly naked. Another procedure. This time a woman searches. I am completely naked. She looks even in my hair, which she orders me to comb finely with her comb. With dirty hands she examines me. I do gymnastics.[39]

Men seem to have performed most of the gynecological searches. The increased humiliation this caused comes through the style used to report them: the descriptions are shorter and vaguer than those of searches performed by women. A clerk from Stanisławów states, "Searches were conducted among us every few days—conducted by men not constrained by the fact that we are women." "A Soviet officer performed the first body search," writes an instructor for a Catholic youth organization, "The search crossed the boundaries of decency. There were no women to do the search."[40] Typically the content is not discussed, no details offered, and no bodily parts or procedures named. The shame left by these ordeals seems to have precluded words.

None of the women report acts of defiance or appeals to higher authorities. Recalling the searches, the women are quiet about their reactions; though shame and disgust come through, anger does not. The fact that the women were alone during the examinations undoubtedly intensified the individual's fear of the outcome of any protest. Naked, vulnerable, subject to the probing of men with apparently unrestricted power, she had nothing to hold onto for support, from which she could speak out and offer resistance. Moreover, the affront proved more devastating, for this invasion targeted her body. The touching, the attention to sexual organs, left a mark on the woman's body and psyche that she could not discard; the victim of the body searches seems to have been branded, in her own mind, with shame and guilt.

Comparison with the statements of Polish men who underwent similar searches makes this readily apparent.[41] They were not searched by female investigators and make a point of stating that Polish women were stripped and searched by men. Male prisoners write of their body searches with disgust and with bluntness unparalleled in women's documents. Unimpeded by shame, men refer to body parts and by-products never named by women. "They meticulously searched each naked prisoner," writes one man, "making them do knee bends, looking in the mouth and even the rectum."[42] They also express anger and a desire for revenge for their humiliation.[43] Men's reactions stem not from shame at the attention to and abuse of their bodies, but their lack of control over them. They bridle at their loss of mastery.

In women's accounts of the baths, the greatest stigma fell on Soviet men for their base behavior. Not feeling any guilt, women remained able to externalize the injury and find anger; in the group setting they could even express it. The more personal and intrusive attack—the body search—entailed a shifting of responsibility for the shame. As isolated individuals, the women did not construe this invasion as an injury done to the Polish nation. Their descriptions rarely contain references to the nationality of victim or perpetrator: only women and men are involved. Furthermore, the searches not only affected the physical body, but especially damaged its social aspects. If women bear a responsibility to hide and protect the female body, to maintain its purity, then violations implicate their propriety; the female whose body is invaded is traditionally considered dishonored. Unable to completely externalize this affront, she becomes more reticent, both at the time of the offense and then in the retelling. One woman recalls her typical reaction to such a search: "I kept silent, but felt as if I had been deprived of all human dignity." Czesława Humaner responded similarly: "I didn't pay any attention at all, with lowered head, with eyes fixed onto space, I acted as if I saw nothing around me."[44] In this context, the notion of suffering for the fatherland was not invoked and national identity offered no solace.

Sexual Exploitation

Rape and forced prostitution constitute the final category of offenses. Poles' accounts of their lives in the USSR depict a world in which sex was forcibly taken or commodified with considerable frequency. Incarcerated women describe arbitrary abuses of police power. Like the searches, this sensitive issue rarely receives detailed or open discussion by those involved. Dorota Majewska notes without explanation that in prison she realized that NKVD agents could do anything they wanted to a defenseless girl. One prisoner recalls that her interrogator, suggesting he could help her out, said he had "special feelings" for her. Maria Norciszek relates that her investigator "in the most shameless manner undressed himself completely, took off his long underwear, and behaved himself like the most shameless pig."[45] In a report rare for its bluntness, Eugenia Swojda declares that her interrogator behaved "scandalously"; she had to defend herself, after he locked the door, from his desire to rape her.[46]

Female prisoners were not free from the threat of sexual abuse once they passed beyond the closed rooms of NKVD interrogators. After summary sentencing, the women were transferred to labor camps throughout the USSR. By all accounts, the camps were harsh and dangerous places, particularly for females. According to Elinor Lipper, a Dutch woman imprisoned in the Gulag, "The Soviet camp . . . is a university of crime; it has become a place of both physical and moral destruction." The criminals, she states, "raped all the women who took their fancy," and gang rape, called "falling under the trolley," was extremely common.[47] In his work on crime in Russia, Valery Chalidze notes that among the professional underworld, "the most highly valued expression of the sexual instinct seems to be rape, especially collective rape."[48]

According to Polish accounts, in some camps women were afraid to leave their barracks at night, "because men attacked them and raped them." Male criminals, the infamous *urki,* made nighttime raids on women's barracks.[49] These powerful criminals habitually played cards for other people's clothing and even lives; "when it came to women, they played for the right to rape."[50] Maria Olechnowicz, incarcerated at Pot'ma, explains this custom: "The winner is the first to commit rape, the others are bound to help him carry out the enterprise." Camp authorities, many former inmates assert, did little to prevent such behavior.[51]

In addition to attacks and coercion, many Poles write scornfully about encountering a form of sexual union involving only a degree of consensus. "The institution of 'camp husbands' is a rather curious phenomenon specific to the closed camps in the USSR," explains Janina Seudek-Malanowicz: "Men and women alike, after arriving, try to contract a concubinage for the period of stay in a given camp."[52] The term "camp husband" (*lagernyi muzh*) is common to the literature of the Soviet labor camps.[53] Also known as "protectors," these men served to improve the daily living conditions of their sexual partners by arranging lighter work, obtaining larger food rations, or providing them with food and material goods unobtainable through normal channels. They also helped ensure that their lovers fulfilled their quota at work, at least on paper. As one Pole relates, the only way a woman could fulfill the work norm was by "becoming the lover of one of the camp functionaries, which was easy to do, as they exchanged her every month or two, when they grew bored."[54]

As the name implies, these men also protected "their" women from the aggression of others. The response of one Pole to what she feared would be a proposition or attack illustrates both the ever-present threat to women and the respect accorded to other men's "property." Approached by a man whose "tiny eyes shone with animal desire," she responded resourcefully: "I do not know what inspired me to say that I was waiting for the superintendent. 'That's all right then,' he said, 'wait for your lover.' And off he went. I was truly lucky. No one acquainted with conditions in the camp would be surprised at my horror." Albertyna Korzeniowska learned of this prevailing "order" from a Russian man who approached her soon after her arrival. "He is grinning and laughing, witty," she recalls, "He tries to explain to me that the position of a woman in a labor camp without a man is very difficult, that he likes me very much, that he is looking for a lady friend." Barbara Szumska relates a similar experience in the camp Vorkuta: "I remember it was in June 1941 . . . some chief engineer-agronomist, a Georgian. He liked my braids, he told me that with defiant frankness, and then proposed transferring me to a better position. They always start that way. I did not agree."[55]

The threat and reality of sexual violation was also a fact of life outside the Gulag. The testimonies of female deportees include incidents paralleling those recounted of the camps, be it abuses of police power, individual and gang attacks, or forced prostitution. Though Poles in "free exile" did not face regular interrogations by the secret police, NKVD agents summoned individuals at will. In some cases their intentions may have been sexual exploitation. Olga Słabowa, deported to Kazakhstan, reports being called to the office of the factory where she worked. There a well-dressed man suggested he could improve her position. "He was an official of the NKVD," she writes, "who offered me his companionship—with the goal of taking me to the barracks." Another young woman describes being taken by an NKVD agent to a dark office. After making sure the building was empty, he assured her that if she got on well with him she would have everything, and he would not submit a complaint against her to his chief.[56] Separated from male family members and little valued by the Soviet government, the women were generally defenseless, if not before the predatory intentions of such men of authority, then before their capacity for revenge.[57]

Women in "free exile" write about pressure for sex from men who commanded their work brigades, directed their schools, issued ration cards, and ran the local administration. Jadwiga Jeleniewrza states that her brigade leader often recorded a lower work output (which determined food rations) than its members actually achieved: "Often the reason for this was the refusal of women-Poles to submit to the brigade leader." A homemaker deported to Kazakhstan writes that "from the side of the members of the administration there were disgusting propositions, even rapes."[58] Deportees also feared drunken males in their settlements. One woman reports several visits her first night in a settlement from inebriated peasants who "wanted to make her acquaintance," which, she learned, meant simply, "I want to spend the night with you."[59] Relocation for temporary job assignments, like tractor crews and haycutting brigades, involved considerable anguish, for the young women shared tents with local males. Some of them report that fear kept them awake all night. Stating simply that these men behaved "very unpleasantly," one deportee writes, "Every night that my sister did not return home was a torture of anxiety for us."[60]

Women in settlements and collective farms in Central Asia report abductions of young girls and the "buying" of wives, perversions of marriage that they describe in the same tone as their incarcerated counterparts discuss "camp marriages." "Frequent cases occurred in the village of wives being bought for a certain amount of provisions," writes a woman who was told that she "could get a lot" for her friend. Most of the young woman's testimony details the terror evoked by local men. She and her sister, alone in exile, allied with two older women "for defense against the attacks of the Kirghiz and the Uzbeks, who in all sorts of ways, by rape and bribery, desired to take advantage of the misery of two hungry girls." The man who controlled bread rationing wanted to "marry" her fourteen-year-old sister, a proposition prompting them to flee the region.[61]

While sexual harassment and the danger of rape were ever-present aspects of their lives in exile, the oblique way the women choose to discuss the issue renders it impossible to estimate the number of women raped.[62] The Poles broach the topic of sexual abuse in such a manner that one cannot escape the suspicion that far fewer women were willing to vocalize the matter than experienced it. The women's writing reveals much about the sexual and moral norms to which they adhered and which formed an important part of their identities.

Discussions of "camp husbands" typically include assertions that while such alliances commonly occurred, Polish women did not avail themselves of the men's costly assistance. In spite of the difficult life in the camp, writes Stanisława Widoła, "No one benefited from any kind of relief, which would have been the result of the favor of the commandant of the settlement and for which one would have had to give up the honor of a Pole or the reputation of a woman."[63] According to their testimonies, Polish women excluded themselves from such arrangements.

Similarly, most references to sexual violence take the form of general statements that such things occurred, or tales of third parties. Irena Czekalowska notes vaguely that at her settlement, "there were even such cases where Polish girls were attacked with force." As a rule, the names of victims do not appear. Polish women working in the local sawmill, a deportee relates, "were constantly exposed to verbal assaults and even rapes from Soviet bandits—*urki.*" Writing about attacks by local men out on the steppe, a young woman recalls, "There were several such incidents, which ended with the girls being killed. I prayed then."[64]

Those who relate such information keep themselves at a distance; it apparently happens only to others. This phenomenon occurs frequently in relation to the subject of widespread rape. In a study of Southern women during General Sherman's march to the sea in the American Civil War, Jane Schultz concludes: "Rape became for them an unspeakable crime—never named but referred to in oblique language as something that happened to other women."[65] Recently, investigators seeking to uncover the story of mass rape in Bosnia-Hercegovina in the 1990s initially found that though everyone knew of someone who had been raped, they met no one who identified herself as a victim. "If they do come forward they try to remain anonymous and avoid being labeled as rape victims," reports a psychiatrist working with these women; "they usually begin by speaking about themselves in the third person (that is, they say that someone else has been raped)."[66] Polish women, too, speak of rape in the third person.

Though some women do describe their own threatening encounters with Soviet men, not one rape victim appears among them. Even the most detailed accounts of coercion and intimidation drop away in the middle of the story, or note the woman's escape, so that none of the authors, it seems, is actually raped. The woman taken at night to the deserted NKVD office managed to run from the building; others fled their localities, illegally, to elude men who continually pressured them for sex.[67]

The most explicit and evocative account of a Soviet man's attempt to force a Polish woman to have sexual relations with him comes from Sabina Ziółkowska. After her arrest for trying to cross the Polish-Romanian border, a male NKVD agent searched her. "One after another he orders me precisely to remove pieces of my clothing," she writes:

> I tremble, he also trembles, I from fear and disgust, he? I still don't know. He starts to speak on *ty* [familiar terms]. See what I'll do for you? I'll write a nice protocol, at 4:00 in the morning there is a train to Białystok. You'll go on it, I'll take you to the station myself. Just stay with me till 4:00 AM, for this one night. In prison there are lice, you won't go there. You'll stay with me. He extends shaking hands for me, or rather at me. How disgusting. Should I scream or beg? Remain silent or persuade? I speak nervously. I think, after all I am alone with him. I tell him—you have your own friends, your own women, what do you want with me? He puts on a record—some pretty, suggestive tango. Why does he put a record on, maybe he thinks that music will put me in the mood, or maybe he thinks that I will scream and he wants thus to cover my cry? Again he speaks, again he trembles. Don't be scared, you won't get pregnant. He takes a bottle of vodka out of the cupboard. I calmly try to persuade again. He understood me, but sent me to prison.[68]

The grammatical tense and pace of her account abruptly change as she endeavors to get out of the situation. She is much less explicit in describing how the episode came to a close. Was something painful omitted between her entreaty and her exit? Ziółkowska suggests that she succeeded in talking her way out of the situation, but she may instead be demonstrating the boundaries of the speakable.

The language used to describe the encounters is telling. Rather than directly stating what happened, the women employ euphemisms and ellipses to express the men's most objectionable behavior, the most distressing moments for themselves. The men "have special feelings" or offer "companionship." They simply behave "shamelessly" or "scandalously."[69] The sexual content of their intentions and behavior remains veiled, and references to the body minimized, if not altogether avoided. For this reason Ziółkowska's description, including the man's trembling and the acknowledgment of the possibility of pregnancy, is highly unusual. Even the verbs "abduct," "attack," and "rape" tend to be used only in abstract comments. For the exiled women, any attention to the femaleness of their bodies, to their sexuality, offends their identity as "proper" women, and becomes unspeakable.[70]

Women also commonly leave gaps in the narrative, so that the ending remains uncertain. It is not clear if the woman was raped. Without explaining what occurred after her investigator removed his clothing, Norciszek states that the interrogation concluded with a beating by another agent. Korzeniowska does not relate what happened with the man who insinuated that he wanted her as his "camp wife."[71] Either the women assert that they refused or escaped, or they fall silent on the outcome of the threatening encounter, gliding past it to other topics.

The report of Zofia Jernsiówna stands out for its focused and detailed expression of emotional trauma connected with sexual coercion. She depicts an incident in Siberia, in which a young deportee faces the choice of having sex with the son of the collective farm chairman, in order to have her desperately ill brother transported to a hospital, or helplessly watching him die. The document also stands out for the distance between its author and the wrenching experience it describes, and thus provides a clear example of how the exiled women deal with the issue of sexual abuse. Jernsiówna's entire documentation of her exile is devoted to the two days surrounding this decision. She depicts the episode vividly and emotionally, but in the third person, with no introduction or explanation of the characters, as if it is about other, unnamed people. It is hard not to assume that the experience is Jernsiówna's own.

Here is her retelling of the proposition made by the chairman's son: "He knows that she has to send her brother to the hospital, knows that she didn't get a horse, he can still save the boy, he can get a horse, but not for free—for a terrible price, the price of her." Given one night to consider, the protagonist sees the decision as one between sacrificing her brother or herself. "To sacrifice the life of the one who, after the death of Mother was the closest person to her, without whom she could not imagine her existence. To sacrifice her honor, and maybe her entire life and future for him." Willing to make that ultimate self-sacrifice, she delivers her brother to the young man so he can take him to the hospital, and then goes to work. She returns home later in great distress, "knowing that disgrace and shame await her." There is no nobility or exoneration for her in this act of caring and sacrifice, only shame, which apparently adheres to the woman, and not the man exacting such a high price. The author avoids the language of the nation and does not cast this sacrifice as one made on the "altar of the Fatherland," which would have granted the protagonist heroic status as a patriot. Instead, she is promised only the shame of a fallen woman. The episode ends similarly to those discussed above. When the man comes to her place to collect his "payment," she continually evades his touch, then begs and pleads with him to leave her alone. By what she terms a "miracle," he understands and leaves. She credits her savior as *Matka Boska*, the Holy Virgin.[72] Perhaps the story could not have been told with a different ending.

Given the widespread violence and sexual coercion, it is hard to believe that none of these women was actually overpowered and raped. These women may in fact be the lucky ones, who managed to escape being raped or selling their bodies. Alternatively, they may have left the most painful facts out of their accounts. These women might have changed the ending to create a memory with which they could comfortably live. "'Remembering' or 'not remembering,'" historian Klaus Theweleit points out, "simply means making decisions about the reality to be produced."[73] This latter possibility cannot be underestimated, for the stigma of rape and prostitution may well have compelled women to censor their narratives. Furthermore, while expressing shame and humiliation, Polish women do not, however, speak of such feelings as anger, hatred, grief, or desire for revenge. Nor do they employ the language of the nation, which would cast the abuse as an injury done to the Polish collective and allow open expression. Instead, in cases involving sexual coercion, the women isolate themselves and internalize the offense. Their Polishness means nothing when they are violated as women; neither does the nationality of the man seem relevant. The incident appears to reflect on the victim, not the perpetrator.

To understand what was at stake for these women, we can return to Jernsiówna's account. Her narrative highlights the supreme importance to Polish women of their sexual honor, which precludes sexual relations for any purpose other than procreation within wedlock. She equates the physical death of the male (the brother) with the implicit moral death of the female. And the moral death results from socially illicit sex—even though coerced. The "price of her" is not literally her life, it is her chastity. The identity of the "proper" woman is thus distilled to her sexual honor, which provides a woman with self-esteem and standing in society. As in other cultures in which rape is treated as a crime against honor, the raped woman is seen as dishonorable.[74]

Valuing a woman's "honor"—her sexual propriety—over her very life has occurred in various societies and across time. Anastasia Pavlova, a Bulgarian, related her ordeal at the hands of Greek soldiers during the Balkan Wars of 1912–1913. Herself badly beaten and raped, she detailed her efforts to prevent her daughter's rape, stating, "My one consolation is that I saved her honor."[75] Studying the mass rape of German women by Soviet soldiers in the aftermath of World War II, Norman Naimark uncovered suicides in response to the threat of rape and humiliation. One document Naimark cites describes the actions of a professor who "killed his wife and daughters and then himself not to have to bear the anguish [of their rape]."[76] This notion is not a relic of the past. Interviewers report that in the recent war in the former Yugoslavia, many Bosnian women stated, "I would prefer to be killed than raped."[77] While this reaction may appear to individuals in some cultures to be so normal as to escape attention, it is a profoundly revealing description of the social identity frequently ascribed to—and internalized by—females. It tells the woman that her sexual honor (which in all too many cases she is powerless to control) determines her own and her family's social standing, and ultimately the value of her life.

The only first-hand reports of rape I have found in the archival collections are not in the testimonies and memoirs, but in two personal letters sent by women who had no hope of rejoining their families and nation. Both letters were written by women stranded in Kazakhstan to their husbands in the Polish army. In the first, the wife of an officer writes: "I was the mistress of thirty herdsmen. I could no longer endure this, so I married the thirty-first herdsman. Now I carry the child of this herdsman in my womb. Life is terribly difficult.

I beg you to forget about me forever." The second letter states: "My life here is hell, but I have not had the courage to kill myself. . . . One day some herdsmen, more than a dozen, one after the other took advantage of me. As one of them showed a desire to keep me close to him I preferred that. I serve him as a wife. I carry a child in my womb . . . I beg you, forget me forever, remake your life."[78]

Given the reticence of Polish women to discuss the issue of rape, it seems that only the desperateness of the situation and the intimacy of the relationship to the addressee made these admissions possible. These women have resigned themselves to their fate; they have no prospect of rejoining Polish society—no need, therefore, to conceal what happened to them. Critically, the assumed audience of the letters were spouses, not the government or any wider public, as was the case for the authors of the testimonies. These women make no attempt to gain anything—sympathy, assistance, revenge—from the status of rape victim. On the contrary, they appear so debased that they see it as cause for the obliteration of the former self. In both letters the woman considers herself defiled by her lot; instead of identifying herself as a blameless victim of a crime, deserving of aid and compassion, she seems to accept guilt and ostracism. Unable to avoid the reality of rape, these women essentially ask, in their very personal entreaties, that they be erased from the past and the consciousness of those with whom they shared it.

The shame resulting from illicit sex and the strength of the taboo against sexual activity outside of marriage are underscored by the way these women depict their plight. They avoid the word "rape" and do not state that they are continually abused or forced to live with a perpetrator. Instead, they redraw the lines of the new situation, so that they serve as "wife" of the man, not his rape victim. Obliterating their past lives but drawing on them to make sense of their predicament, they cast their new status in terms with which they can live. The status of wife and mother, though out of compulsion, replaces the intolerable label of rape victim.

The women disclosing that they had been raped write while trapped in the consequences of the events described. In contrast, those women recording their experiences after evacuation from the USSR write from the memory they constructed, in the hope of reintegration into their society. Some women may have changed the endings to their stories about sexual violation because they could not face the consequences the admission of rape would have for their social standing among compatriots. For them, the shame associated with rape could be left behind—at least publicly. Rather than recount actual incidents of rape or fill in the blanks of their vague descriptions, they can be silent and avoid that reality. Similarly, the paramount value placed on one's overlapping "honor as a Pole" and "reputation as a woman" may have barred those women who submitted either to dire need or physical threats from admitting that they had a camp husband. Such silences enable them to remain innocent Polish women, unstained by the stigma of rape, with their sexual honor intact.

Polish men frequently echo their female compatriots' self-depiction, emphasizing Polish women's virtue and heroism. Piotr Cichocki describes the situation of the women of various nationalities in his camp: "These women were used in many ways by the managers of different work divisions. One of the Polish women (I forgot her name) did not want to submit herself to the *prorabovi* who divided work into brigades, so she was kept in the *kartser* for seven days, with only 300 grams of bread and 3/4 liter of thin soup once a day." According to a male deportee, "None of the girls would have anything to do with Soviets . . . our girls didn't talk to the collective farm men."[79]

One can only wonder about the accuracy of such assertions. Descriptions of Soviet penal institutions by some Polish men suggest that many Polish women did not manage to maintain their "virtue" while confined there. Male prisoners recall overhearing the rapes of Polish women through the walls during interrogations.[80] The male author of a report written for the intelligence section of the Polish army states: "Generally speaking, however, a woman in the camps for the most part very easily and quickly succumbs to forced prostitution. The question of food plays a large role here."[81] Another man imprisoned in the Gulag, in a rare discussion of the sexual lives of Polish females there, states:

> The lot of women in the work camps was horrible. I can say that it was worse than that of animals. They were treated like "goods" to be used, traded for a piece of bread. If one didn't want to have a "protector"—a so-called camp husband—then she was ill-treated, her life made disgusting, so that we really must give the greatest credit to those not numerous Polish women who came through the hell clean.[82]

The picture this man paints challenges the self-representation of the Polish women. At the same time, it confirms the culturally accepted notion of dishonor. Those women who succumbed, out of grim necessity or force, to the Soviet "hell," became dirty, their bodies and social identities stigmatized. This man's characterization of the plight of women in the camps makes it clear why the women themselves would choose, even *had* to choose, to remain silent. Apparently, to use the words of a woman who works with rape victims, "there was no discourse available to them in which the women could have revealed their experiences while preserving their dignity."[83] They not only felt that others would see them as defiled but believed that of themselves. The experiences of rape victims or camps wives contradicted their identities as proper Polish women.

The women's documents suggest that collectively and individually they were not able to make a "conscious separation of the feminine body and the sense of self," which would have enabled them to demystify the notion of defilement and reject the burden of shame.[84] The female body, wrapped in traditional taboos, stayed at the core of their sense of self, their sexuality a source of guilt and shame. Unable to separate their sexual honor from their identity, these Polish women consequently did not find a voice that would have enabled them to talk openly of all they suffered at the hands of Soviet males.[85] In cases of sexual exploitation, even their national identity was overridden by their sexual one.

Any victimization by Polish men was doubly silenced. If traumatized by rape or forced prostitution, women felt compelled to remain silent. For them, the story of the nation in exile had no space for such suffering.

Conclusion

Once taken from their homes in eastern Poland, the exiled women faced conditions and treatment ranging from uncomfortable to lethal. Some of the hardships and violence they endured can be called generic, as they did not concern the sex of the individual. Such afflictions as hunger and disease, or beatings, were shared by male and female Poles, who interpreted them according to a similar framework. Drawing on past experiences of their nation under Russian domination, Poles cast their agony in both historical and religious terms that rendered it explainable and bearable. When describing their physical suffering, individuals of both sexes expressed their connection to a common national history, which helped shape a sustaining identity. Poles tended to see themselves as part of one family, engulfed in the historic struggle of their nation. "The road to Siberia was difficult and it seemed that it might be without return," writes one woman, "we were tracing the steps of our forefathers, who also were heroes exiled to Siberia for the cause of Poland."[86] Women too considered themselves martyrs for Poland. Dorota Majewska recalls the moment the NKVD arrived at her home: "I endured the arrest calmly. Mama didn't cry either. It was as if she turned into stone. She said only, 'Yet another flame on the altar of the Fatherland.' "[87] Describing the calamity of the Poles, one woman employs a common metaphor: "We traveled a real Golgotha."[88]

The nation provided women a space and a language for expressing "generic" physical suffering. Importantly, none of this pain called attention to their female bodies. Women located the reason for their starvation or beatings in their Polishness—which only intensified their sense of national identity—and could talk about these trials as the story of the victimized Polish nation. Other forms of indignity and violence, however, contradicted their identities as Poles: gendered offenses, which targeted them precisely as women, did not seem to fit into the tragedy of the nation.

Polish cultural norms of proper womanhood required detachment from the body and silence on its particular needs and agonies. Life in exile rendered this difficult: mixed living conditions and bathing facilities turned the spotlight on their femaleness. Women could recall these uncomfortable scenes because they befell them as part of a group and left their individual bodies untouched. In such cases they could still cast the indignity as an injury done to the Polish collective, and one that reflected on the base nature of their national enemy. The shame they expressed about mixing confirmed their identities as modest Polish females.

The more individualized and invasive offenses isolated women from the collective. In other words, the nation lost its relevance to the women the more they suffered as females. Those who endured the transgressions of gynecological searches and sexual coercion progressively internalized the offenses. Cultural norms regarding the female body intensified the injuries, so that what was done to a female by others tainted her body and compromised her identity as a woman. She became stigmatized, even in her own mind, by the acts of others upon her body. Feeling herself dishonored, she could no longer speak of the offense as a crime of the enemy. If she revealed herself to be a victim of rape, the transgression would be attached to her, more than to the perpetrator, damaging both her self-esteem and her social standing.

Describing their travails in the USSR, it was clearly easier for women to say "he beat me," or "he made me starve," than "he raped me." The former statements include a conviction that "he did this to me as a Pole," which gives a group allegiance that both upholds the individual and provides the room and language for voicing outrage. Sexual violation, however, contains a more secreted knowledge that "he did this to me as a woman," an identity that, on its own—deprived of the shoring up effect of national identity—apparently did not extend to the victims a sense of support and legitimate outrage. While Soviet men could be presented as uncivilized brutes who did not respect the norms regarding sexual difference, the fact that they raped women could be told only in the abstract. Women could only publicly present the story as a crime of Soviet men when it was (seemingly) about other, unnamed victims.

If we consider how damaging rape typically appears to the victim or potential victim, so much that she might choose death as her only recourse, then the silencing of the violation can be seen as the solution to that dilemma. At a time of extreme chaos, involving total dislocation, uprooting from all the mainstays of "home," she needed those identities that were imbued with honor and esteem, that assured her place in a society she knew and longed for, and that gave her a sense of difference and superiority from the individuals and the nation seeking to degrade her.

Since the wounding of the body occurred as a result of the women's displacement at the hands of a national enemy, it helped—in the cases of "generic" bodily hardships and mixing—to mobilize their outrage and their resistance as a *nation*. But the more personal and invasive the attack on female bodies, the less this seemed possible. Ultimately, the concept of the nation proved so masculinized that it had no room for women to talk about specifically female suffering. Women could appeal to the fatherland for understanding and expressing their pain only when it fell into masculine categories of suffering. Their objections to mixing in the transports and the baths, to the searches, and to the sexual abuse, contain no articulation of their position vis-à-vis men in general. They equate the pain that they are able to discuss solely with Soviet domination, marginalizing their experiences as females apart from the "Polish" qualifier. The women's statements suggest that all that is needed to alleviate their suffering is a return to home, to Poland. Any struggles that they faced there as women, at the hands of Polish men, were even less permissible in the story of the nation.

Notes

Some of this material is from *Exile and Identity: Polish Women in the Soviet Union during World War II*, by Katherine R. Jolluck, © 2002 by University of Pittsburgh Press. Reprinted by permission of the University of Pittsburgh Press.

1. English-language discussion of women's roles in Polish national struggles includes Rudolf Jaworski and Bianka Pietrow-Ennker, *Women in Polish Society* (Boulder, Colo.: East European Monographs, 1992); Robert Ponichtera, "Feminists, Nationalists, and Soldiers: Women in the Fight for Polish Independence," *International History Review* 19, no. 1 (1997): 16–31. For Mickiewicz's poem "To a Polish Mother," see *Konrad Wallenrod and Other Writings of Adam Mickiewicz* (Westport, Conn.: Greenwood Press, 1975), 128–29.

2. For the best expression of this idea: Adam Mickiewicz, *Księgi narodu polskiego i pielgrzymstwa polskiego* (Cracow: n.p., 1922).

3. Initial calculations of the total number of deportees by the wartime Polish government, and subsequently émigré historians, reached nearly one million. Citing documents from recently opened Soviet archives, some historians now suggest a range of 315,000 to 380,000. The revised data have prompted debate among historians, some of whom find the new figures unreliable and incomplete. For early estimates: Bronisław Kuśnierz, *Stalin and the Poles* (London: Hollis & Carter, 1949), 80; Władysław Wielhorski, *Los Polaków w niewoli sowieckiej, 1939–1956* (London: Rada Ziem Wschodnich R. P., 1956), 11–15. For revised estimates: Aleksander Gurjanow, "Cztery deportacje 1940–41," *Karta* 12 (1994): 114–36; Albin Głowacki, "Widmo Berii w statystyce," *Polityka* 6 (5 February 1994). Challenging the revised figures: "Sprawozdanie z dyskusji dotyczącej liczby obywateli polskich wywiezionych do Związku Sowieckiego w latach 1939–1941," *Studia z dziejów Rosji i Europy Środkowo-Wschodniej* 31 (1996): 117–48; Małgorzata Giżejewska, "Deportacje obywateli polskich z ziem północno-wschodnich II Rzeczypospolitej w latach 1939–1941," in Tomasz Strzembosz, ed., *Studia z dziejów okupacją Sowiecką* (Warsaw: Biblioteka Ziem Wschodnich, 1997), 85–103.

4. See, for example, Hoover Institution Archives, Władysław Anders Collection 1939–1946 (hereafter AC)/box 38/vol. 5/no. 5637 (subsequent references to this collection will include box/volume/number); AC/45/13/14214; AC/52/31/R6081.

5. Many scholars consider 8 to 10 percent a reasonable estimate of the death rate among the deportees before the amnesty. See Grzegorz Hryciuk, "Deportacje ludności Polskiej," in Stanisław Ciesielski et al., eds. *Masowe deportacje radzieckie w okresie II wojny światowej* (Wrocław: Instytut Historyczny Uniwersytetu Wrocławskiego, 1994), 61; Andrzej Paczkowski, "Poland, the 'Enemy Nation,'" in Stéphane Courtois et al., eds., *The Black Book of Communism: Crimes, Terror, Repression*, trans. Jonathan Murphy and Mark Kramer (Cambridge, Mass: Harvard University Press, 1999), 372. The overall death rate in the Gulag was 6.7 percent in 1941, shooting up to 17.6 percent in 1942. V. N. Zemskov, "GULAG (Istoriko-sotsiologicheskii aspekt)," *Sotsiologicheskie issledovaniia* 6 (1991): 14–15.

6. The majority of these documents are housed in the Hoover Institution Archives, in the Władysław Anders Collection; Records of the Polish Embassy in the Soviet Union (hereafter AMB); and Records of the Polish Ministry of Information and Documenta-

tion (hereafter MID). Subsequent references to AMB and MID will begin with box/folder.

7. AC/36/2/1554.

8. AC/43/10/11896; AC/43/11/12173.

9. AC/48/20/R1568.

10. AC/48/20/R1583.

11. See AC/53/34/R7094; AC/39/6/7628; AC/38/5/6281.

12. AC/41/8/10685.

13. AC/36/2/1969; AC/36/2/1948; AC/42/9/11190; AC/40/7/8995.

14. AC/38/5/6082; AC/44/13/14008.

15. AC/40/7/9590; AC/36/3/2208; AC/44/13/14005.

16. AC/36/2/1561; AC/45/13/14189.

17. AC/41/8/10059.

18. AC/41/8/10052.

19. AC/39/5/7348; AC/43/10/11711.

20. AC/50/25/R3589.

21. AC/39/5/7109.

22. AC/42/10/11377.

23. AC/42/10/11330; AC/41/8/9966.

24. AC/35/1/482.

25. AC/41/8/10623; MID/91/12, Besiadowska.

26. AC/41/8/10691.

27. See AC/38/5/6102; AC/55/39/R8585.

28. MID/91/12, Besiadowska; AC/42/9/10754.

29. AC/43/10/11686; AC/41/8/10623; AC/42/10/11677.

30. Gérard Vincent, "A History of Secrets?" in Antoine Prost and Gérard Vincent, eds., *A History of Private Life*, vol. 5, *Riddles of Identity in Modern Times*, trans. Arthur Goldhammer (Cambridge, Mass.: Belknap Press, 1991), 171.

31. The isolation of the female body from the traditional undefined body occurred as part of the creation of the modern body, beginning in the late eighteenth century. See Barbara Duden, *The Woman Beneath the Skin: A Doctor's Patients in Eighteenth-Century Germany*, trans. Thomas Dunlap (Cambridge, Mass.: Harvard University Press, 1991), 17–41.

32. The most popular journal in Poland, the Catholic monthly *Rycerz Niepokolanej*, devoted much attention to this issue: "Biskupi przeciw dekoltom," *Rycerz Niepokalanej* 5, no. 9 (1926): 275; "Krótkie sukienki i tańce powodem gruźlicy," *Rycerz Niepokalanej* 7, no. 3 (1928): 78; J., "Ważne słowa lekarzy," *Rycerz Niepokalanej* 6, no. 10 (1927): 308.

33. A. K., "Przykre, ale konieczne . . . ," *Rycerz Niepokalanej* 7, no. 10 (1928): 294; "Rezolucje diecezjalnego Kongresu Eucharystycznego w Łódzi," *Rycerz Niepokalanej* 7, no. 9 (1928): 259.

34. AC/41/9/10722.

35. AC/48/21/R1980; AC/53/32/R6336.

36. AMB/33/A, Eugenia Pióro.

37. AC/39/5/7109; AC/42/10/11638. Polish men also note the search of women by males. See AC/36/2/2126. It is unclear if this practice represented a deliberate attempt to humiliate Polish women. Contrary to Polish accounts, other women report that only female guards searched females. Elinor Lipper, *Eleven Years in Soviet Prison Camps* (Chicago: Henry Regnery, 1951), 6, 205; Margarete Buber-Neumann, *Under Two Dictators* (New York: Dodd, Mead & Co., 1949), 27.

38. AC/40/7/9590.

39. AC/41/8/10691.

40. AC/38/5/6335; AC/53/32/R6337.

41. AC/36/2/2126; AC/41/8/10687.

42. AC/35/1/835; also AC/41/8/10172. One man recalls being "startled and embarrassed" by an anal inspection. Janusz Bardach and Kathleen Gleeson, *Man is Wolf to Man: Surviving the Gulag* (Berkeley: University of California Press, 1999), 198.

43. AC/64/66/R15704; AC/66/71/16068.

44. MID/91/12, Besiadowska; AC/42/9/10756.

45. AC/43/10/11942; AC/41/8/10623; AC/41/8/10059.

46. AC/53/34/R7094.

47. Lipper, *Eleven Years,* 150, 95, 157.

48. Valery Chalidze, *Criminal Russia: Essays on Crime in the Soviet Union,* trans. P. S. Falla (New York: Random House, 1977), 64. Also, Robert Conquest, *The Great Terror: A Reassessment* (New York: Oxford University Press, 1990), 315; Aleksandr Solzhenitsyn, *Arkhipelag Gulag 1918–1956,* 2 vols. (Moscow: Sovetskii Pisatel'-Novyi Mir, 1989), 2:214.

49. AC/44/12/12598; AC/36/2/1610; AC/44/13/13971.

50. AC/44/13/13971.

51. AC/38/5/6111. Chalidze confirms this point. Chalidze, *Criminal Russia,* 70.

52. AC/44/12/12598.

53. Solzhenitsyn, *Arkhipelag Gulag,* 2:208–14; Buber-Neumann, *Under Two Dictators,* 69, 82; Lipper, *Eleven Years,* 118–19, 159–61; Zoe Zajdlerowa, *The Dark Side of the Moon* (London: Faber and Faber, 1946), 155; Hilda Vitzthum, *Torn Out by the Roots: The Recollections of a Former Communist* (Lincoln: University of Nebraska Press, 1993), 134.

54. AC/43/10/11698.

55. MID/91/12, Besiadowska; AC/42/10/11658; AC/43/10/11698.

56. AC/38/5/6103; AC/48/20/R1617.

57. One woman writes that when she went to the police after local Kazakhs raided her hut, she was arrested for making a false report. AMB/33/A, Janina Dukjetowa.

58. AC/41/8/9966; AC/53/34/R7104.

59. MID/91/12, Besiadowska; also AC/40/6/8413.

60. MID/198/8, Halpern; also AC/48/20/R1898.

61. MID/91/12, Besiadowska; AC/43/10/11941. For "marriage by abduction": Gregory Massell, *The Surrogate Proletariat: Moslem Women and Revolutionary Strategies in Soviet Central Asia, 1919–1929* (Princeton: Princeton University Press, 1974), 114. For the subjection of Polish women to this practice: Stanisław Ciesielski, *Polacy w Kazachstanie w latach 1940–1946* (Wrocław: Wydawnictwo Uniwersytetu Wrocławskiego, 1996), 273–74.

62. This holds true for the incidence of rape in the USSR, in general, as the Soviet government ceased publishing criminal statistics in 1928. Chalidze, *Criminal Russia,* 198.

63. AC/39/5/7365. Similar reports come from earlier occupations. Sophie Nowosielski stresses that during World War I, as a Polish woman, she rejected all advances and courtesies from German and Russian officers; patriotism and honor rendered flirting with the enemy inconceivable. Nowosielski, *In the Hurricane of War: Memoirs of a Woman Soldier* (N.p.: The Author, 1929), 37, 40, 44.

64. AC/48/21/R1914; AC/44/13/13971; AC/43/10/11940.

65. Jane Schultz, "Mute Fury: Southern Women's Diaries of Sherman's March to the Sea, 1864–1865," in Helen Cooper et al., eds., *Arms and the Woman: War, Gender and Literary Representation* (Chapel Hill: University of North Carolina Press, 1989), 60.

66. Vera Folnegovic-Smalc, "Psychiatric Aspects of the Rapes in the War against the Republics of Croatia and Bosnia-Herzegovina," in Alexandra Stiglmayer, ed., *Mass Rape: The War against Women in Bosnia-Herzegovina* (Lincoln: University of Nebraska Press, 1994), 176.

67. AC/48/20/R1617; AC/42/10/11637.

68. AC/41/8/10691.

69. AC/43/10/11898; AC/38/5/6310; AC/48/20/R1898.

70. The authors of the testimonies are reticent to discuss topics connected with the female body. They avoid the issue of menstruation; I have found only two references to it in the women's statements—one of which is oblique and purely incidental. See AC/41/8/10691; MID/91/12, Besiadowska. Nor do they express any anxiety connected with amenorrhea, which likely accompanied their near-starvation. The issues of unwanted pregnancy and abortion do not appear in the documents.

71. AC/41/8/10059; AC/42/10/11658.

72. AC/43/10/11705.

73. Klaus Theweleit, "The Bomb's Womb and the Genders of War (War Goes on Preventing Women from Becoming the Mothers of Invention)," in Miriam Cooke and Angela Woollacott, eds., *Gendering War Talk* (Princeton: Princeton University Press, 1993), 308.

74. See discussion in Rhonda Copelon, "Surfacing Gender: Reconceptualizing Crimes against Women in Time of War," in Stiglmayer, *Mass Rape*, 200.

75. Appendix C, Document No. 43, in *The Other Balkan Wars: A 1913 Carnegie Endowment Inquiry in Retrospect* (New York: Carnegie Endowment for International Peace, 1993), 304–305.

76. Norman Naimark, *The Russians in Germany: A History of the Soviet Zone of Occupation, 1945–1949* (Cambridge, Mass: Harvard University Press, 1995), 86, 81.

77. Slavenka Drakulic, "Women Hide Behind a Wall of Silence: Mass Rape in Bosnia," *The Nation* 256, no. 8 (1993): 271.

78. MID/91/5, L.dz.1036/Tj.41, Defense Minister Sosnkowski to Minister Professor Stronski, 4 April 1941; U.S. Department of State, Records of the Department of State, Reel 73, 860c.48/710, item 193. The letters, reproduced in Polish government reports, and the issue of the rape of Polish women in Soviet Central Asia, captured the attention of the highest Polish authorities, who recognized their propaganda value. Using condescending terms to denote the peoples of Central Asia—Mongols, Asiatics, and nomads—government documents stress the victimization of Polish women, hence the Polish nation, at the hands of savages. The message to the British and Americans, who considered the USSR an ally: the Soviets are delivering our women to the wild "Asiatics" who rape; the representative of culture and civilization is at the complete mercy of barbarians. Men use the incidents as a clarion call for sympathy, outrage, and action on the part of Polish soldiers and foreign opinion. The masculinized concept of the nation has space for women's violation when told in this symbolic way. See MID/2/6, Zdisław Łecki, "Działalność Związku Sowieckiego na terenie okupowanych ziem Polski od dnia agresji 17.9.39 do lipca 1941," 57; MID/91/3, N4/2B, "Polacy na Syberii."

79. AC/37/3/2555; AC/35/1/482.

80. AC/36/2/1393; AC/44/12/12583; AC/45/15/15051.

81. MID/98/6, Prof. Świaniewicz, "Więziennictwo Sowieckie," 16. Reproduced under the name Ernst Tallgren in David Dallin and Boris Nicolaevsky, *Forced Labor in Soviet Russia* (New Haven: Yale University Press, 1947), 17. Translation mine.

82. AC/52/29/R5337.

83. Ruth Seifert, "War and Rape: A Preliminary Analysis," in Stiglmayer, *Mass Rape,* 68.

84. Annemarie Tröger, "Between Rape and Prostitution: Survival Strategies and Chances of Emancipation for Berlin Women after World War II," in Judith Friedlander et al., eds., *Women in Culture and Politics: A Century of Change* (Bloomington: Indiana University Press, 1986), 111.

85. This idea comes from Margaret Miles, who writes that adequate self-representation requires two conditions: public space and collective voice. Margaret Miles, *Carnal Knowing: Female Nakedness and Religious Meaning in the Christian West* (Boston: Beacon Press, 1989), 84.

86. AC/53/34/R7148.

87. AC/43/10/11942.

88. AC/52/31/R6091.

11 "The Alienated Body": Gender Identity and the Memory of the Siege of Leningrad

Lisa A. Kirschenbaum

Leningrad during World War II, a "city front" where it was possible to travel to the front lines by urban tram, constitutes a particularly rich site for an examination of gender identity during wartime. Not only did the war disrupt traditional gender roles; in the besieged, starving city, bodies lost the visible signs of sex differences. Blockaded for almost three years, subject to German bombing and artillery fire as well as brutal cold and starvation in the winter of 1941–1942, Leningrad was a place where the "distinct bodily experiences of trenches and home front" existed side by side. In Leningrad, both men and women experienced not only the "hunger, overwork, illness and immiserisation" associated with the female home front but also the "dismemberment and death" usually reserved for male soldiers at the front.[1]

The effects of starvation further blurred the border between male and female. With much of its adult male population in the army or evacuated with the war industry, Leningrad became predominately a city of women, children, and old people. It also became, as survivor Lidiia Ginzburg has emphasized, a city where the most mundane and denigrated of "women's work"—finding and preparing food—became the central preoccupation of all inhabitants, male and female.[2] In November 1941, the daily bread ration for dependents and children fell to a low of 125 grams, and even after the ration increased slightly a month later, thousands died of starvation every day. The cruel fact of hunger not only effaced the distinctions between men's and women's preoccupations, it also created what Ginzburg described as the "alienated body" stripped of the markers of human as well as gender identity.[3]

While survivors' narratives of the siege often emphasized disruptions of traditional gender roles—notably the emergence of female "soldiers on the city front"—they rarely detailed the bodily effects of starvation. It is perhaps not surprising that wartime accounts of the siege and those produced in the postwar years by or with the authorization of the Soviet state minimized both the horrors and the extent of starvation, preferring to represent the civilians trapped in Leningrad as "heroes of the Leningrad front."[4] More surprising is that so many narratives produced or published beyond the reach of the Soviet censor demonstrated a similar tendency to detail the wartime blurring of gender roles but to treat starvation in abstract terms, ignoring or downplaying starvation's erasure of the physical markers of gender identity. How survivors represented—or declined to represent—the bodily effects of starvation suggests both the continuing resonance of Soviet myths for people who lived through the siege and the danger of reading gaps and omissions in narratives produced during the Soviet period as straightforward evidence of the coercive power of the state.

Soldiers' Bodies, Civilians' Bodies

Wartime narratives that portrayed women at once as vital to the war effort and as indestructibly feminine and inextricably tied to the world of family and children drew on and substantially modified earlier representations of women in Soviet political art. The "unwomanly" work of young women who entered the war industry or served in the local air defense recalled early Soviet images that emphasized women's status as workers rather than mothers; it also blurred the recently articulated boundaries between appropriate roles for men and women codified in 1936 legislation that restricted divorce, outlawed abortion, and fostered an unabashed sentimentalization of motherhood.[5] However, the press also represented women's war work as constituting a necessary and direct defense of hearth and home. The Soviet press depicted Leningrad women, like their sisters elsewhere in the Soviet Union, as combining the steadfastness (*stoikost'*) and courage (*muzhestvo*—from *muzh,* man) of (male) soldiers with a Soviet femininity that was austere, nurturing, and unfailingly chaste.[6] Picturing women as saving children from the ruins of bombed buildings, nursing orphans, and "substituting" at the factory bench for husbands and fathers who had left for the front, wartime accounts recognized women's war work while defining women as the embodiments of the domestic values for which men were expected to sacrifice their lives.

When wartime accounts of the siege focused on female fatalities in Leningrad, they emphasized that women were victims of Nazi bombs and artillery and downplayed or completely ignored the far larger death toll taken by starvation. According to wartime press coverage, women on the city front died the violent deaths of soldiers. One typical example is novelist Vera Ketlinskaia's story of the first year of the war, which appeared in *Komsomol'skaia pravda.* Ketlinskaia, who lived through the period of mass death due to starvation of the winter of 1941–1942, mentioned hunger, but minimized its impact. The young woman who was the protagonist of Ketlinskaia's story, looked at herself in the mirror and saw a "thin, dulled face, thin, bony arms—was it really her, Olia?" The recognition of the effects of hunger was followed by the statement that "Olia found out about the death of her father after he had already been buried. She did not cry." The proximity of the description of Olia's face and arms and the news of the father's death invited the conclusion that he died of starvation, but the cause remained unspecified.

By contrast, Ketlinskaia rendered in relatively graphic detail the violent death of a woman working alongside Olia digging antitank trenches. As Ketlinskaia described the scene, airplanes with clearly visible iron crosses on their tails swooped down over the young women working in the open. Digging alongside Olia, her friend Niura was killed—"the bullet hit her in the back of the head. Besides her, there were three others killed and ten wounded in that sector." All four were buried in a communal (*bratskoi*) grave, under a marker that read "Here lie Leningraders killed by the Germans. Comrade fighters, do not allow the fascist murderers into Leningrad. Avenge our comrades with blood." The marker listed the women's full names. The women digging trenches became the first casualties on what would soon become a more traditional battlefield. Buried at the front like soldiers, the dead women also would remind male soldiers of the threats to their mothers, daughters, and sisters back home.[7]

In wartime accounts of the siege, the beginning of bombing raids on the city cemented its status as a front, where, under enemy fire, civilians—specifically women and children—became indistinguishable from soldiers. In Ketlinskaia's story, Olia watched the first bombing raids of September 1941 from her civil defense post on the factory roof. Bombs dropped in the neighboring district, the sky filled with black smoke, and Olia pledged to herself to remain at her post and put out fires if the bombs dropped in her district. Nikolai Tikhonov's 1943 book *Geroicheskaia zashchita Leningrada* (*The Heroic Defense of Leningrad*) focused on the military aspects of the battle for the city, and, even more explicitly than Ketlinskaia's story, treated the city front as a seamless extension of the battle front. He quoted with approval the declaration of a Leningrad worker: "My field of battle is the factory shop!" That "women and teenagers entered industry" did not diminish the factory's status as a battlefield. Tikhonov characterized the civil defense brigades as "a numerous army" that "defended the city from air raids, put out fires, tore down ruined buildings, defused delayed-action bombs, and rendered aid to the wounded." He did not mention that this "army" was constituted mainly of young women. Making no distinction between men, women, and children, Tikhonov asserted that "All of the city's inhabitants maintained the strict discipline of siege conditions, continuing work for the strengthening of Leningrad."[8] In wartime accounts of Leningrad, the city was peopled with steadfast and courageous soldiers—in the factories and on the rooftops—not with starving women and children.

The decision to avoid discussions of the extent of starvation in Leningrad may be understood as stemming from a desire to deflect attention from uncomfortable questions about the Soviet failure to stockpile food in the city and to evacuate civilians from front areas. Only in 1943, after the worst period of the siege had passed, did official accounts begin to portray the effort to starve the city as a Nazi war crime. The 125-gram daily bread ration of the starving winter and images of corpses being transported on children's sleds eventually became icons of the siege. Hunger became an essential element of the Leningrad myth. While Leningraders starved, however, the press preferred to blame German bombs and artillery, rather than the lack of food, for civilian suffering.

The absence of images of starving mothers in initial wartime accounts of the city may also be understood as part of a propaganda effort that favored the most straightforward images of Nazi barbarity and of female vulnerability as a means of mobilizing support for the war effort.[9] Soviet wartime accounts employed images of women and children as victims of bombs and artillery shells that could be unproblematically traced to their Nazi source.

The Soviet state's refusal to acknowledge the extent of starvation in Leningrad functioned as part of the strategy of representing Leningraders as soldiers on the city front. The dismembered civilian—man, woman, or child—could be and was represented as a "heroic defender." As Elaine Scarry has argued in her study of the "body in pain," the "idiom of 'heroism,' 'sacrifice,' 'dedication,' 'devotion,' and 'bravery' " has been "conventionally invoked to describe the soldier's individual act of consent over his own body." Scarry asserts that this language of heroism is "neither inappropriate nor false" since the soldier "agree[d] to go to war, agree[d] to permit this radical self-alteration to his body."[10] In the case of Leningrad, the conventional language of "heroism" and "sacrifice" was applied to civilians, and could seem both "appropriate and true" when describing civilians on rooftops or at the factory bench under German artillery fire. By contrast, starving civilians stood not only as a potential reproach to the state that lacked the means to feed them, but also as a potential challenge to the notion of heroic and meaningful sacrifice.

Moral Starvation

The wartime Soviet state had a clear interest in representing the starving citizens of Leningrad as heroic defenders on the "city front," the home front that became a battle front for the duration of the blockade. In a letter to her cousin Boris Pasternak, Ol'ga Freidenberg, the organizer of the first department of classical philology during the Soviet period, underscored precisely this state interest when she condemned the language of heroism as the worst sort of Soviet hypocrisy and deception. The important point for Freidenberg, as for Scarry, was the act of consent over one's own body. She argued that "[n]ot the agony of the living, nor the murder of them, nor the starving of them, could move our heads of state to surrender the city, nor even to open negotiations with the enemy so as to achieve some small alleviation of the suffering. . . . It was dubbed valor, the heroism of the besieged, the *voluntary* sacrificing of one's own life for one's country."[11] Freidenberg disputed the propaganda claim that Leningraders trapped in the city voluntarily sacrificed their own bodies for the cause.

What Freidenberg's criticism ignored was the resonance of the language of heroism, steadfastness, and courage among other survivors of the siege. As the memoirs and interviews discussed below demonstrate, the official story provided not only a convenient but also a comforting framework for constructing personal memory. While starvation was arguably the essential fact of life for Leningraders in the first winter of the war, survivors' accounts of that period often accepted the notion that Leningraders—men, women, and children—should be understood as active soldiers rather than civilian victims. This was the case not only in Soviet-era accounts, where one might reasonably assume that Soviet censorship and self-censorship were at work, but also in glasnost'-era, post-Soviet, and émigré accounts of the siege. Even survivors who criticized or condemned the Soviet state often employed the rhetoric of heroism, steadfastness, and bravery as a way of making sense of their experiences and of representing themselves as something other than victims of starvation.

In some cases, silences about the injuries done to the body can be understood as a reflection of the sensory numbness, the alienation from their own bodies, that survivors portrayed both as a physical consequence of starvation and as a means of coping with trauma. In a memoir published when she was in her sixties and living in New York, Elena Kozhina, who was eight years old when she was evacuated from Leningrad in February 1942, remembered that for over a year her experiences remained frozen out of her consciousness. "I did not cry, did not grieve, did not fear, and did not complain. It was as if I was frozen inside a glacier. Perhaps I simply had no strength to respond to what was happening around me." Only in the summer of 1943 did "bats"—dark memories of the siege—begin to haunt her. Kozhina emphasized the searing power of these memories, "pictures" that suddenly and unexpectedly broke into her consciousness. Yet while the images she recounted—corpses blocking the entrance to her apartment building, a neighbor predicting that her older brother would die soon—were often horrifying, they reveal very little of the girl's own physical struggles.

Scarcely mentioning her own body or physical sensations, Kozhina experienced—or at least remembers experiencing—starvation primarily as a sort of psychic struggle: "We are drying our food ration for the day on the chimney pipe—miniscule slices of bread, 'eighths.' We look at them and cannot tear our eyes away, we cannot think of anything else."[12] The emphasis on the moral strength needed to survive constituted a recurrent theme in survivors' memoirs. Essayist Vladimir Daev, who has little patience for the myths of the siege and has insisted that "the time has come to wipe off some of the syrup," nonetheless presented the suggestion that the selfless survived better as a law of the siege. "The person whose actions did not have a moral foundation more quickly gave in to depression; he was capable of stealing a piece of bread from his own brother, taking a crust from a child's hand. In order to extinguish the feeling of hunger, he did not distract himself with the struggle, but drank water, deceiving his stomach. Before others he collapsed in bed, his body swollen, and in the final analysis, he died earlier than active citizens supplied with the exact same ration."[13] In short, throwing oneself into the struggle provided a means of coping with the horrors and hardships of the siege. Leningraders seemed to find solace in doing—or in representing themselves as doing—exactly what official narratives described them as doing.

The recourse to the state narrative can be read as an effort to avoid recalling the worst of the siege and to emphasize instead that the struggle had meaning.

In a short memoir included in a post-Soviet collection of reminiscences by survivors who worked at Leningrad State University during or after the war, E. P. Gruzdeva, an administrator at the university, noted that the difficult conditions of work on the city's defenses led to her admission into the hospital "with the diagnosis 'DYSTROPHY,'" the euphemism for starvation employed during the siege. After three months in the hospital, she was again mobilized to work on the city's defenses. Declining to "continue to enumerate the episodes and facts of our bitter life," Gruzdeva emphasized that "all the comrades dear to me throughout the blockade had the highest level of moral purity, at the foundation of which was decency, honesty, and benevolence. We were united by the general cause of the fight for Victory over fascism, a firm belief in the inevitable end of the war. With the humble work, courage, steadfastness, and patience of soldiers in civvies we struggled, with our last strength, to do what we could to help the front."[14] She spent less time telling the story of her own suffering than affirming that her actions fit into the public narrative of heroism and self-sacrifice for the cause. By the end of her account, the official story of soldiers on the city front has overshadowed her own experience of "hunger, cold, bombs, and fire."

The state's representation of the siege as an opportunity for purposeful action and of Leningraders as determined and selfless reappeared in memoirs as part of an active and effective coping strategy, an effort to endow suffering with meaning. Gruzdeva's recollection of a feeling of unity in the cause suggests that Soviet propaganda may have resonated with Leningraders struggling to "preserve social connection" and to find a higher meaning for the death that surrounded them—both highly adaptive coping mechanisms.[15] Similarly Rimma Neratova, an émigré whose memoir often criticized the Soviet state, described her ability to survive in terms that would not have been out of place in a Soviet-era account of the siege. Neratova, who spent the early months of the siege working at a hospital where she treated wounded soldiers, noted that she, her sister, and her mother "stopped going to the hospital at the end of December 1941: already we didn't have the strength, we turned into dystrophics, although still only first stage. We were terribly tired; small edemas appeared on our faces, and our legs swelled." Still, Neratova emphasized, "our thoughts were always occupied with someone else's troubles, preventing us from concentrating on our own. This helped to keep us from turning into moral dystrophics."[16] The use of the medicalized "dystrophic"—a term that soft-pedaled civilian starvation—and the distinction between physical and moral starvation suggests both an unwillingness to recount bodily injury and the strategies of preserving social connection and moral values that allowed Neratova to cope with trauma.

Gender has significance in these descriptions of the moral strength and fighting spirit of Leningraders because they drew, implicitly and sometimes explicitly, on the notion of the soldier on the city front. Effacing the distinction between the struggles of the largely female city and the predominantly male front, the "soldier in civvies" suggests that there is little reason to remember or commemorate a distinctively urban, female experience of the war. Tikhonov's wartime call for a postwar monument to the "unknown female worker" that would mirror monuments to the "unknown soldier" valued women's wartime contributions by emphasizing the parallels with male heroism.[17] That female heroism on the city front often failed to neatly fit the pattern of the battle front is suggested by Neratova's validation of her mother's predawn departures to wait in line for bread as "quiet and unnoticed heroism."[18] Despite the fact that the her mother's "quiet" civilian heroics had little in common with the soldier's, Neratova adopted the rhetoric of heroism, steadfastness, and courage as a means of endowing female and civilian sacrifice with meaning and importance.

Profaned Bodies

For survivors of the blockade, remembering the body threatened to destabilize not only the Soviet myth of heroic Leningrad but also survivors' own stories that incorporated any components of that myth. Representing Leningraders as soldiers on the city front entailed a blurring of gender roles, an identification of civilians with soldiers. Starvation, however, obliterated the visible bodily markers of gender identity and turned civilians not into soldiers but into personifications of war's destruction of civilized values. The starving body complicated, even contradicted, "heroic" narratives told by the state and often adapted by survivors seeking to endow their sufferings with historical or moral significance. N, the depersonalized, gender-neutral protagonist of Ginzburg's account of the siege experienced starvation as an alien and "agonizing fleshiness" and as a "maniacal concentration" on food that was "humiliating and bestial."[19] Rendered in these terms, the starving "siege person" not only suggested that even the most effective coping strategies were bound to fail but also potentially refuted the most comforting of Soviet myths. If the dismembered body corporealized the (male) heroism of the front, the starving body enacted the most profane and senseless horrors of a war that turned women and men into sexless inhuman beings.

Many survivors, including those who published memoirs in the post-Soviet period and those interviewed in the 1970s and 1980s, have attempted to represent the unspeakable horrors of starvation by visualizing the pain of starvation as the obliteration of the physical markers of gender.[20] *Blokadnaia kniga* (The Book of the Blockade), a collection of diaries and oral histories published in the late 1970s, "marked a turning point in the official Soviet accounts of 1941–1944."[21] Rejecting sanitized representations of the siege, the collection's editors, Ales' Adamovich and Daniil Granin, argued that while it might have once made sense for "those hurt by the war to spare the hearts of their fellow countrymen," forty years later "it is absolutely vital that the postwar generations should know as much as possible, in all its details, about what happened before their time, that they should get the feel of it all."[22] The increasing realism of accounts of the siege, the editors hoped, would ensure that the younger generation would remember and value the sacrifices of the aging war generation. Focusing on individual stories allowed the editors to include the ugliest details of their still essentially heroic story—to emphasize both sacrifice and victory. One interviewee, E. S. Liapin, recalled that under starvation conditions, "the appearance, the face changed, the person became in the nature of an animated corpse, and it's well known that a corpse is a grim spectacle. . . . The yellow face, fixed stare, a noticeable loss of voice—you couldn't tell from the voice if it was a man or a woman, a quavering voice—the voice of a person who had lost age and sex."[23]

Other male survivors emphasized that starvation, by destroying the visible markers of gender identity, undermined "natural" male views of women as objects of desire. In a diary entry from early January 1942 reproduced in *Blokadnaia kniga,* Georgii Kniazev portrayed his fifty-one-year-old wife as a "delicate, thin girl" who had "not lost her femininity or her exceptional feminine neatness." By late February, her face had become "little, wrinkled, old-womanish (!)"—a diminution if not complete loss of attractiveness and embodied sexual identity.[24] One of the editors, who had been a soldier on the Leningrad front, remembered the visit of a contingent of women workers from the city in December 1941. Soldiers received almost double the civilian food ration, and such visits were vital to the survival of many Leningraders.[25] After a dinner of kasha, salted beef, bread, and a lump of sugar—far richer fare than they had become accustomed to—the young women fell asleep in the soldiers' bunks. Callers from the neighboring units stopped by to witness the unusual sight. "It seemed like years since we had seen women in dresses. But what women these were—thin, worn out, grown ugly. Crowding into the entrance of the dugout, the soldiers looked at the sleeping women not with masculine feeling, but with pity."[26]

Such discussions of the bodily effects of starvation called into question a key element in the official narrative of the siege; the spring of 1942 as a moment of rebirth, a victory over the death and cold of the previous winter that presaged recovery and ultimate Soviet victory. The myth had a basis in fact. The spring of 1942 had brought many of the outward signs of normalcy, from renewed public transit to running water. Accounts of the siege published from the early 1960s through the early 1980s recognized that deaths due to prolonged malnutrition persisted into the spring. However, these accounts emphasized that by April 1942 rations had increased, and a mood of optimism reigned in the city. A massive effort on the part of the city's women to clear the streets of snow—and more specifically of the slops and corpses that had been frozen in the snow—brought the city back to something approaching normal. A 1972 history of the city entitled *Heroic Leningrad* is typical of the genre:

> By 15 April [1942], the inhabitants had tidied up over 12,000 courtyards, cleaned up more than three million square meters of streets, squares and embankments, and removed almost a million tons of debris and snow. The city was literally transformed [*preobrazilsia,* also: transfigured]. On 15 April, after a long interruption, Leningraders once again heard tram bells, which that spring were for them, if you please, more dear than the nightingales' trills.[27]

This official history of "heroic Leningrad" did mention that Leningraders continued to die, but the emphasis was squarely on recovery, on the reopening of movie theaters and concert halls, the establishment of dining rooms to provide extra rations to the most seriously malnourished, and the planting of vegetable gardens.

Discussions of the bodily effects of starvation threatened to undermine this rosy picture. The return of warm weather occasioned the confrontation with a body whose strangeness had been at least partly concealed under layers of clothes and blankets. Many Leningraders did not undress during the entire course of the starvation winter. As Ginzburg noted, with spring "the body was coming up to the surface again."[28] Rather than representing the return of better conditions as a relief, memoirists who paid attention to the body often underscored the painful realization of the degree to which survivors had had to abandon traditional norms, especially traditional *female* gender identities that had been undermined by the physical obliteration of the "female" body. With spring came not relief, but the shame, despair, and horror of having managed to set aside "civilized" standards and live through the catastrophe of the starvation winter.

Such shame or survivor guilt is a widely observed consequence of traumatic events, a response to "helplessness, the violation of bodily integrity, and the indignity suffered in the eyes of another person."[29] It is perhaps not so surprising that survivors of the siege, who experienced some degree of helplessness, violation, and indignity, might feel such shame and that they might prefer to emphasize steadfastness, courage, and the cause. Adamovich and Granin made explicit their efforts as editors to include both interviewees who viewed the spring as a moment of renewal and those who experienced shame. The editors explained that survivors, like the apostles, told the same stories from different points of view—a situation that created the paradoxical characterization of the spring of 1942 as a period both of joy and of despair.[30]

The accounts of the first hot baths in the spring of 1942 included by Adamovich and Granin attempted to balance the promise of renewal with the shock of seeing naked bodies after the starvation winter. Elena Nikolaevna Aver'ianova-Fedorova recalled that demand for a chance to visit the baths was high, and tickets were given only "to the best workers." Maiia Ianova likewise remembered that on the first day, people queued up for eight hours or so for the opportunity to take a bath. When two weeks later she finally succeeded in getting in, the experience proved painful:

> It was so horrible, when they were all naked and kept falling—they didn't have the strength to carry the wash basins. My god! What a nightmare you could see there. Many didn't have soap, but some rubbed and rubbed themselves even without soap. And they fell down right there. The line moved slowly, they washed themselves slowly, but there was hot water.[31]

Ianova distanced herself from the scene and the "nightmare"—"*they* fell down."

In the reminiscences collected in *Blokadnaia kniga,* the shame of starvation was also defused by an emphasis on the return to normalcy as embodied by the return of clearly gendered and desirable female bodies. Galina Bobinskaia, who described spring 1942 as a moment of "heedless, unreasoning joy," emphasized in her diary that "now some people are smartly dressed" and "the hairdressers are full of women getting manicures and hot waves—they bring their own paraffin."[32] A demobilized officer evacuated his fiancée from Leningrad in March 1942. He remembered her then as an

> old woman—gray, shriveled, hunched. She could hardly walk. Bones covered with skin. I took her with me to the 'mainland.' There, in the space of six months, she gained strength, straightened up, and grew younger month by month. He eyes shone, no longer sunk in their sockets. Her hair also came back to life, got thicker. Her skin tightened. Then her rosy complexion returned. She grew young again. She was transformed from an old woman into a pleasing woman, and as time went on she became still younger, turning into such a young and beautiful girl that I felt uncomfortable marrying her.[33]

In Adamovich and Granin's collection, recovery from starvation was marked by the return of femininity and youth and of male desire.

Ginzburg, who wrote about the physical effects of starvation, provided no such happy endings, but she too recognized that the starving body potentially subverted the comforting conclusion that even as they starved, Leningraders served a larger purpose. On the one hand, Ginzburg presented a powerful account of the shame of the survivor who felt "the inadequacy of the sacrifice . . . (I survived—that means I didn't sacrifice enough), and along with the inadequacy, remorse." On the other hand, she adopted a point of view very close to the state's narrative of heroism and meaningful sacrifice. As Saul Friedlander has argued with regard to the Holocaust, "individual *common* memory, as well as collective memory, tends to restore or establish coherence, closure, and possibly a redemptive stance."[34] This tendency toward a "redemptive stance" is clearly visible even in Ginzburg's frank account of the effects of starvation. She argued that the "people of besieged Leningrad worked (while they could) and saved (if they could) both themselves and their loved ones from dying of hunger. And in the final reckoning that was also essential to the war effort, because a living city barred the path of an enemy who wanted to kill it."[35] Sensitive to the shame of survival, Ginzburg suggested that it could be overcome with the recognition that starving civilians participated in a meaningful struggle. The narrator's "detached and analytic point of view" recognized the shame of surviving starvation, but also provided enough distance from this shame to allow the siege to be constructed as a meaningful experience.[36]

In reminiscences written in 1962 but published only in 1990, Ol'ga Berggol'ts, a poet and survivor of the siege, suggested that starving bodies ruled out such compromises with the myth of shared struggle. Berggol'ts made the disappearance of the gendered body a measure of the degradation caused by war. She described the scene at a Leningrad bathhouse in the spring of 1942, when warmer weather allowed survivors to enjoy their first hot bath in months.

> Then I looked at the women . . . The blemished, stretched, rough skin of the women's bodies—no, not even women—they had ceased to resemble women. Their breasts had disappeared; their stomachs were shrunken; the purple and

> blue stains of scurvy crawled across their skin. A few had horribly distended stomachs on top of skinny legs—legs without calves, where the fattest part was the ankle. These black or bluish-white phantoms did not resemble women. On repulsively thin legs, they had been stripped of all womanly charm, all the womanly essence that humanity idolizes and admires—its highest delight, Madonna, its holy mother, its lover. Womanly beauty—what has become of it?! Into what horror and despair and shame had humanity sunk if its women became like this, if it allowed such a distortion of woman! I repeat, torn off arms and legs are nothing compared to these bony bodies: You know, missing arms do not deform Venus. Here everything was in place and nothing was missing. One should sob, looking at the multitude of these women; one should be amazed, that they decided to bare in the light of day so profaned, emaciated, blemished, and spotted a body.[37]

The wounds she saw in the warmth and safety of the bathhouse were, Berggol'ts argued, more horrifying than the dismemberment of the soldier at the front.[38] The disfigured soldier, like Venus, might still embody godlike heroism, bravery, and dedication. The starving woman projected only horror, shame, and despair.

Still, Berggol'ts, like other survivors who talked less frankly about the starving body, hesitated to identify herself as among the wounded. Describing the woman that she saw at the bath, Berggol'ts did not describe her own body, although there is every reason to believe that it was no less "profaned, emaciated, blemished, and spotted" than the others.[39] Distancing herself from the bodies she described, declining to directly describe her own pain, Berggol'ts suggests the alienation that Ginzburg identified as central to the experience of malnutrition: "the sensations were alien, as if they were being experienced by someone else altogether."[40] The pain of starvation was seen rather than felt—was felt only because it could be visualized as the "woman who no longer resembles a woman." Even as she described the effects of starvation and suggested its senselessness, Berggol'ts retained her silence about her own body, remained alienated from her own pain.

The absence of graphic descriptions of starving bodies in the oral histories and diaries can be understood not only as an editorial decision designed to shore up the official myth of "heroic Leningrad" but also as an artifact of survivors' silences. In a recent interview, Adamovich admitted that the editors of *Blokadnaia kniga* had decided not to include the most horrifying stories they heard, particularly survivors' accounts of cannibalism—perhaps the ultimate defilement of human flesh.[41] Moreover, they interleaved reminiscences that emphasized horror—for example the "nightmare" of the bathhouse—with stories of victory, heroism, and survival. Yet, as Catherine Merridale has argued in her study of "death and memory" in the Soviet Union, "the denial of death . . . was not simply imposed by the state."[42] When in 1992 the editors finally published interviewees' stories of cannibalism, they did so with reservations, fearing that such stories might make it impossible "to talk and write about the heroism of the blockade, about the exceptional virtue with which they held out and died in unbearable conditions, about the high cultural level [*intelligentnosti*] of this city."[43]

Survivors told of the degradation of the human body, but they also told stories that affirmed the resilience and sanctity of the human body as a seat of gender identity and represented Leningraders not as victims of starvation but as soldiers under enemy fire. The original edition of *Blokadnaia kniga*, published in 1979, and the first section of the longer 1982 edition ended with a lengthy interview with Mariia Ivanovna, who, as a civil defense worker, saved an injured woman and her newborn baby from the rubble, even as German shells continued to fall.[44] That the editors chose to emphasize such stories does not negate the fact that survivors—seeking to make sense of their experience, to evade the memory of horror, despair, and shame—told them. The injured mother, with beautiful fair hair that reached her knees, who gave birth in the midst of an air raid, constituted a less painful memory, for both the state and survivors, than the sexless bodies of the women in the bathhouse. The state did not need to impose silence in the face of the degradation and destruction of the human body—especially one's own body. Survivors often did that on their own.[45]

Notes

1. Kathleen Canning, "The Body as Method? Reflections on the Place of the Body in Gender History," *Gender and History* 11, no. 3 (November 1999): 508. Canning is summarizing Elisabeth Domansky's argument in "Militarization and Reproduction in World War I Germany," in Geoff Eley, ed., *Society, Culture, and the State in Germany 1870–1930* (Ann Arbor: University of Michigan Press, 1996), 427-64.

2. Lidiia Ginzburg, *Blockade Diary*, trans. Alan Myers (London: Harvill Press, 1995), 42–43, 71. The most exhaustive account of the siege of Leningrad in English remains that of journalist Harrison Salisbury, *The 900 Days: The Siege of Leningrad* (New York: Harper and Row, 1969). Recent scholarly works in English include Richard Bidlack, "Survival Strategies in Leningrad during the First Year of the Soviet-German War," in Robert W. Thurston and Bernd Bonwetsch, eds., *The People's War: Responses to World War II in the Soviet Union* (Urbana: University of Illinois Press, 2000), 84–107; Bidlack, "The Political Mood in Leningrad during the First Year of the Soviet-German War," *The Russian Review* 59, no. 1 (January 2000): 96–113.

3. Ginzburg, *Blockade Diary*, 10.

4. There are numerous wartime and postwar examples of the representation of civilians as "heroic defenders"; for example, Nikolai Tikhonov, *Geroicheskaia zashchita Leningrada* (Moscow: Gosudarstvennoe izdatel'stvo politicheskoi literatury, 1943). Postwar examples include N. A. Manakov, *V kol'tse blokady: Khoziaistvo i byt osazhdennogo Leningrada* (Leningrad: Lenizdat, 1961); V. E. Zubakov, *Geroicheskii Leningrad* (Moscow: Voennoe izdatel'stvo ministerstva oborony SSSR, 1972).

5. Victoria Bonnell, "The Representation of Women in Early Soviet Political Art," *Russian Review* 50, no. 3 (1991): 275; Jeffrey Brooks, "Revolutionary Lives: Public Identities in *Pravda* during the 1920s," in Stephen White, ed., *New Directions in Soviet History* (New York: Cambridge University Press, 1992), 34; Elizabeth A. Wood, *The Baba and the Comrade: Gender and Politics in Revolutionary Russia* (Bloomington: Indiana University Press, 1997), 47; Elizabeth Waters, "The Female Form in Soviet Political Iconography, 1917-32," in Barbara Evans Clements et al., eds., *Russia's Women: Accommodation, Resistance, Transformation* (Berkeley: University of California Press, 1991), 235-37. Early in the war, the press characterized women in the war industry as "substituting" for men at the front. By 1945 women's war work became "unwomanly" (*delo ved' ne zhenskoe*); *Komsomol'skaia pravda* (hereafter *KP*) (30 April 1945), 2. On the "resurrection" of the family: Wendy Z. Goldman, *Women, the State, and Revolution: Soviet Family Policy and Social Life, 1917–1936* (Cambridge: Cambridge University Press, 1993), 296-336; Elizabeth Waters, "The Bolsheviks and the Family," *Contemporary European History* 4, no. 3 (1993): 275-91; Lisa A. Kirschenbaum, *Small Comrades: Revolutionizing Childhood in Soviet Russia, 1917–1932* (New York: Routledge Falmer, 2001), 133-59.

6. Kirschenbaum, "'Our City, Our Hearths, Our Families': Local Loyalties and Private Life in Soviet World War II Propaganda," *Slavic Review* 59, no. 4 (Winter 2000): 840. On the relationship between masculinity and courage: Karen Petrone, "Masculinity and Heroism in Imperial and Soviet Military-Patriotic Cultures," in Barbara Evans Clements et al., eds., *Russian Masculinities in History and Culture* (New York: Palgrave, 2002), 172-93.

7. Vera Ketlinskaia, "Rasskaz o prostoi devushke," *KP* (23 June 1942), 3.

8. Tikhonov, *Geroicheskaia zashchita Leningrada,* 19–20. Other wartime press accounts that emphasize deaths resulting from artillery and bombs, rather than starvation, include: "Leningradtsy," *KP* (11 December 1943), 4; "Studenty Leningrada," *KP* (1 November 1941), 2; "Leningradskaia zhenshchina—boets goroda-fronta," *Leningradskaia pravda* (hereafter *LP*), (23 July 1942), 1; Nikolai Tikhonov, "O muzhestve i skromnosti," *LP* (1 January 1942), 2.

9. In her study of representations of women during the Irish famine, Margaret Kelleher has argued that "images of starving mothers and children spell famine's worst horrors, but the affective response thus generated may also involve a passivity and fatalism which works against real understanding." While the Soviet state may have had little interest in "real understanding," it had little use for representations that fostered "passivity and fatalism." Margaret Kelleher, "Woman as Famine Victim: The Figure of Woman in Irish Famine Narratives," in Ronit Lentin, ed., *Gender and Catastrophe* (London: Zed Books, 1997), 251.

10. Elaine Scarry, *The Body in Pain: The Making and Unmaking of the World* (New York: Oxford University Press, 1985), 112.

11. Cited in Cynthia Simmons, "Lifting the Siege: Women's Voices on Leningrad (1941-1944)," *Canadian Slavonic Papers* 40, no. 1-2 (1998): 60. Margaret Wettlin, an American who lived in the Soviet Union for nearly fifty years, including the war years, made a similar point, emphasizing that the people of Leningrad "were victims. They were trapped in the city. No other choice was offered them. A hero is one who chooses to sacrifice himself for something he holds dearer than his own life, be it the life of another, or a cause, or a cult. For me, the entrapping of the citizens of Leningrad was a war crime"—whether Soviet or Nazi remains unclear. Wettlin, *Fifty Russian Winters: An American Woman's Life in the Soviet Union* (New York: Pharos Books, 1992), 72.

12. Elena Kozhina, *Through the Burning Steppe: A Memoir of Wartime Russia, 1942–1943,* trans. Vadim Mahmoudov (New York: Riverhead Books, 2000), 122, 123.

13. Vladimir Daev, *S distantsii poluveka: Ocherki blokadnogo Leningrada* (St. Petersburg: Sudarynia, 1998), 89, 85.

14. Emphasis in original. E. P. Gruzdeva, "I golod, i kholod, i bomby, i pozhari—vse vynesli," in *Universitet v blokadnom i osazhdennom Leningrade 1941–1944: Sbornik ofitsial'nykh dokumentov, pisem, fotografii i drugogo fakticheskogo materiala* (St. Petersburg: TOO "Gippokrat," 1996), 108.

15. Judith Herman, *Trauma and Recovery: The Aftermath of Violence—from Domestic Abuse to Political Terror* (New York: Basic Books, 1997), 58–59.

16. Rimma Neratova, *V dni voiny: Semeinaia khronika* (St. Petersburg: Zhurnal "Zvezda," 1996), 55.

17. Tikhonov, "O muzhestve."

18. Neratova, *V dni voiny,* 60.

19. Ginzburg, *Blockade Diary,* 9, 62.

20. Simmons, "Lifting the Siege," 58.

21. Ibid., 48.

22. Ales' Adamovich and Daniil Granin, *Blokadnaia kniga* (Moscow: Sovetskii pisatel', 1982), 22.

23. Ibid., 49.

24. Ibid., 369, 390.

25. Bidlack, "Survival Strategies," 91.

26. Adamovich and Granin, *Blokadnaia kniga,* 312.

27. Zubakov, *Geroicheskii Leningrad,* 96–97.

28. Ginzburg, *Blockade Diary,* 11.

29. Herman, *Trauma and Recovery,* 53. Primo Levi's discussion of shame stands as among the most eloquent and moving descriptions of survivor guilt. His contention that "the worst survived, the selfish, the violent, the insensitive, the collaborators" (82) constitutes a chilling rejoinder to the Leningrad story of moral strength. Levi, *The Drowned and the Saved,* trans. Raymond Rosenthal (New York: Vintage International, 1989), 70–87.

30. Adamovich and Granin, *Blokadnaia kniga,* 193.

31. Ibid., 68–69.

32. Ibid., 186.

33. Ibid., 338.

34. Saul Friedlander, "Trauma, Memory, and Transference," in Geoffrey Hartman, ed., *Holocaust Remembrance: The Shapes of Memory* (Cambridge, Mass.: Blackwell, 1994), 254.

35. Ginzburg, *Blockade Diary,* 62, 8, 3.

36. Boris Gasparov, "On 'Notes from the Leningrad Blockade,'" *Canadian American Slavic Studies* 28, no. 2–3 (Summer-Fall 1994): 217.

37. Ol'ga Berggol'ts, "Dnevnye zvezdy," *Ogonek,* no. 19 (5–12 May 1990), 16.

38. Katharine Hodgson offers a similar reading of the bathhouse in "Under an Unwomanly Star: War in the Writing of Ol'ga Berggol'ts," in Rosalind Marsh, ed., *Women and Russian Culture: Projections and Self-Perceptions* (New York: Berghahn Books, 1998), 139.

39. Adamovich and Granin, *Blokadnaia kniga,* 329–32.

40. Ginzburg, *Blockade Diary,* 9.

41. Simmons, "Lifting the Siege," 43–65.

42. Catherine Merridale, "Death and Memory in Modern Russia," *History Workshop Journal*, no. 42 (Autumn 1996): 2.

43. Ales' Adamovich and Daniil Granin, "Blokadnaia kniga: Glavy, kotorykh v knige ne bylo," *Zvezda*, no. 5–6 (1992): 8. Also Simmons, "Lifting the Siege," 49, n. 26.

44. Ales' Adamovich and Daniil Granin, eds., *Blokadnaia kniga* (Moscow: Sovetskii pisatel', 1979), 287. Adamovich and Granin, *Blokadnaia kniga* (1982), 193–97.

45. On "the impossibility of telling" as a central experience of Holocaust survivors: Shoshana Felman and Dori Laub, *Testimony: Crises of Witnessing in Literature, Psychoanalysis, and History* (New York: Routledge, 1992), 79–80, 190–91.

Select Bibliography

Bokovoy, Melissa. "Scattered Graves, Ordered Cemeteries: Commemorating Serbia's Wars of National Liberation, 1912-1918." In *Staging the Past: the Politics of Commemoration in Habsburg Central Europe, 1848 to the Present,* ed. Maria Bucur and Nancy M. Wingfield. West Lafayette, Ind.: Purdue University Press, 2001.

Bucur, Maria. "Between the Mother of the Wounded and the Virgin from Jiu: Romanian Women and the Gender of Heroism during the Great War." *Journal of Women's History* 12, no. 2 (Summer 2000): 30–56.

Burke, Joanna. *Dismembering the Male: Men's Bodies, Britain and the Great War.* London: Reaktion Books, 1996.

Cooke, Miriam, and Angela Woollacott, eds. *Gendering War Talk.* Princeton: Princeton University Press, 1993.

Darrow, Margaret H. *French Women and the First World War: War Stories of the Home Front.* New York: New York University Press, 2000.

Davis, Belinda J. *Home Fires Burning: Food, Politics, and Everyday Life in World War I Berlin.* Chapel Hill: University of North Carolina Press, 2000.

Deák, István et al., eds. *The Politics of Retribution in Europe: World War II and its Aftermath.* Princeton: Princeton University Press, 2000.

Diamond, Hanna. *Women and the Second World War in France 1939–1948: Choices and Constraints.* London: Longman, 1999.

Domansky, Elisabeth. "Militarization and Reproduction in World War I Germany." In *Society, Culture, and the State in Germany 1870–1930,* ed. Geoff Eley. Ann Arbor: University of Michigan Press, 1996.

Eksteins, Modris. *The Great War and the Birth of the Modern Age.* New York: Anchor, 1990.

Frommer, Benjamin. "Expulsion or Integration: Unmixing Interethnic Marriage in Postwar Czechoslovakia." *East European Politics and Societies* 14, no. 2 (2000): 381-410.

———. *National Cleansing: Retribution against Nazi Collaborators in Postwar Czechoslovakia.* New York: Cambridge University Press, 2004.

Fussell, Paul. *The Great War and Modern Memory.* Oxford: Oxford University Press, 2000.

Gillis, John R., ed. *Commemorations: The Politics of National Identity.* Princeton: Princeton University Press, 1994.

Gullace, Nicoletta. *The Blood of Our Sons: Men, Women, and the Renegotiation of British Citizenship During the Great War.* London: Palgrave Macmillan, 2003.

Gullickson, Gay. *Unruly Women of Paris: Images of the Commune.* Ithaca: Cornell University Press, 1996.

Hagemann, Karen, and Stefanie Schuler-Springorum, eds. *Home/Front: The Military, War and Gender in Twentieth-Century Germany.* Oxford: Berg, 2002.

Hanisch, Ernst. "Die Männlichkeit des Kriegers: Das österreichische Militärstrafrecht im Ersten Weltkrieg." In *Geschichte und Recht: Festschrift für Gerald Stourzh zum 70. Geburtstag,* ed. Thomas Angerer et al. Vienna: Böhlau, 1999.

Healy, Maureen. *Vienna and the Fall of the Habsburg Empire: Total War and Everyday Life in World War I.* Cambridge: Cambridge University Press, 2004.

Heineman, Elizabeth D. *What Difference Does a Husband Make? Women and Marital Status in Nazi and Postwar Germany.* Berkeley: University of California, 1999.

Higonnet, Margaret R., ed. *Lines of Fire: Women Writers of World War I.* New Haven: Yale University Press, 1987.

Higonnet, Margaret R. et al., eds., *Behind the Lines: Gender and the Two World Wars.* New Haven: Yale University Press, 1987.

Hodgson, Katharine. "The Other Veterans: Soviet Women's Poetry of World War 2," in *World War 2 and the Soviet People,* ed. John Garrard and Carol Garrard. New York: St. Martin's Press, 1993.

Hynes, Samuel L. *The Soldiers' Tale: Bearing Witness to Modern War.* New York: Penguin, 1998.

Ignatieff, Michael. "Soviet War Memorials." *History Workshop* 17, no. 3 (1984): 157-163.

Jolluck, Katherine R. *Exile and Identity: Polish Women in the Soviet Union during World War II.* Pittsburgh: University of Pittsburgh Press, 2002.

Kirschenbaum, Lisa. "'Our City, Our Hearths, Our Families': Local Loyalties and Private Life in Soviet World War II Propaganda." *Slavic Review* 59 (Winter 2000): 825-847.

Klein, Yvonne M. *Beyond the Home Front: Women's Autobiographical Writing of the Two World Wars.* New York: New York University Press, 1997.

Landes, Joan B. *Visualizing the Nation: Gender, Representation, and Revolution in Eighteenth-Century France.* Ithaca: Cornell University Press, 2001.

Leed, Eric J. *No Man's Land: Combat and Identity in World War I.* New York: Cambridge University Press, 1979.

Melman, Billie, ed. *Borderlines: Genders and Identities in War and Peace 1870–1930.* New York: Routledge, 1998.

Mosse, George L. *Fallen Soldiers: Reshaping the Memory of the World Wars.* New York: Oxford University Press, 1990.

——. *The Image of Man: The Creation of Modern Masculinity.* Oxford: Oxford University Press, 1996.

Pollard, Miranda. *Reign of Virtue: Mobilizing Gender in Vichy France.* Chicago: University of Chicago Press, 1998.

Rachamimov, Alon. *POWs and the Great War: Captivity on the Eastern Front.* Oxford: Berg, 2002.

Roberts, Mary Louise. *Civilization without Sexes: Reconstructing Gender in Postwar France, 1917–1927.* Chicago: University of Chicago Press, 1994.

Rousso, Henry. *The Vichy Syndrome: History and Memory in France since 1944,* trans. Arthur Goldhammer. Cambridge, Mass.: Harvard University Press, 1991.

Sherman, Daniel. *The Construction of Memory in Interwar France.* Chicago: University of Chicago Press, 2001.

Simmons, Cynthia, and Nina Perlina, eds. *Writing the Siege of Leningrad: Women's Diaries, Memoirs, and Documentary Prose.* Pittsburgh: University of Pittsburgh Press, 2002.

Smith, Angela K. *The Second Battlefield: Women, Modernism and the First World War.* Manchester: Manchester University Press, 2000.

Stockdale, Melissa K. "'My Death for the Motherland is Happiness': Women, Patriotism, and Soldiering in Russia's Great War, 1914-1917." *American Historical Review* 109, no. 1 (February 2004): 78-116.

Summerfield, Penny. *Reconstructing Women's Wartime Lives.* Manchester: Manchester University Press, 2000.

Theweleit, Klaus. *Männerphantasien,* 2 vol. Vol. 1*: Frauen, Fluten, Körper, Geschichte.* Vol. 2: *Männerkörper—zur Psychoanalyse des weißen Terrors.* Paperback ed. with new epilogue by the author (Munich: Piper, 2000). In English: *Male Fantasies,* 2 vols., trans. Stephen Conway. Minneapolis: University of Minnesota Press, 1987.

Tumarkin, Nina. *The Living and the Dead: The Rise and Fall of the Cult of World War II in Russia.* New York: Basic Books, 1994.

Watson, Janet. *Fighting Different Wars. Experience, Memory, and the First World War in Britain.* Cambridge: Cambridge University Press, 2004.

Winter, Jay. *Sites of Memory, Sites of Mourning: The Great War in European Cultural History.* Cambridge: Cambridge University Press, 1995.

Winter, Jay, and Jean-Louis Robert, eds. *Capital Cities at War: London, Paris, Berlin, 1914–1919.* Cambridge: Cambridge University Press, 1997.

Winter, Jay, and Emmanuel Sivan, eds. *War and Remembrance in the Twentieth Century.* Cambridge: Cambridge University Press, 1999.

Woollacott, Angela. *On Her Their Lives Depend: Munitions Workers in the Great War.* Berkeley: University of California Press, 1994.

Contributors

Eliza Ablovatski is Assistant Professor of History at Kenyon College. She has published articles on the post–World War I revolutions in Germany and Hungary, as well as on the history of the Jewish community in Czernowitz/ Cernăuţi.

Melissa Bokovoy is Associate Professor of History at the University of New Mexico and author of *Peasants and Communists: Politics and Ideology in the Yugoslav Countryside, 1941–1953,* winner of the AAASS 1999 Barbara Jelavich Prize.

Maria Bucur is Associate Professor of History and John V. Hill Chair in East European History at Indiana University. She is author of *Eugenics and Modernization in Interwar Romania,* as well as articles on gender, war, and memory.

Melissa Feinberg is Assistant Professor of History at the University of North Carolina, Charlotte. She is author of *Elusive Equality: Gender, Citizenship and the Limits of Democracy in Czechoslovakia, 1918–1950.*

Benjamin Frommer is Associate Professor of History at Northwestern University. He is author of *National Cleansing: Retribution against Nazi Collaborators in Postwar Czechoslovakia.*

Maureen Healy is Assistant Professor of History at Oregon State University and author of *Vienna and the Fall of the Habsburg Empire: Total War and Everyday Life in World War I.*

Katherine R. Jolluck is Senior Lecturer in the Department of History at Stanford University. Author of *Exile and Identity: Polish Women in the Soviet Union during World War II,* she has also published articles on gendered nationalism and anti-Semitism.

Lisa A. Kirschenbaum is Associate Professor of History at West Chester University. In addition to *Small Comrades: Revolutionizing Childhood in Soviet Russia, 1917–1932,* she is author of *The Legacy of the Siege of Leningrad, 1941–1995: Myth, Memories, and Monuments.*

Mara Lazda holds a Ph.D. from Indiana University. Her article "Latvia" appeared in *Women, Gender and Fascism in Europe, 1919–45,* edited by Kevin Passmore.

Alon Rachamimov is Lecturer at Tel Aviv University. He is author of *POWs and the Great War: Captivity on the Eastern Front,* winner of the Fraenkel Prize in 2001.

Nancy M. Wingfield is Associate Professor of History at Northern Illinois University. She has published articles and books on the history of Habsburg Central Europe.

Index

References to illustrations appear in italics.

Lightning Source UK Ltd.
Milton Keynes UK
UKHW021825080322
399764UK00007B/262